POSTCARD HISTORY SERIES

Iowa City

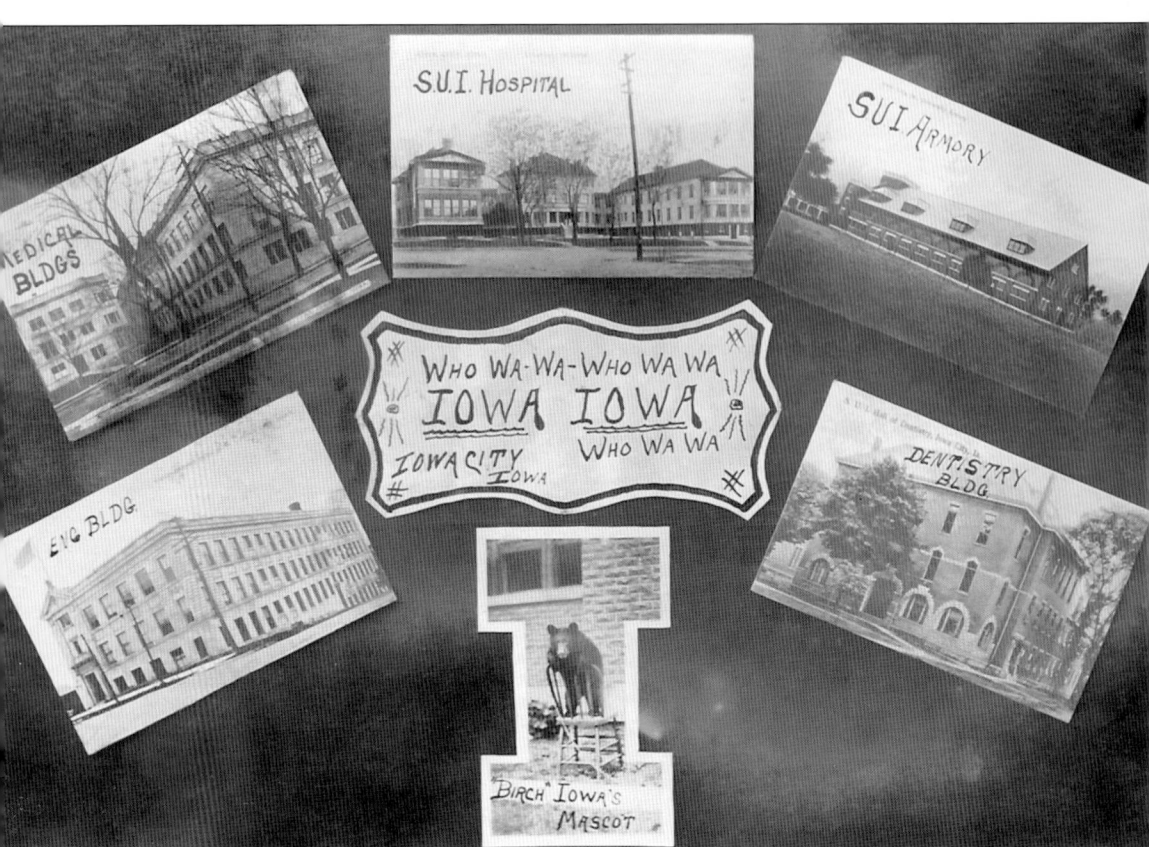

This 1909-postmarked card, in which an unidentified "Dear Kid" is greeted on the reverse face of the card at an address at Cedar Rapids, Iowa, presents a now-vintage University of Iowa collage that includes the then-current Iowa mascot Birch the bear cub, plus a collegiate "yell." In 1909 terminology, a yell is a Native American chant, which is probably politically out of favor today. The university was in the process then of discarding an "Iowa State University" name in favor of "State University of Iowa," or SUI, on this century-old card.

POSTCARD HISTORY SERIES

Iowa City

Bob Hibbs

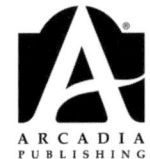

ARCADIA
PUBLISHING

Copyright © 2010 by Bob Hibbs
ISBN 978-0-7385-8402-7

Published by Arcadia Publishing
Charleston SC, Chicago IL, Portsmouth NH, San Francisco CA

Printed in the United States of America

Library of Congress Control Number: 2010930148

For all general information contact Arcadia Publishing at:
Telephone 843-853-2070
Fax 843-853-0044
E-mail sales@arcadiapublishing.com
For customer service and orders:
Toll-Free 1-888-313-2665

Visit us on the Internet at www.arcadiapublishing.com

On the Front Cover: Parades on Clinton Street in Iowa City remain at least an annual event with University of Iowa homecoming activities. In years past, the parade was an ubiquitous part of the warm seasons, particularly including Independence Day, when an "ice cream" sign near the closest streetlamps identified a door that would have been a popular threshold. This May 1915 image features the Association of Commerce from Peoria, Illinois.

On the Back Cover: The first trolley car to clamor along Iowa City streets is heralded in 1908 at the Clinton and College Streets intersection with what appears to be Mayor George W. Ball waxing eloquently above the crowd, from the front (right) conductor's station in the car. Service blossomed into five routes to Rundell Street, Oakland Cemetery, North Dodge, Manville Heights, and the Rock Island depot, plus most intervening points, before being supplanted by "go anywhere" buses.

Contents

Acknowledgments		6
Introduction		7
1.	Heart and Soul: Old Town Center, Hospitals, and Churches	9
2.	Shops and China Closets: Store Interiors Including Dresden China Shop	23
3.	Fun and Frolics: Chautauqua, Theaters, and Sports	33
4.	Business and Weather: Hatchery, Banks, and Weather Station	47
5.	On the Avenues: Streetscapes, Including a Double-Page Spread	57
6.	Friends and Neighbors: Coralville, River, City Park, and Lover's Leap	67
7.	One-Night Stands: Motels and Hotels	77
8.	The Common Good: PO, Courthouse, Schools, Firemen, and Military	85
9.	Sightseeing: Out and About, Including Two Double-Page Spreads	101
10.	Lies and Shenanigans: Phony Images, Including "Night" Scenes	117
Index		126

Acknowledgments

One does not undertake a project of this nature without incurring debts, or using resources gained through the good graces of others. Such is the case here, with special thanks to fellow local history writer and friend Tim Parrott for editorial consultation and proofreading. A special thanks as well to longtime friends Charles and Anna Mae Miller for the continuing loan of reference materials, which I have used yet again in the preparation of this volume.

Reference materials are important. It always has been true, and remains particularly so today, that any modern espouser of any body of facts stands on the shoulders of all predecessors in the field. Such is the case with this work, for it is based extensively on the past writings and musings of those former writers of Iowa City history and its panorama of then-current events.

Particularly, I feel indebted to Lolly Parker Eggers for her 1997 *A Century of Stories*, to the late John C. Gerber for his 1988 *Pictorial History of the University of Iowa*, to Gerald Mansheim for his 1989 *Iowa City, an Illustrated History*, to Hiram A. Reid for his *1883 History of Johnson County Iowa*, and to many others, including Irving Weber, who have added greatly to the fabric of local history with their church and lodge histories, articles in newspapers, and pamphlets outlining their service, issue, or event. This mountain of historic material, much of it amassed in my personal library, plus immediate access to the State Historical Society of Iowa and its vast resources in Iowa City, gives this work whatever veracity it may possess.

Lastly, one typically is motivated by personal encouragement and support. Such is my case with my wife, Margaret Kincheloe Hibbs, who has put up with me now for 47 years and counting. She just smiled, perhaps knowingly, for she too is a collector, when I began a quarter-century ago spending a dime, or a quarter, and occasionally even a dollar for an antique Iowa City postcard. Postcards now typically sell for many times those amounts. So, to my wife, Margaret, the love of my life, I dedicate this little volume in the hope she will continue to tolerate my idiosyncrasies. For Margaret's encouragement and support, I am most grateful.

Visit Bob Hibbs on the Internet at www.iagenweb.org/johnson/opostcardindex.htm.

INTRODUCTION

From politicians to professors, residents and visitors alike have thoroughly enjoyed themselves through 17 decades of swing and sway, the Iowa City way.

Smug, liberal Iowa City likes to think of itself in straightforward terms—the writing capital of America, Big 10 party university, Frank Gehry architecture, Broadway plays, concert hall music, and world-class medical center. There are no comparable communities in Iowa.

No one claims Iowa City is humble. In fact, local venerable sages have said of Iowa City: "Just as New York City is not New York State, so Iowa City is not Iowa." It's too naughty, too intellectual, too highly paid, and most of all, far too liberal to be Iowa.

And not only is Iowa City a misfit, it is the seat of a county named for U.S. vice president Richard Mentor Johnson (1780–1850), a Kentucky war hero, U.S. senator, and congressman. As a successful politician from a southern state, Mr. Johnson spent his entire adult lifetime with just one wife, who just happened to be African American—a wonderful incongruity that almost perfectly characterizes Iowa City.

From other environs, too, but particularly from across the state, folks come to Iowa City to be healed, to play, or to be educated. And, if Iowa City plays hard, it also works hard. Ten and twelve-hour days are not uncommon for the researcher, the insurance agent, the operating room physician, or the writer alike. And for the student, too—at least during exams week!

Kinnick Stadium on a football Saturday takes on a festive celebratory atmosphere from tailgate to traffic jam. Traffic jam, in Iowa? Well, yes, for 15 minutes. After all, Iowa City is in Iowa; and it brags that locally there is no such thing as rush hour. Rather, workdays begin and end with "rush minute."

Life is good; everyone has a say, from the lively newspaper editorial page to the endless committee meetings of an academic community. There is a club or focus group tailored to every interest or need, including some not yet identified. It is said that there are four distinct seasons in Iowa City, and someone to criticize them all.

Parks are plentiful—even for your dog, off leash and all! From twin, 13-floor condominium towers at the center of town, it's a five-minute drive to open countryside, 10 minutes to the winery, 15 to the lake, or 30 to family-style dinner in the nationally renowned Amana Colonies.

The opera and rock music extravaganza, Joffrey Ballet, the legitimate stage both big-city born or as often-raunchy experimental student theater all burst forth regularly from the venues of Iowa City. Venues include an open-air "Shakespeare Festival Stage" in City Park modeled after The Bard's original located back across the pond in the old country.

But, Iowa City didn't happen overnight; it has a long history that it treasures. The only person memorialized by a life-sized outdoor bronze statue anywhere in town is beloved dead historian Irving Weber. Heisman Trophy winner Nile Kimmick is memorialized by a twice-life-sized bronze statue in an entrance courtyard at the university football stadium that bears his name.

From its beginnings during 1839 as the fledgling capital of the Territory of Iowa through a decade of statehood, politicians were the centerpieces of a raucous pioneer town at the end of the railroad on the western frontier. Then, as the financial panic of 1857 decked the country, Iowa City was sent cartwheeling by the added blow of removal of the capital to Des Moines.

If the political heyday had produced the headline "Drunk or Rich in Iowa City," it soon became just "Drunk" as Iowa City featured "the longest bar west of Chicago" in McInnerny's, whose watering trough stretched continuously from the front window back 150 feet to the alley door.

And, Iowa City shared its wealth barreling forth from three breweries along a two-block stretch of Market Street that produced sufficient suds daily to drown the thirsts of half of eastern Iowa—from the middle of the 19th century until 20th-century Prohibition!

With the capital whisked away to "some foreign location nearer the center of the state," Iowa City settled down to be an industrial center. But this didn't work and didn't suit it, at least not until Proctor and Gamble decided more than a half-century ago to deposit a huge toothpaste plant on the outskirts of town, and American College Testing (ACT) became a giant in college entrance examinations.

Meanwhile, the University of Iowa crawled beyond its initial decade as a paper tiger—when it existed in state law but didn't offer classes—into a fledgling science and classical center. "Athens of Iowa" the local wags proclaimed to snickers from around the state breathing "Johnson County High School" in deference to the fact the university had more pupils in prep classes than were enrolled at college level.

A 1938 *Chicago Tribune* article described Iowa City as offering "culture in a cornfield," marking announcement that the university would offer graduate degrees with theses based in plays, paintings, novels, and other works of art, a radical idea which broke new ground nationally.

As years waxed and waned, university enrollment grew as its faculty matured and its reputation flowered. The end of World War II saw enrollments spike from 3,700 during the fall of 1944, to 9,800 by 1946, with some 6,000 funded by grants under a federal G.I. Bill. About 30 percent were married and lived in "temporary" duplex barracks complexes, housing hordes of kids and featuring shared-shower sheds. The military-type housing communes were hurriedly erected in the open patches of grass across a 300-acre campus.

Today's herd of more than 30,000 students is mostly single, living in rented quarters off campus, and grazing in local eateries, often fueled mostly by Pell grants and credit cards.

Iowa City had forever changed, completing a transition from politicians to professors. Many locals now claim Iowa City got the better of that bargain.

The growth of the University of Iowa Hospitals and Clinics at Iowa City was even more improbable. Told a century ago that there wasn't enough "clinical material" to sustain a teaching hospital in a small town in a rural state, a few shrewd locals successfully lobbied Iowa's farmer-dominated legislature to pay for the treatment of poor kids from across the state in Iowa City. That was in 1915, exactly a half-century before Medicaid put every other hospital in the state on equal footing.

Five years after children opened a door, the program was expanded to cover adults as "indigent care" for all deserving Iowans, paid entirely from state tax revenues. For the first time, University Hospitals had guaranteed patient loads and a steady income stream.

The mid-1920s produced another far-fetched effort. A new generation of smooth talkers with connections convinced the giant Rockefeller Foundation to provide half the cost of an entirely new hospital complex on open land at the western edge of Iowa City. More fast-talking produced the other half from Iowa taxpayers, and University Hospitals claimed a new incarnation during 1928.

It certainly took advantage. Today a trillion-dollar medical complex in a town of 67,000 pays top-notch wages, with benefits, to more than 7,500 who provide care and treatment to 650,000 patients annually from every state and many foreign locales.

But, then, that's Iowa City—with its audacity, its brains, and determined drive. The following pages explore the sense that this is a community with something special to offer. Please take a look; and, if you're inclined, let us know what you think at hibbs@mchsi.com.

The images in this book are taken entirely from the author's personal collection of 3,200 postcards, all offering views in Iowa City or from the immediately surrounding area.

One

HEART AND SOUL
OLD TOWN CENTER, HOSPITALS, AND CHURCHES

Iowa City physically and emotionally revolves around its principal industry, the University of Iowa, which typically is represented by Old Capitol, a small stone statehouse constructed during the 1840s in a frontier wilderness to house the seat of government of the Territory of Iowa. "Old Cap," as it is affectionately called, subsequently served as the first home of government for the state of Iowa. It now stands at the core of "Pentacrest," a four-square-block area at the heart of both campus and community. This image of the Pentacrest was taken about 1950 and looks east across the Iowa River from what now is site of the university's College of Nursing building.

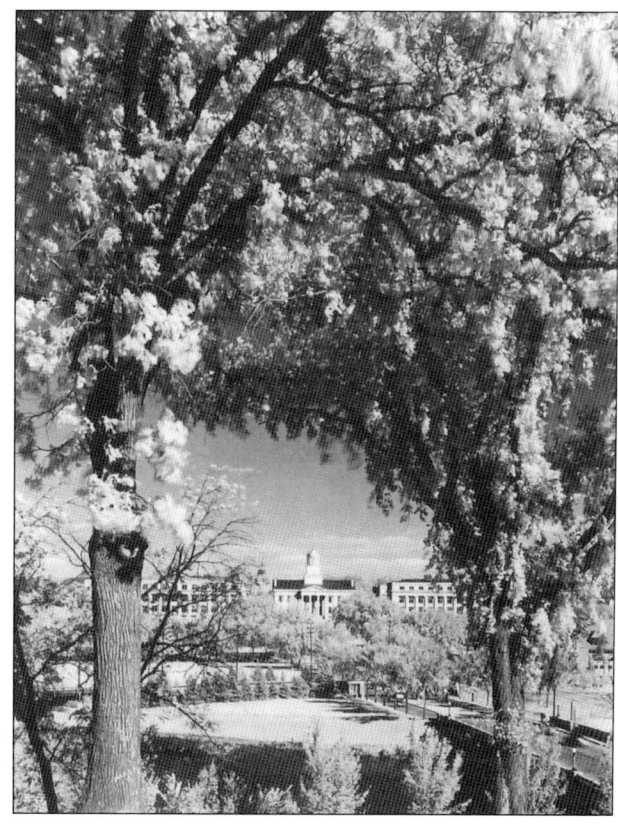

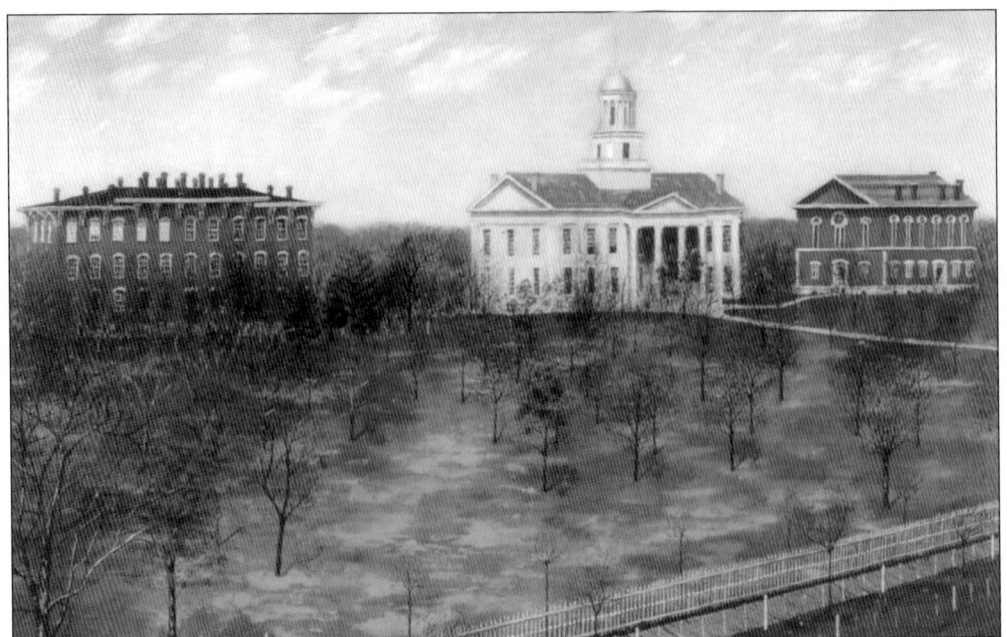

The above image from an oil painting by Frank Bond displays the university campus about 1880, featuring Old Capitol and companions South Hall (left) and North Hall. These are the earliest of five red brick halls that grew in a row flanking Old Cap before a late 19th-century plan called for the four larger stone structures that now surround the original statehouse.

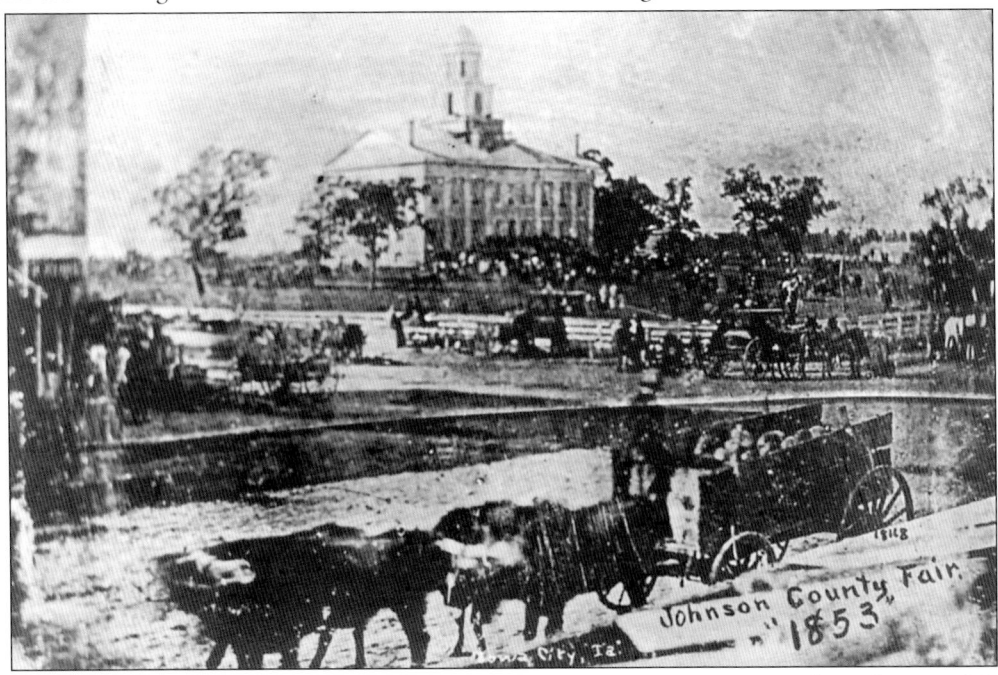

This is perhaps one of the two oldest surviving outdoor Iowa City images, taken of county fair activity in 1853 while state government still occupied Old Capitol before its 1857 move to "a more central location." The Civil War (1861–1865) produced the first widespread use of outdoor photography, making this image a real pioneer presentation of frontier life.

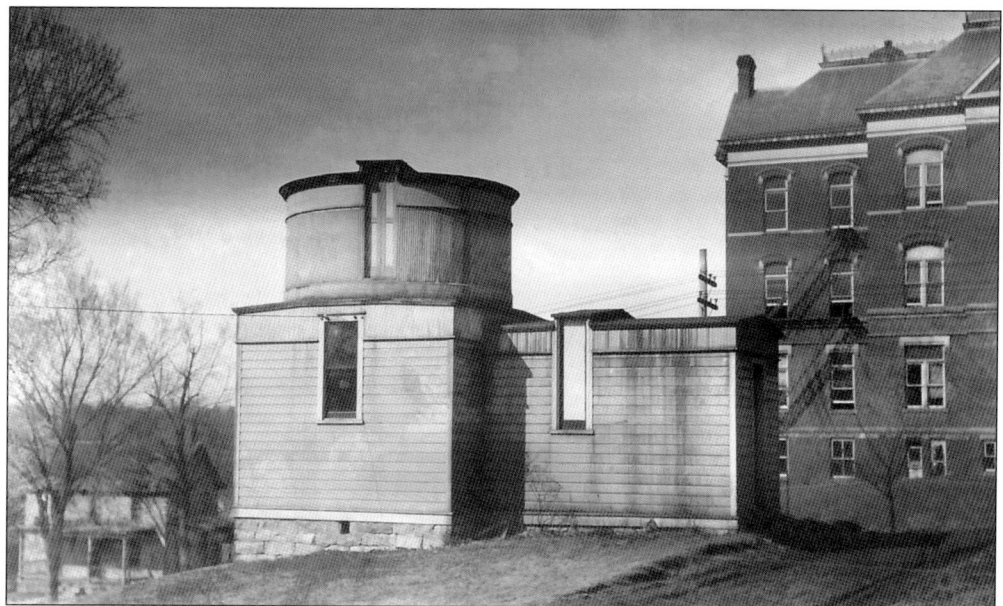

"The Observatory" was bounced about the campus for a half-century, then off campus to southern Johnson County, and finally split in the modern era between Van Allen Hall in Iowa City and the Arizona desert. Here it houses its telescopes on Pentacrest, where it landed to make way for the president's house on its Observatory Hill site in 1909. From here it went to what is now the South Quad Residence Hall site, until its World War II–era demise there, too.

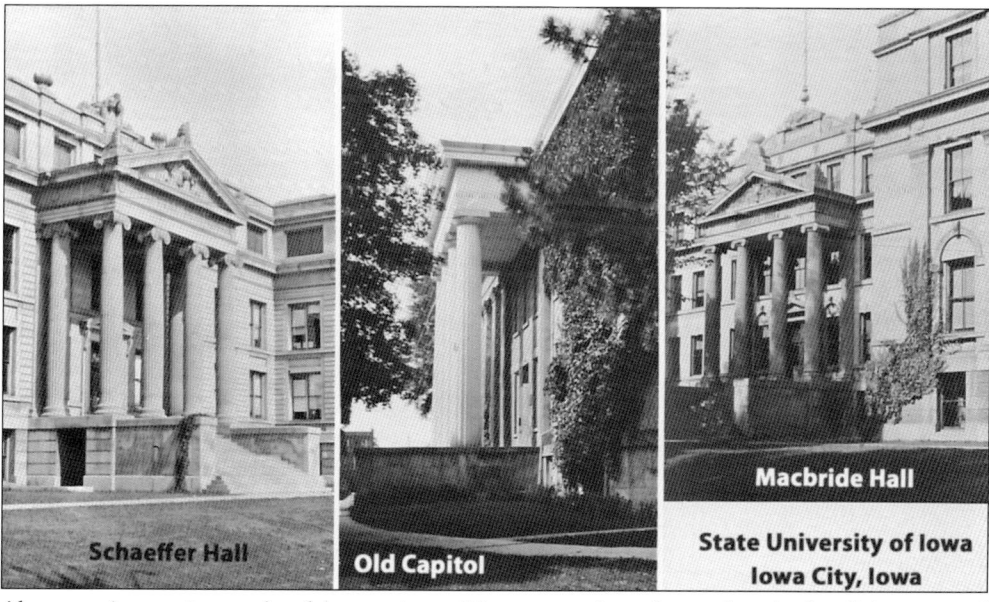

Above, an interesting study of the porticos of Pentacrest, sisters but unique in detail, is presented in this postcard collage created soon after Macbride Hall was completed during 1908. Current building names were added by the author. Macbride, christened in the name of the university's 10th president Thomas Houston Macbride, began life as "Hall of Natural Science," which, with its classic marble interior, makes it among the fanciest of university structures. Schaeffer Hall is named for the university's seventh president Charles Schaeffer.

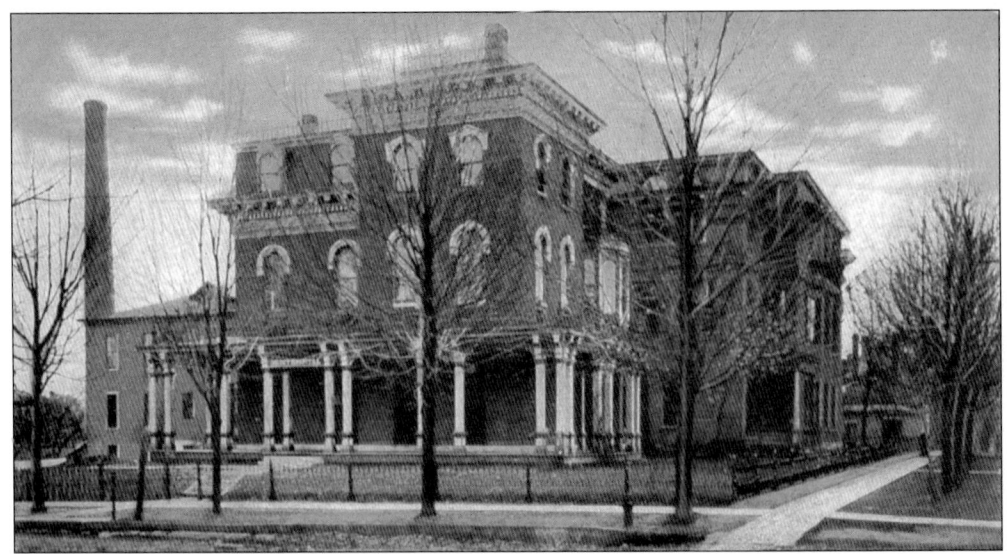

Mercy Hospital, about 1906, was housed in the former mansion of beer-brewing magnet John Dostal, shown here with multiple additions. Sisters of Mercy first journeyed to Iowa City in 1872 to staff the first University Hospital in the Mechanics Academy on Linn Street, just north of Iowa Avenue. Friction caused the 1885 mansion acquisition and a start "on their own."

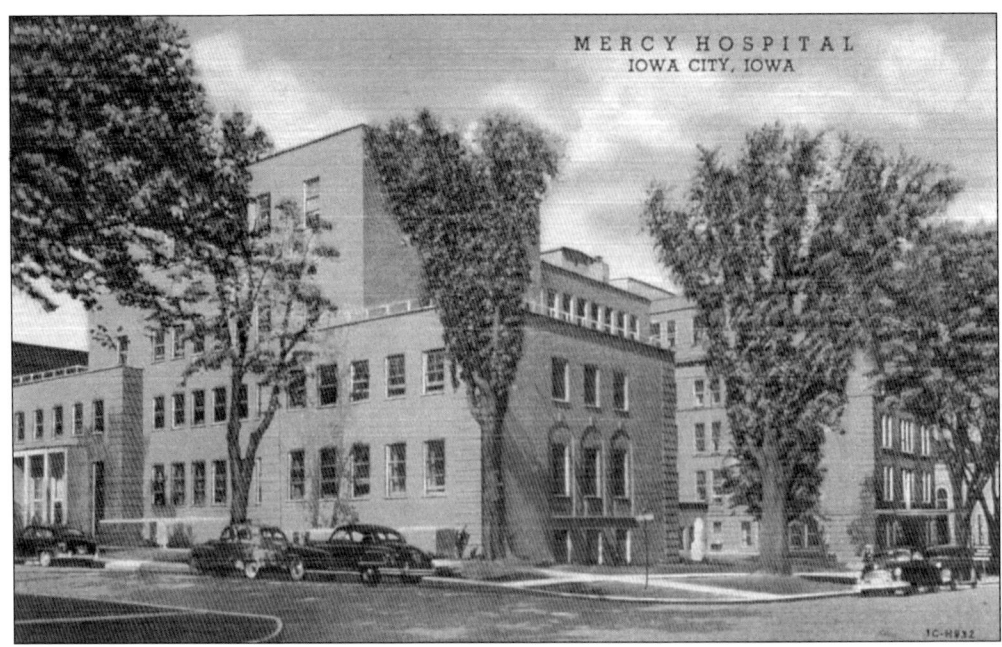

By the 1940s, Mercy Hospital had expanded south along Van Buren Street, now closed through the hospital site, and east along Market Street in space that has since been rebuilt. Stately elms, shown here, which dominated the local landscape until the Dutch elm disease scourge of the 1960s that wiped out virtually all of them, heavily topped out. Vintage cars line the streets.

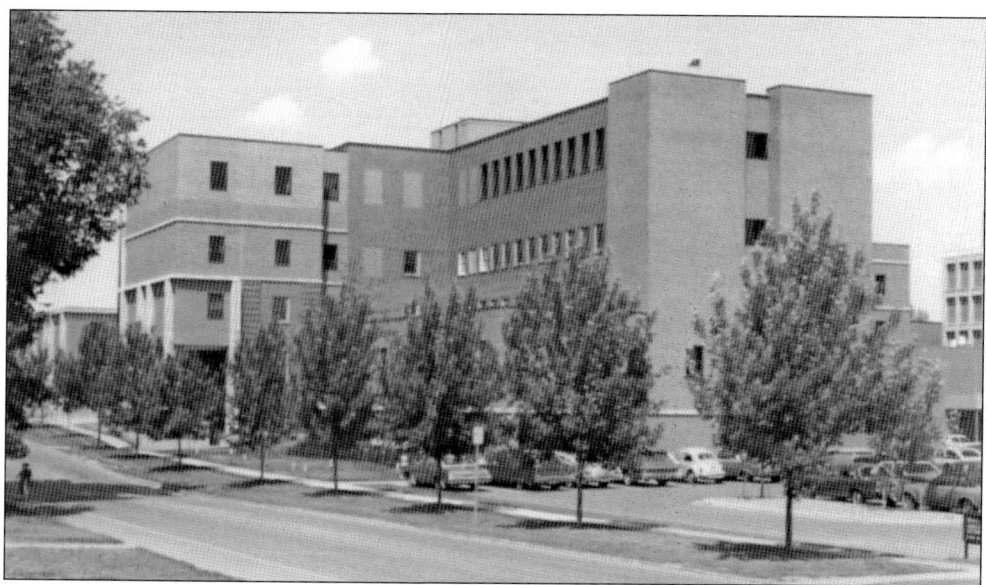

By the 1980s, Mercy Hospital had again rebuilt its space along Market Street. Since then it has bought the old school block across Market and constructed a doctors' clinic building and a parking ramp complete with skywalk across Market to the main building. Its school of nursing, once called Lourdes Hall and now used as administration space, peeks in at far right.

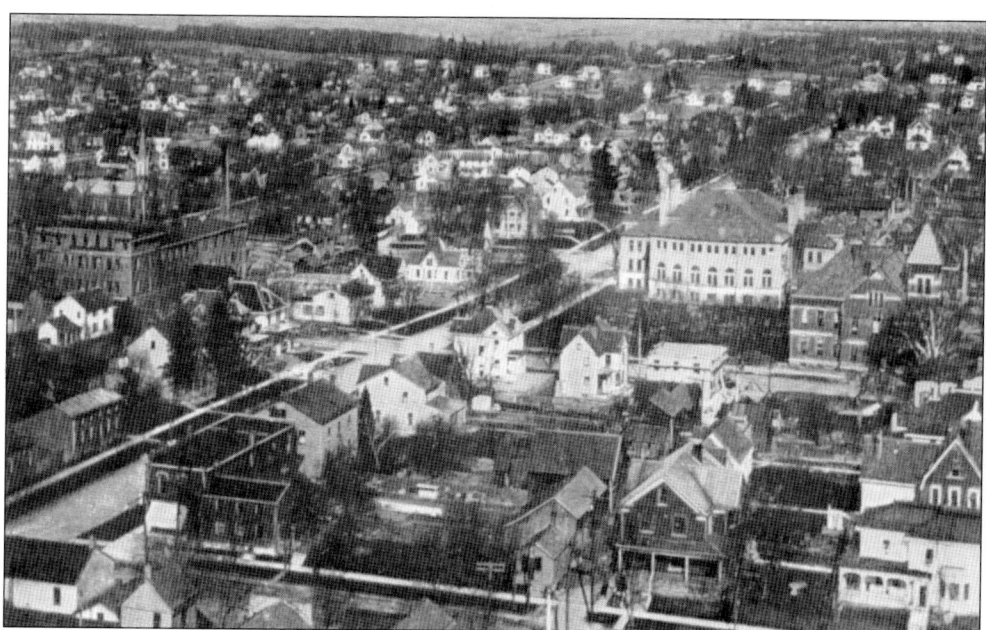

Above, oriented from the Market-Gilbert Streets intersection at lower left, home now to John's Grocery, this pre-1920 view from the steeple of St. Mary's Church shows Mercy Hospital, near the center of the image's left edge; and, across the image, a larger City High building can be seen, later called Central Junior High, next to what had been the previous cycle of class space.

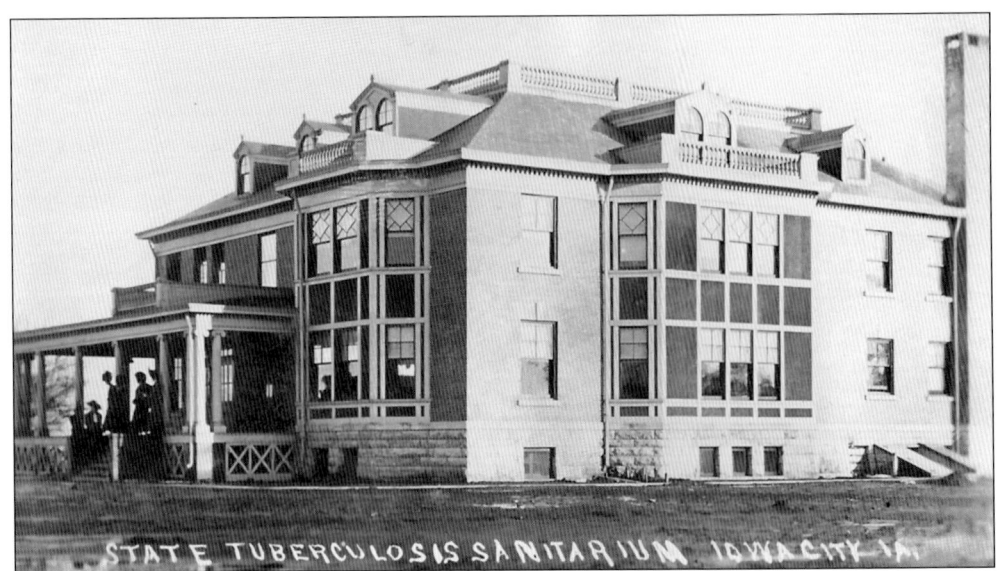

The Oakdale Campus of the University of Iowa has a convoluted history. Acquired as open farmland through which the CRandIC "Interurban" Railway passed between Iowa City and Cedar Rapids, it was first opened in February 1908 as shown above as a tuberculosis sanatorium with a state-wide service area. It morphed into an alcoholic treatment program site about 1965. The university now uses 197 of the 497-acre grounds, which is nearly 5 miles from the main campus, as site to its business incubator park. The state's prisons entry and evaluation unit is located across the road, an old Highway 218 route to nearby North Liberty.

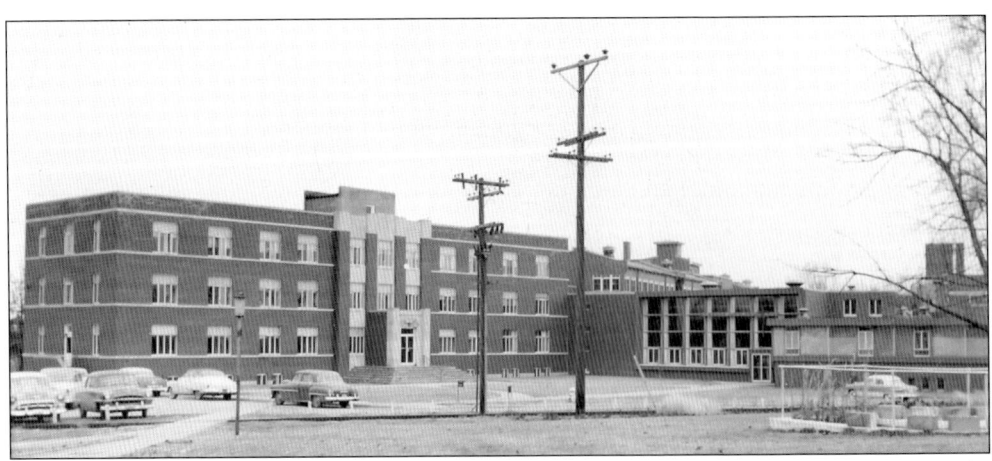

Above, the sanatorium's last built facilities, imaged about 1950, were converted about 1975 for use as the State Hygienic Lab, a public health and communicable diseases testing unit, which by law is structurally separate from the university. The lab, which now employs more than 200, currently is erecting a replacement state-of-the-art facility on the Oakdale Campus along old Highway 218, a half mile from the imaged structure, whose future is uncertain.

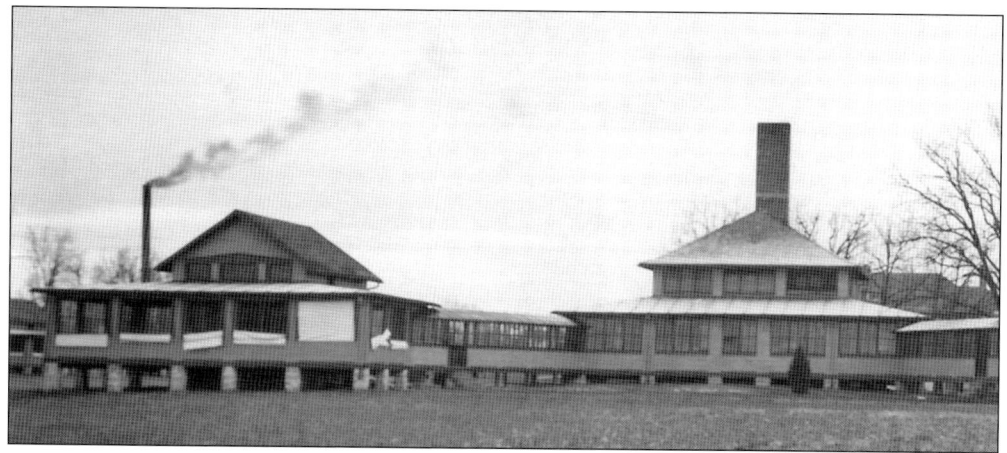

Treatment of tuberculosis before modern drug therapies evolved seems weird if not downright cruel. Separation and isolation were considered essential, thus these "cottages" were erected at the state tuberculosis hospital at Oakdale, a self-contained residential facility set in a farming environment apart from any town, but along a rail line to facilitate public access. Staff also lived on the site, where even outgoing mail, like the postcards carrying these images, was viewed with suspicion for spread of the deadly and dreaded disease. Some were lacquered to seal in "germs," and recipients were advised to burn them after viewing.

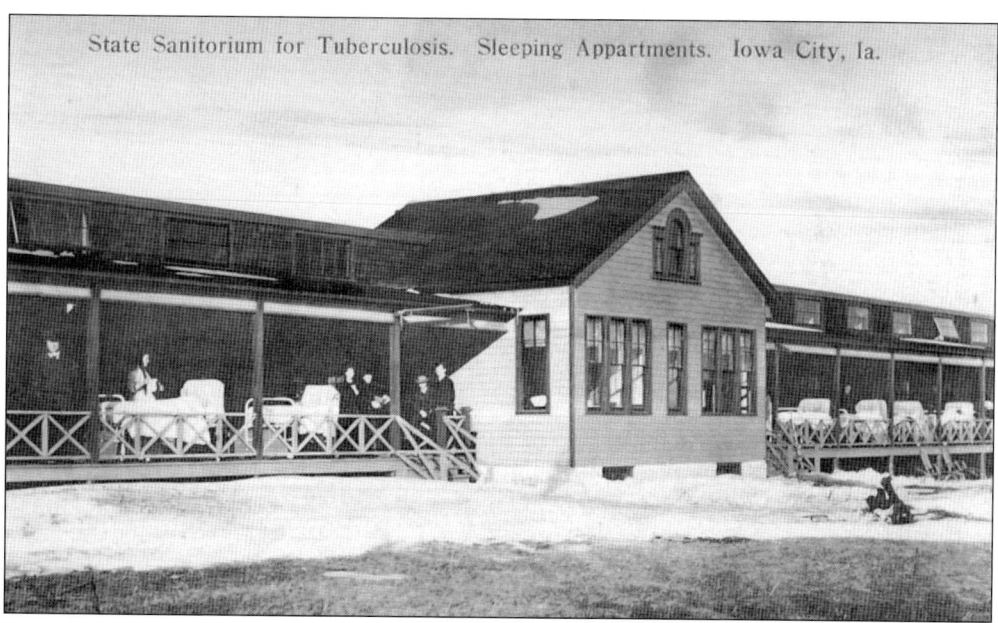

Sunshine and fresh air were requisites to good treatment, based on protocols at that time. In the extreme, seriously ill patients were housed on "sunporches" even with snow on the ground, as shown above. In the image, a nurse at left serves a beverage to a patient in bed virtually buried in white linens. Children frolic in the snow at lower right.

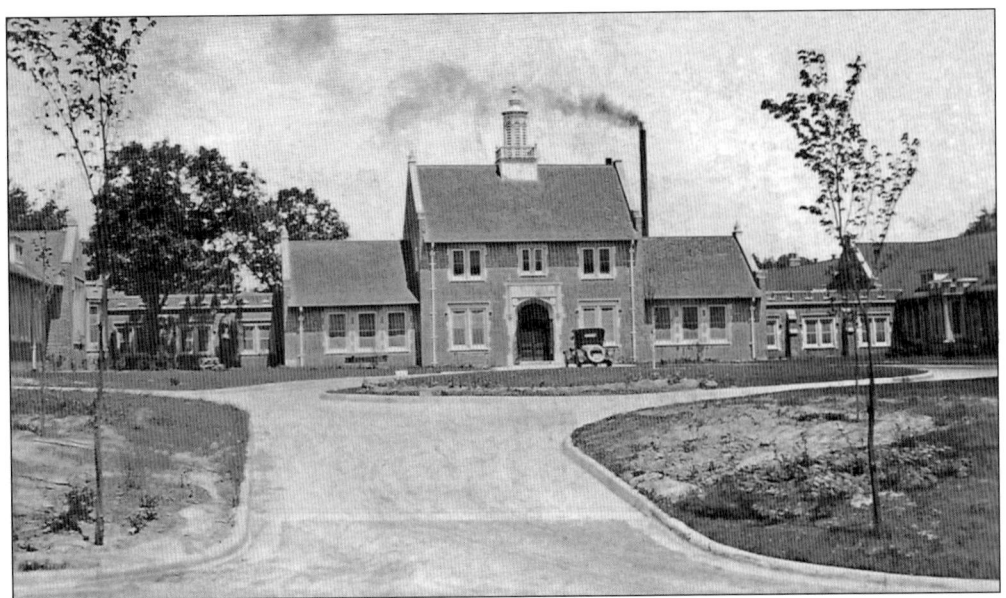

Children's Hospital, the first substantial University of Iowa structure west of the Iowa River, was opened to rave reviews in 1919. Dr. Albert Steindler, a European-trained physician, had convinced the farmer-dominated Iowa legislature that it should pay to treat poor children from any Iowa locale in Iowa City. Expanded 5 years later to cover indigent adults, it represented a Medicaid-type program 50 years before that phenomenon blossomed at hospitals statewide.

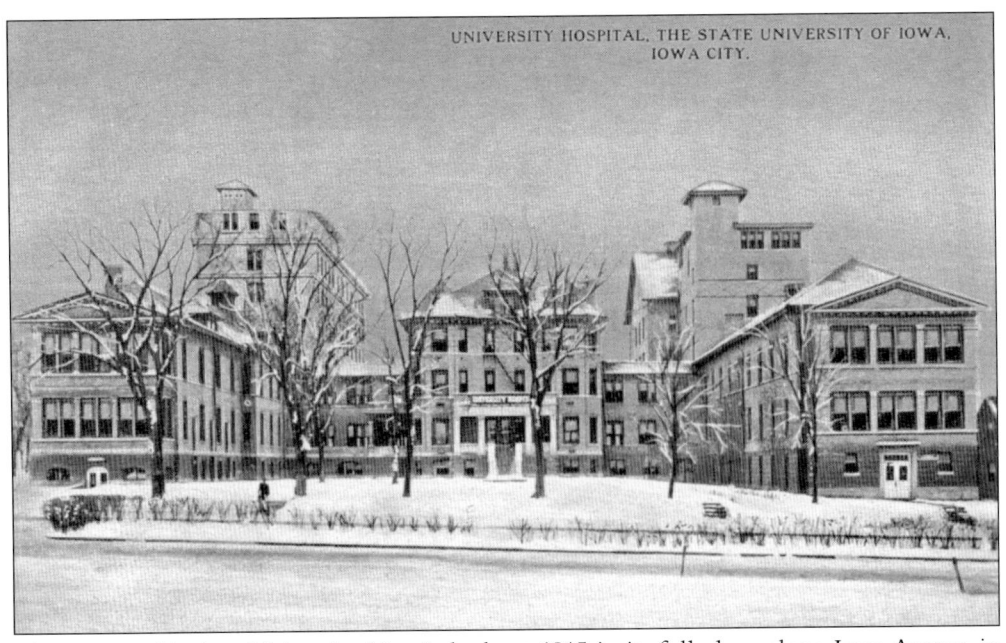

Above, snow blankets University Hospitals about 1915 in its full glory along Iowa Avenue in central Iowa City, two blocks east of Old Cap. Much of the structure still exists in other uses, but is hidden by a major subsequent street-facing addition called Spence Psychology Labs.

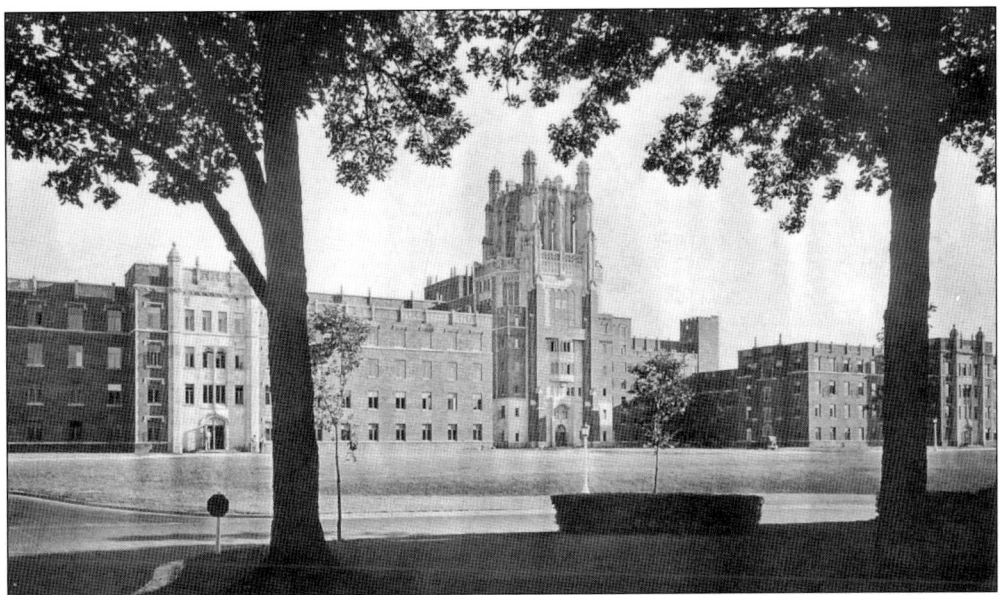

As unlikely as it is to find a widely reputed trillion-dollar medical complex in a little Iowa town, it is even more unlikely that half the $5-million price tag of its original 1928 Gothic tower incarnation, shown above west of the river, was paid for by the giant Rockefeller Foundation. But it is true.

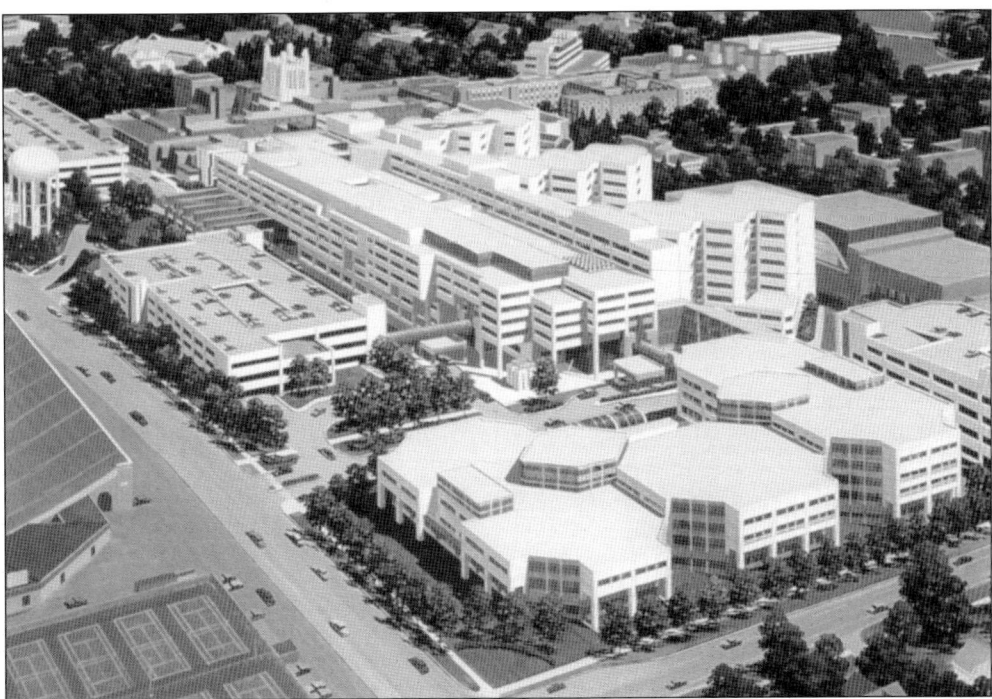

The Gothic tower of the 1928 hospital is barely visible at the distant end of the modern facility, which stretches a quarter mile toward the viewer. The tower stands on an east-west axis from the dome of Old Capitol a half-mile to the east. Now, some 7,500 people work here.

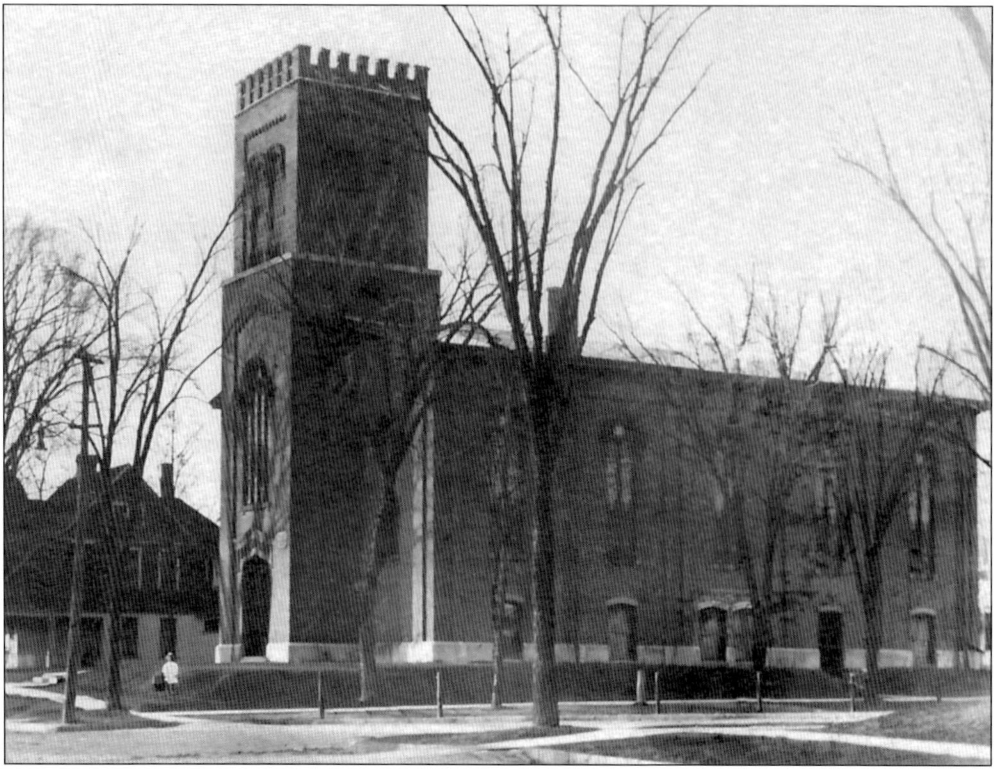

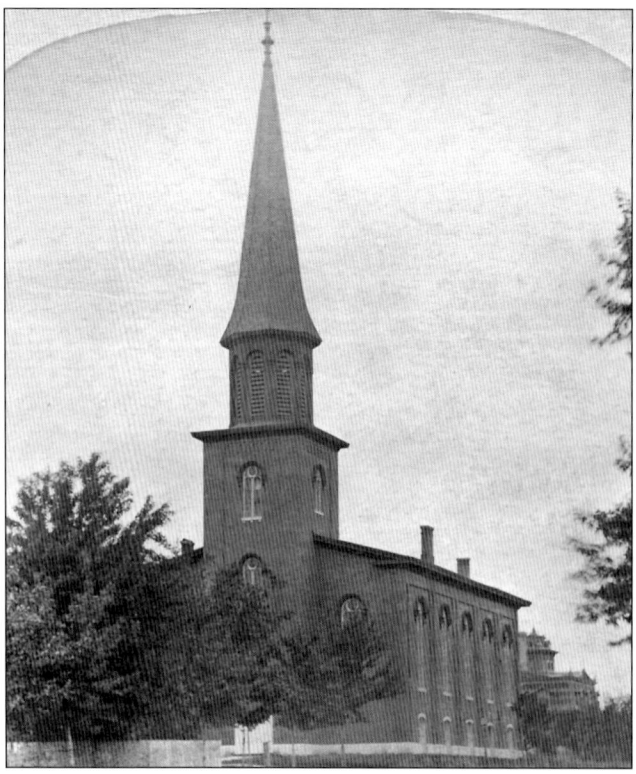

Old Brick Church is presented above in a 1910 postcard that still offers a good representation of its modern profile, although the neighborhood has changed dramatically. Town founder and church member Chauncey Swan donated the lot to First Presbyterian Church in 1843. Sold by the Presbyterians during 1975, the building has a pre–Civil War cornerstone dated 1856, but it wasn't yet complete when dedicated in 1865 without a spire as the Civil War was ending. The image at left of the same structure, taken by Iowa City photographer Timothy Townsend about 1875, represents its original planned appearance with a 153-foot spire constructed in 1869 and blown off a mere eight years later.

Various strains of the Methodist Protestant denomination have illustrious histories in Iowa City emanating from various pioneer congregations. They include both the Methodist Protestants (later the longtime Christian Church site in the 200 blocks of Iowa Avenue), and the Methodist Episcopal Church, which now uses the name First United Methodist Church in Iowa City. It was under the Methodist Episcopal name that the congregation built in 1842, then enlarged in 1863, and rebuilt in 1884 after a fire. This structure faced west onto Dubuque Street and is shown in a postcard image reproduced at right. It was destroyed by fire on April 22, 1906. During worship service on that Sunday, fire broke through the Methodist roof, as a morning Mass was letting out at neighboring St. Mary's Catholic Church, which shares the same half-block. Catholics flooded the Methodist sanctuary through several access doors to warn of the danger; and, although the building was a total loss, no one was reported to have been seriously injured.

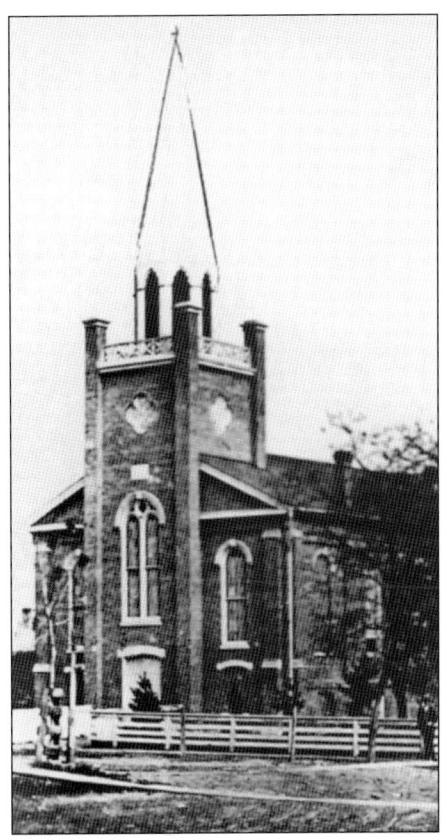

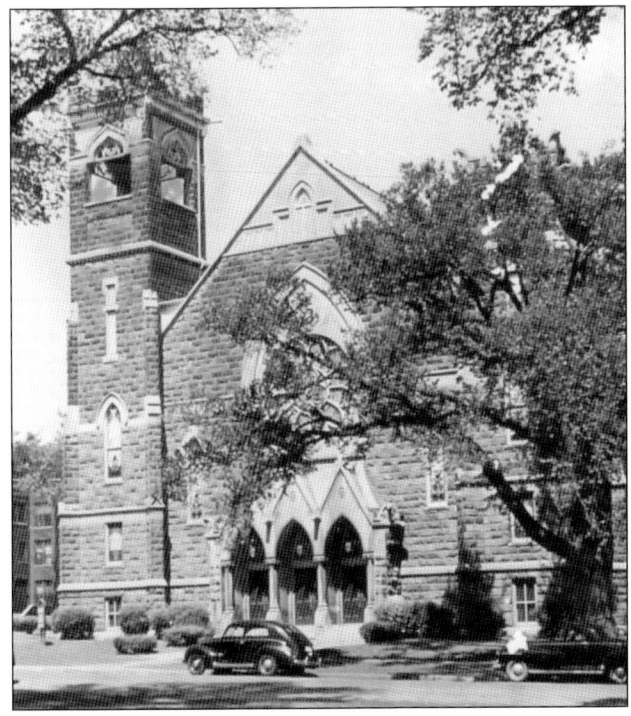

A replacement structure, shown in the 1930-era image at left, was dedicated two years after the fire. The structures rest on the same lot, one shown as a church site on the original town plat located across Jefferson Street from "City Park"—a square-block area that Iowa City gave to the university more than a century ago to help inhibit political grumblings of moving the university elsewhere.

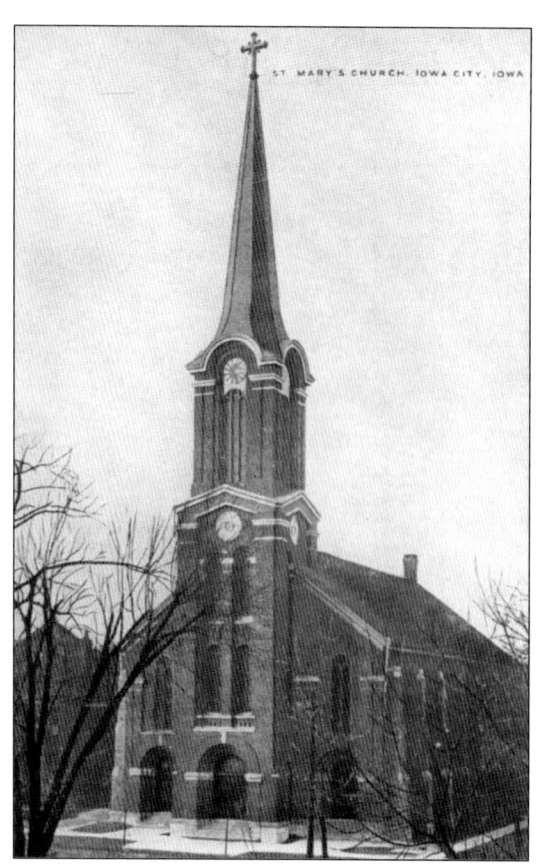

St. Mary's parish, the first Roman Catholic congregation in Iowa City, was organized in 1841 by itinerant Italian immigrant Order of Saint Dominic friar Samuel Mazzuchelli, who had arrived in Iowa City to say a first Mass the previous December. This priest was "venerated" by his church during 1993, nearly 130 years after his death, as a step toward possible sainthood. He is also now credited with giving counsel that elevated the design of Iowa City's Old Capitol from ordinary to outstanding; that is, from stepsister to Cinderella. During five years of church training in Italy, Father Mazzuchelli had studied some architecture. This was before his 1828 migration to America. He designed and commissioned the first St. Mary's edifice, but it proved too small and was replaced by the current facility, shown left about 1910 as it still appears today.

It is also shown as it looked during its 1869 dedication before the 196-foot spire was added during 1872. This building was constructed around the original St. Mary's stone church while the old one still was in use. As the new altar area was ready, the end wall of the old structure was taken out to allow use of the new chancel. Finally the roof and walls of the old building were taken down inside this fully enclosed edifice and carried out, piece by piece, through the front entry doors. Just imagine all the dust and debris to be cleaned up almost daily for regular use.

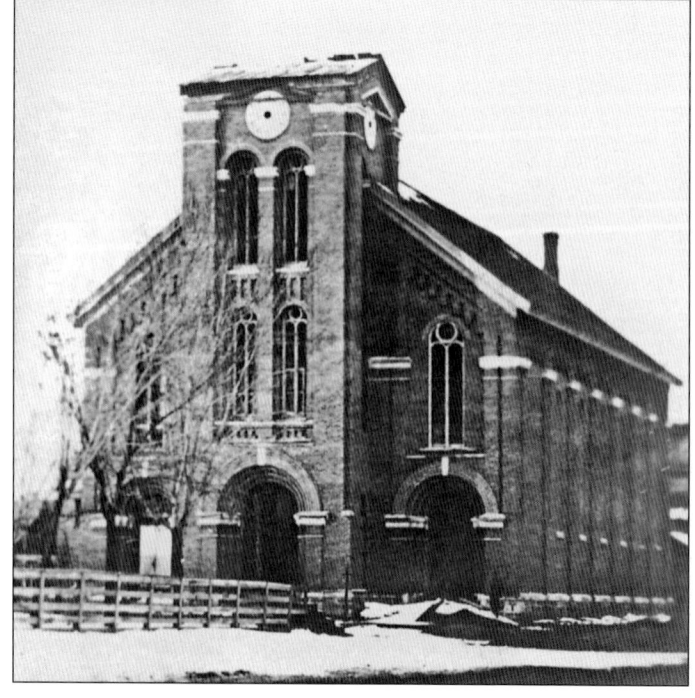

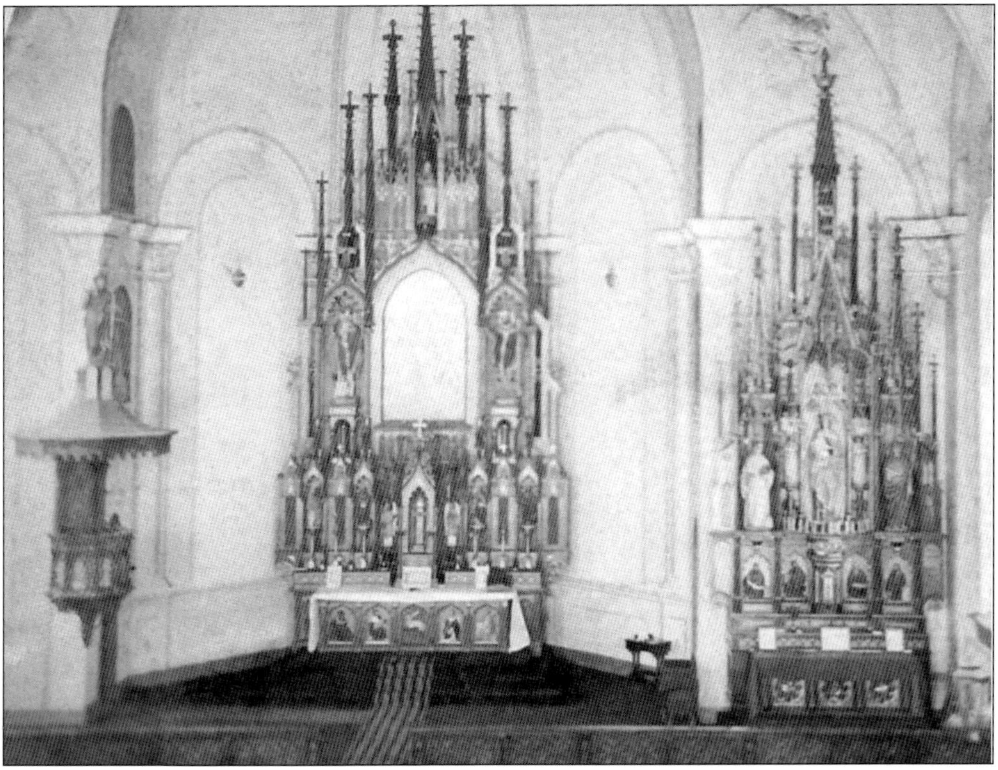

Both two-altar and three-altar chancels have existed at St. Mary's Catholic Church in Iowa City. Although no date is available for the above image of two altars, it was recorded as a stereographic slide, probably dating from the 1870s, now in the author's personal library. Available church records, including full-blown parish histories written by Joseph Fuhrmann in 1916 and a second by Francis Lalor in 1991, do not record a date for addition of the third altar. The postcard image below was published about 1910.

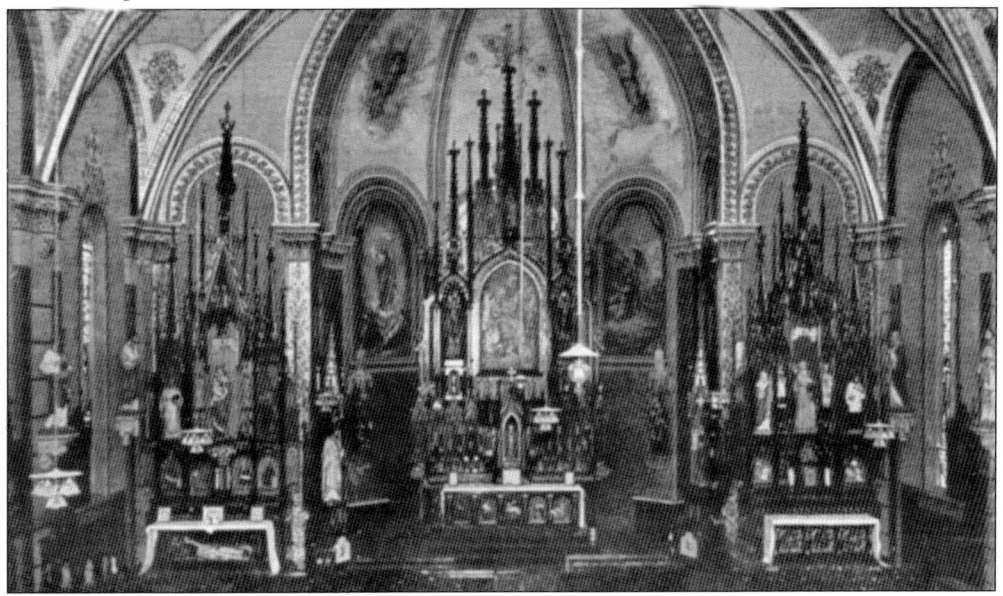

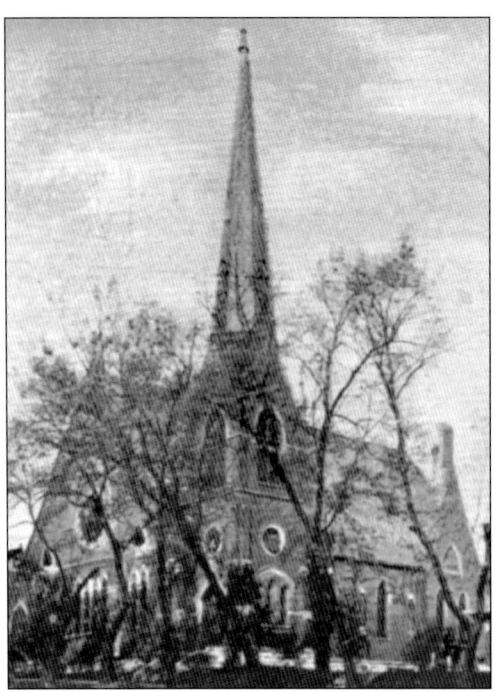

St. Patrick's Catholic Church in central Iowa City appears in the image at left recorded about 1910. A tornado destroyed the structure in 2006, as it passed along a narrow path through Iowa City, only the second such storm to strike the town in 170 years. A replacement facility has been erected in eastern Iowa City.

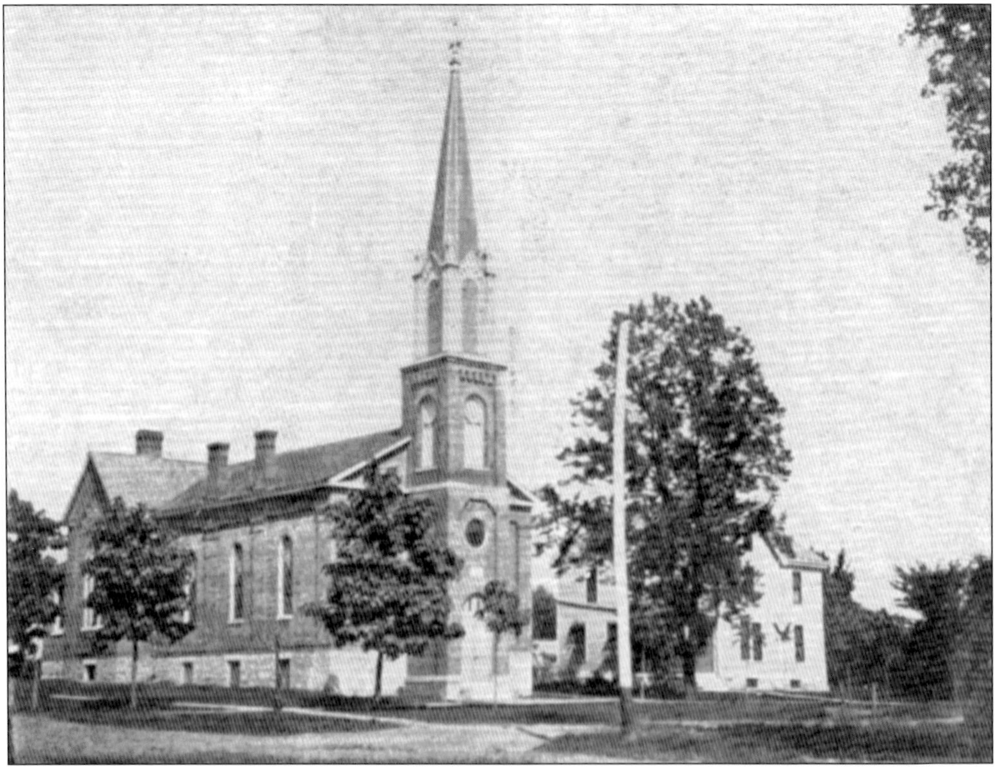

German Protestants organized the Zion Lutheran congregation during 1857 and erected the facility shown above on the northeast quadrant of the Bloomington-Johnson Streets intersection in 1861. It was demolished during 1964 and replaced with the current facility.

Two

Shops and China Closets
Store Interiors Including Dresden China Shop

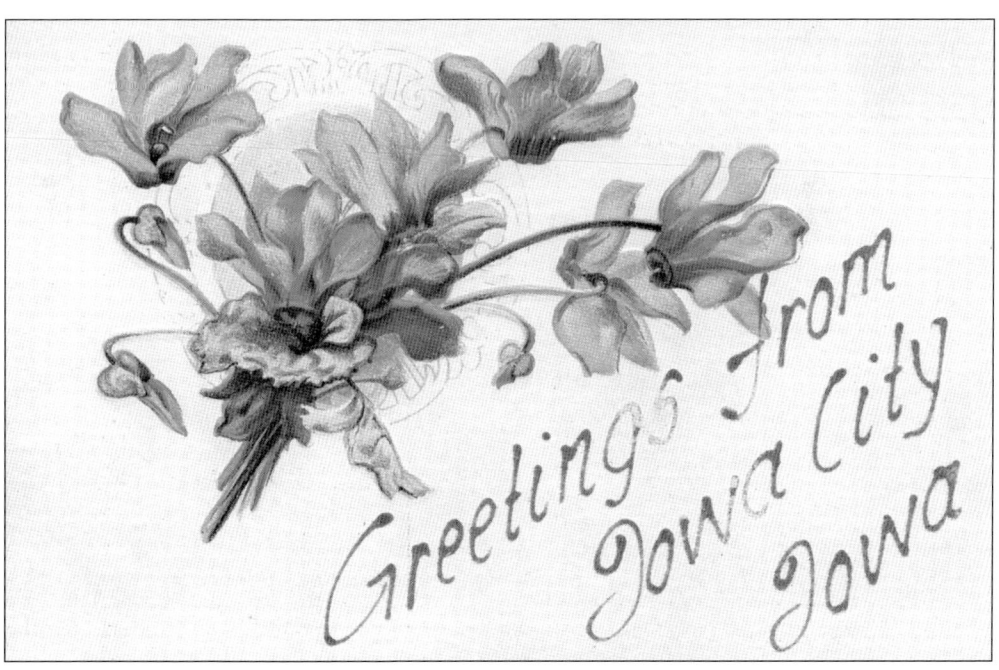

Image from card postmarked in 1908, from Will in Iowa City to Ellis in Cedar Rapids.

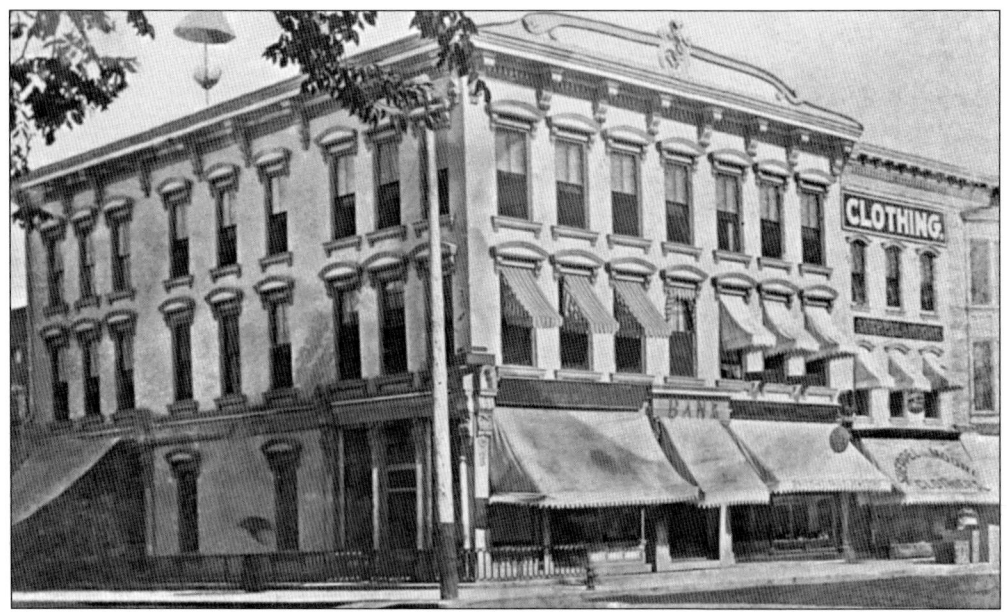

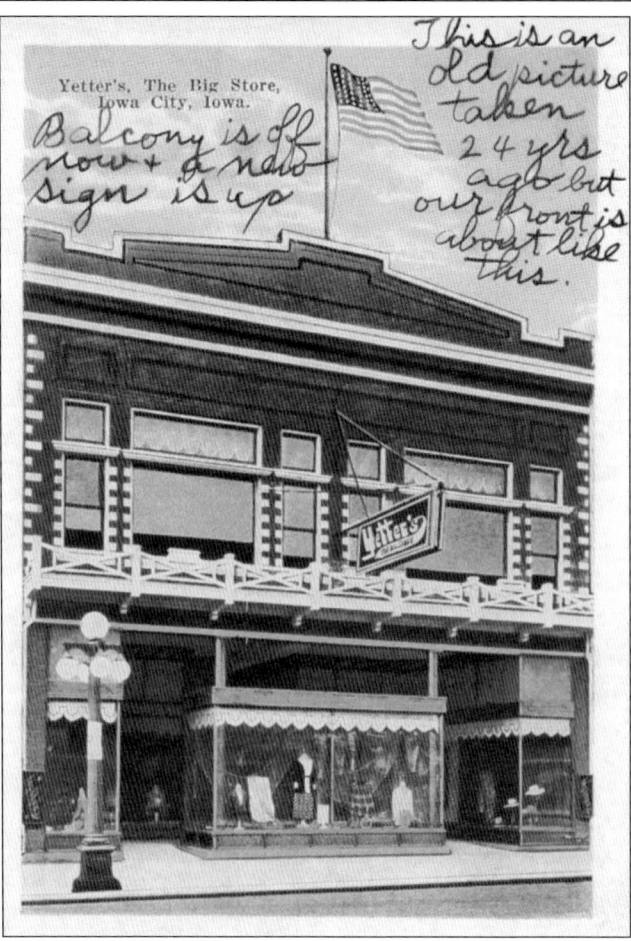

Pioneer Iowans hated banks; too many failed and left folks with worthless paper, feelings reflected early in constitutional prohibition of banks. "Money houses" came after a new state constitution. Such is the "bank" visible as a small storefront imaged above about 1906 crowded into a now extant "bank corner" structure at Clinton and Washington Streets in Iowa City, replaced in 1913 by a six-story bank building.

Yetter's local department store owner Chris Yetter jotted a 1947 note on a 1923 postcard image, at left, of his family's storefront along Clinton Street, now part of the site of what was called Iowa State Bank. Yetter's had a 60-year run, ending during the 1950s with consolidation into Younkers.

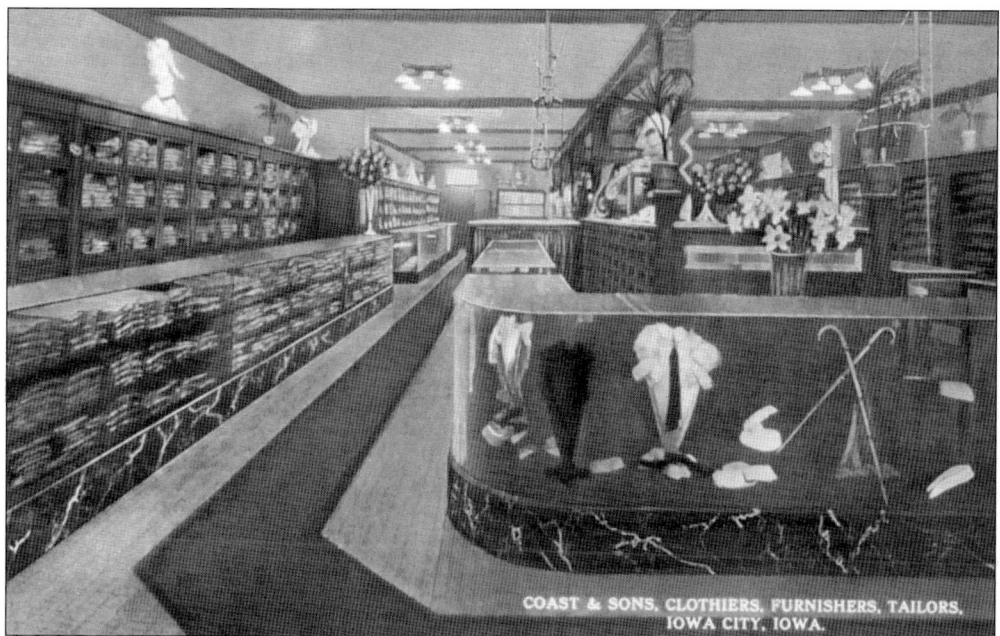

A century ago, William and sons Bill and Preston Coast, or "Coast & Sons, Clothiers, Furnishers, Tailors," offered their wares at 10 and 12 South Clinton Street as imaged above, claiming in advertising to be the "most beautiful small store in the United States."

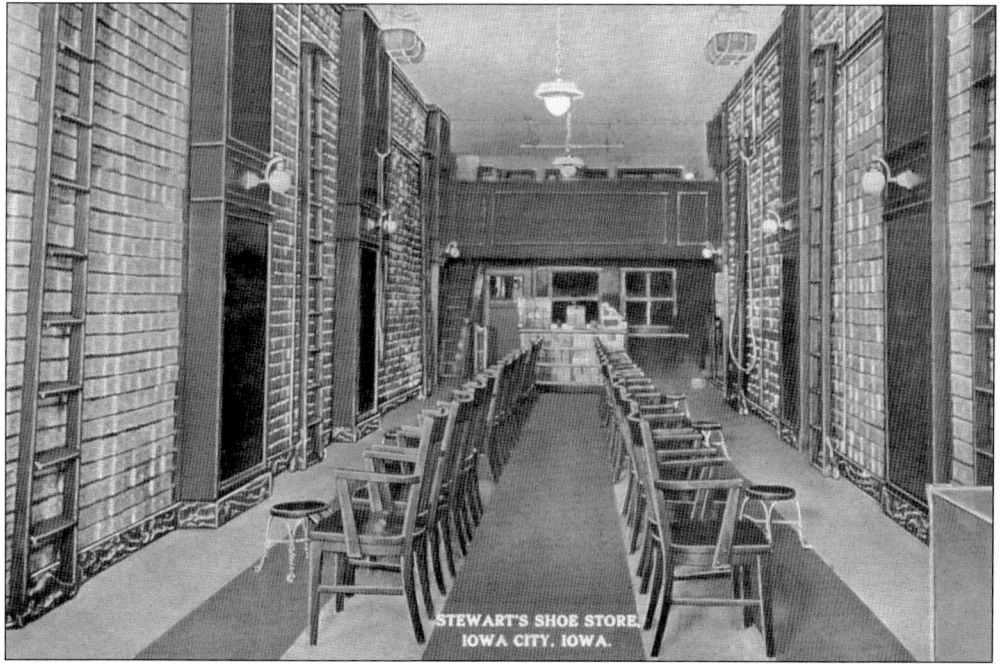

Above, Stewart's Shoes in the Hotel Jefferson building at 125 East Washington Street featured ceiling-high displays accessible by rail-guided ladders, as seen at far left and in other locations, in this 1920s image. Mark and Hal moved on as the Great Depression struck. Hal became an officer at a prominent bank, which closed later in those financially catastrophic years.

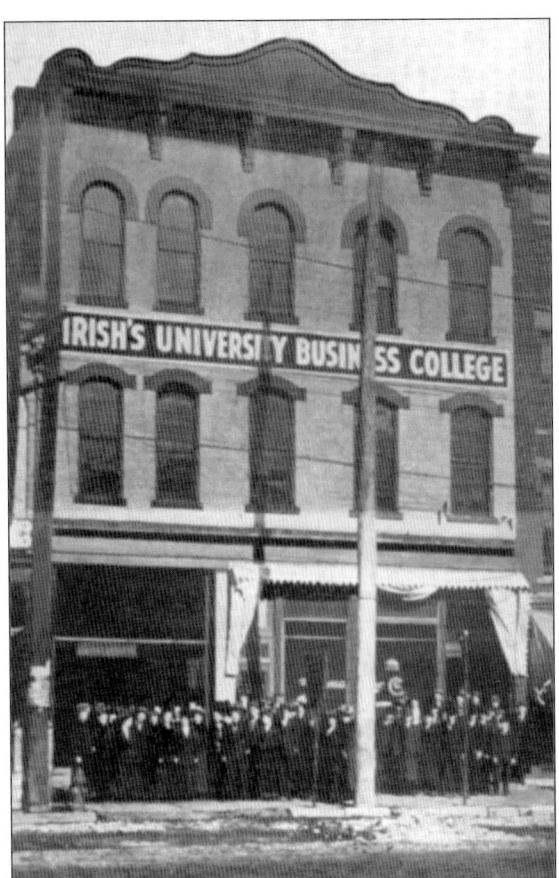

A great-grandmother to the local women's movement and child of a prominent local pioneer and newspaper family, Ms. Elizabeth Irish started offering shorthand and typing in 1895, with one of her classes shown in the 1905-era image at left. She added college prep classes for both sexes, finally retiring in 1940 at age 84.

Below, an Iowa City institution called Prairie Lights (a play on earlier Pacific Lights) is shown about 1980 in its 102 Linn Street location, before owner Jim Harris moved it to a double storefront along Dubuque Street. In this UNESCO-designated world-class "City of Literature" and home to the renowned Writers Workshop, book readings and signings at Prairie Lights have become a stop for local notables and classy writers from everywhere else.

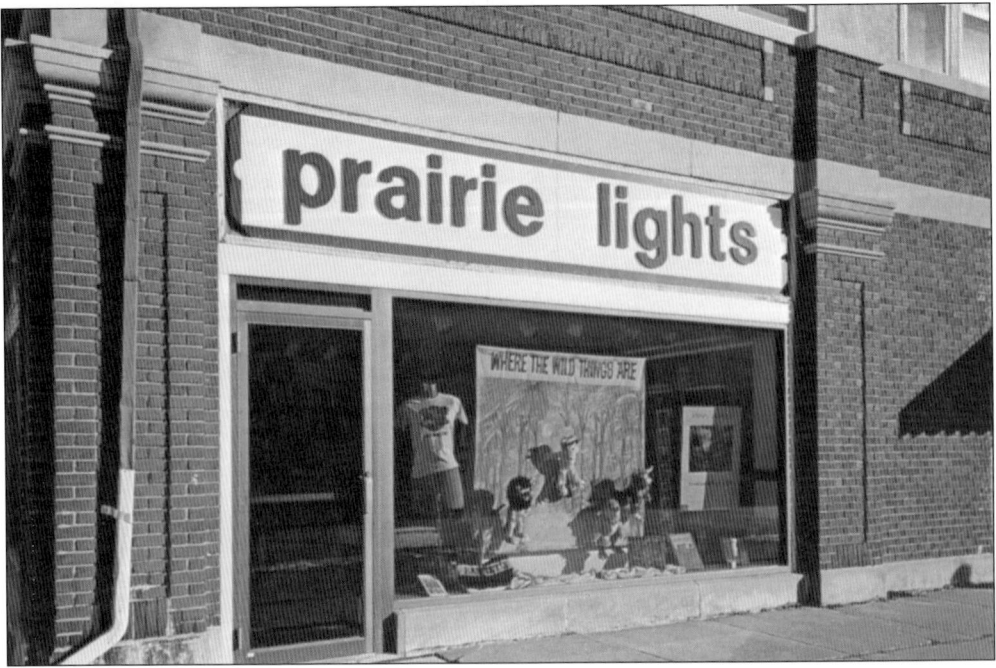

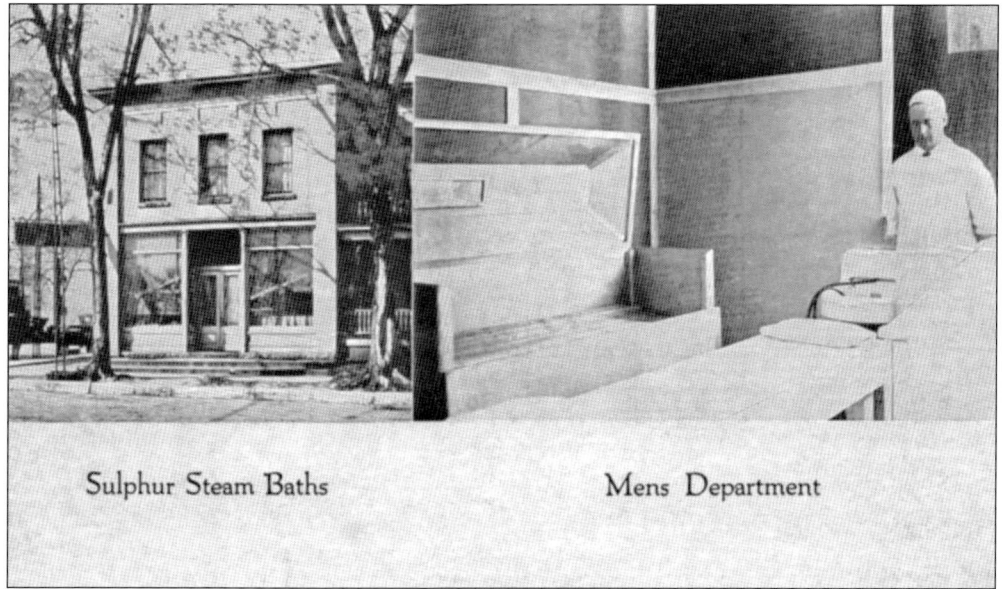

Sulphur Steam Baths   Mens Department

During the middle of the 19th century in Iowa City, natural springs, near what is now College Green, were piped into a facility near Iowa Avenue and Van Buren Street that offered "therapeutic mineral baths." Above, an image from 1917 offers "New and Improved Turkish Bath" a block south of Old Capitol at College and Capitol Streets. The bath "relieves rheumatism, lumbago, kidney troubles and other ailments," according to its postcard ad, mailed to Joe Anciaux on Route 9, Iowa City.

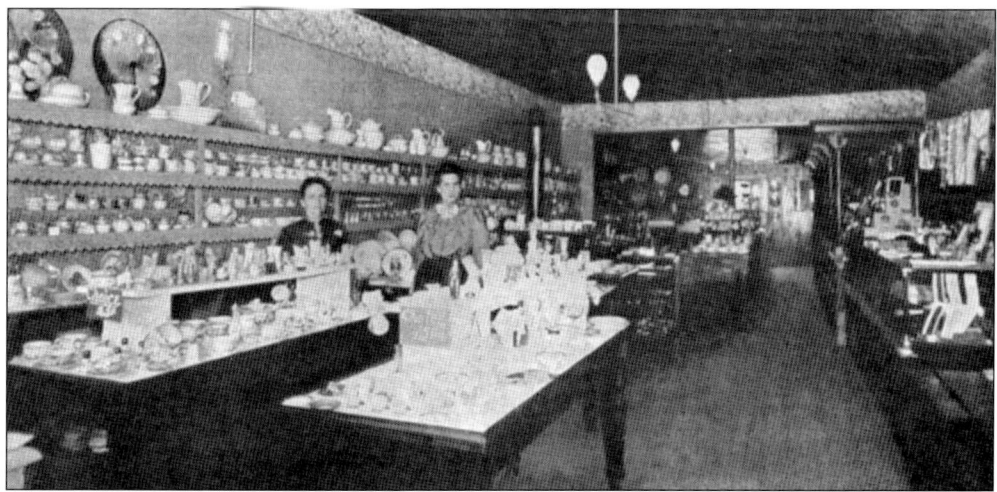

Above, Wallick's five-and-dime didn't last long after its opening about 1910, and it might have fallen below history's radar screen altogether had it not put out this postcard. It was in a good location at 118 East Washington Street, where it advertised: "We are growing slowly in our little place of business, and ask you kindly to help us grow. We have hundreds of 5 cent and 10 cent things and hundreds of better things." By 1922, barber John McGruder had moved his shop into this location from his 14 South Clinton Street location in 1920.

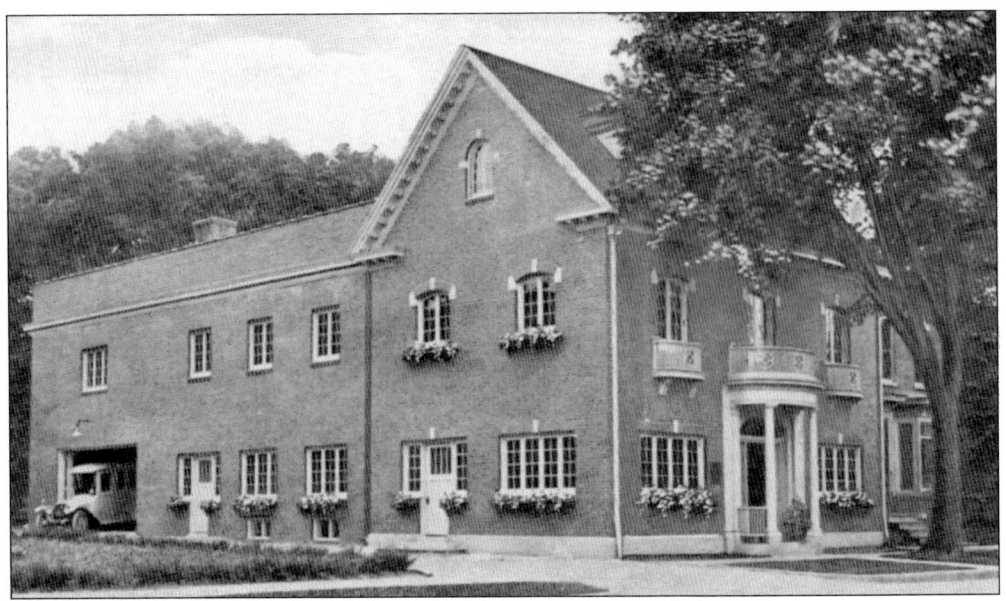

Hohenschuh's Mortuary at 7 South Linn Street speaks through this 1920-era postcard of its importance among the local Catholic community during half the 19th and early 20th centuries. Owner Will Hohenschuh, who also offered furniture in his earlier site on Dubuque Street, was heralded internationally for textbooks and his wide teaching and demonstration of embalming techniques. He also was an instigator and substantial investor in erecting Hotel Jefferson during 1912–1913. Subsequent owners of this funeral home included John Donohue, and later his son Walter Donohue, and then Mike Lensing.

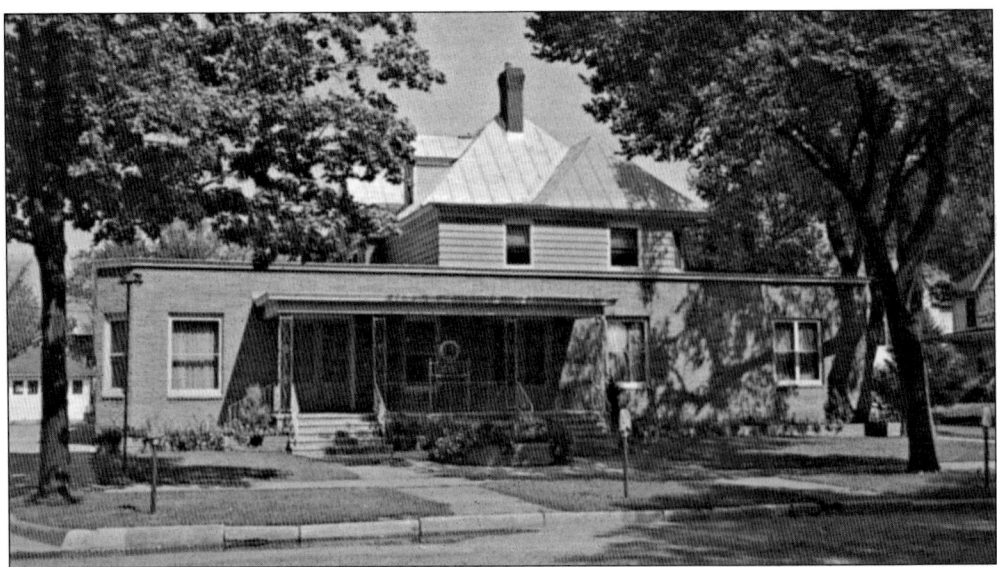

A 1962 fire razed the Oathout Funeral Home, seen below at 336 South Clinton Street, killing a 53-year-old overnight caretaker. Redeveloped as the Rebel Motel, it morphed into offices and was razed after being damaged by a 2006 tornado. Located just across the street from both post office and courthouse, it now boasts a new commercial building.

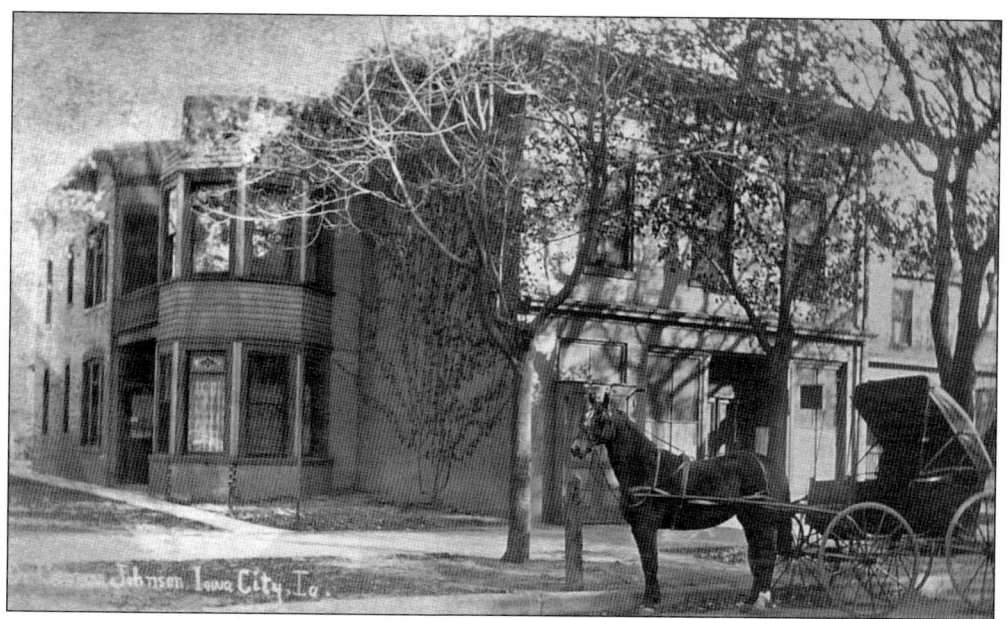

A plethora of physicians now ply their trade in Iowa City. It has been so during much of the town's 170-year history. A pair who did so a century ago is represented by these two postcard scenes, rare in the fact that they preserve moments of history often lost in the midst of time. Above, Leora Johnson at 22 North Clinton Street is represented, and below likewise for an unidentified "MBL" who signed a 1907 holiday greeting addressed to Worchester, Massachusetts.

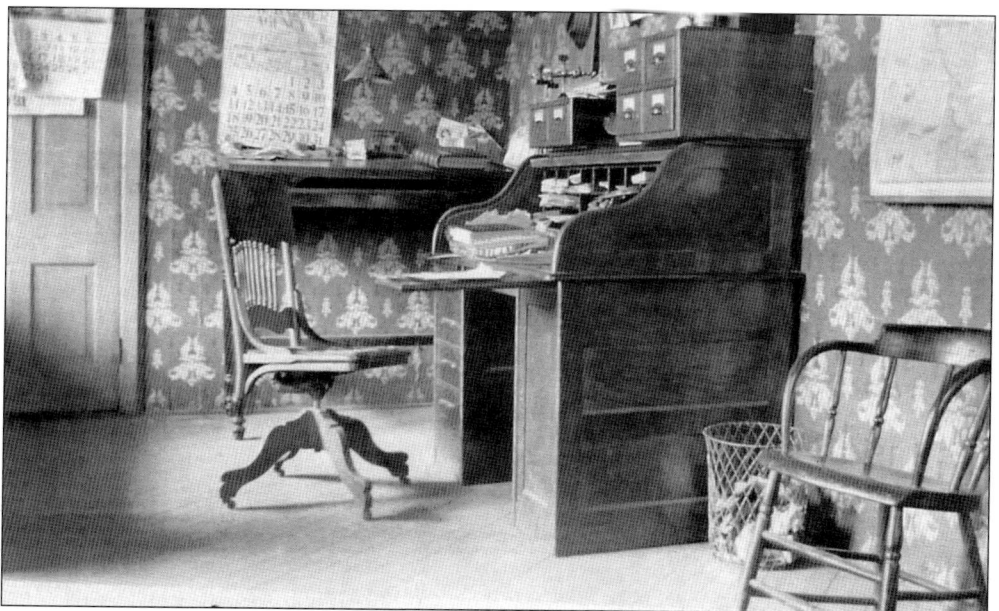

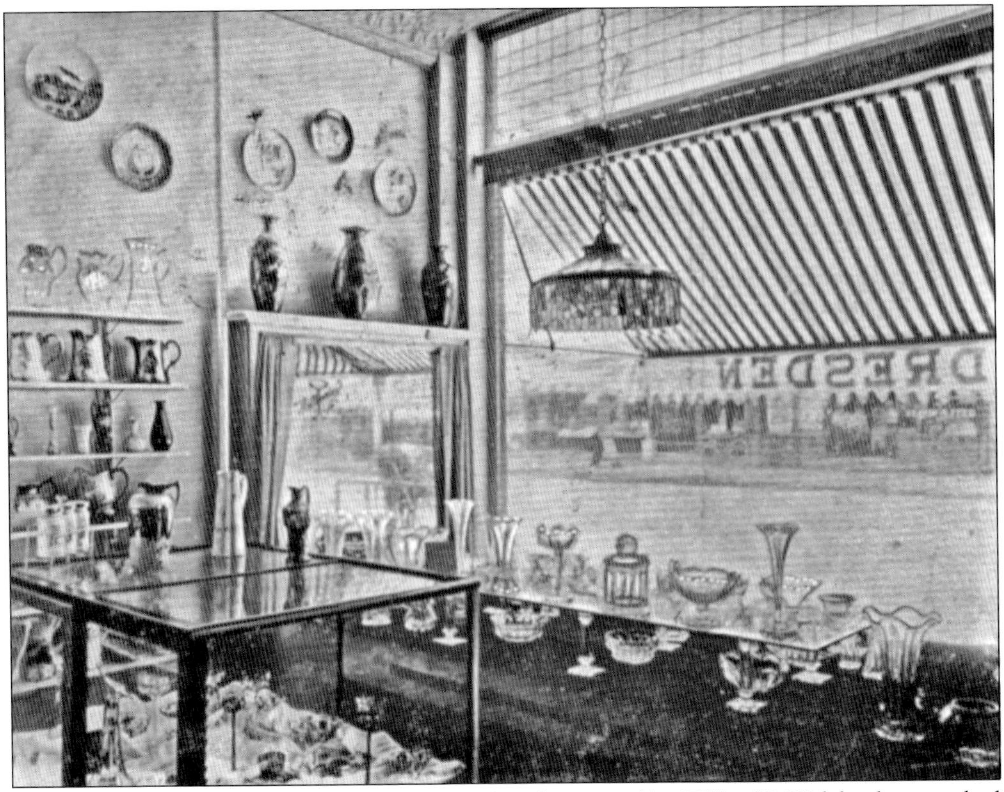

The Dresden China Shop was an Iowa City landmark operated by Willard J. Welch who morphed his grocery business into glassware during the final quarter of the 19th century. Dresden refers to quality glassware produced in a German city of that name. The world wars reduced Dresden to rubble, forever ending its supply to Iowa City.

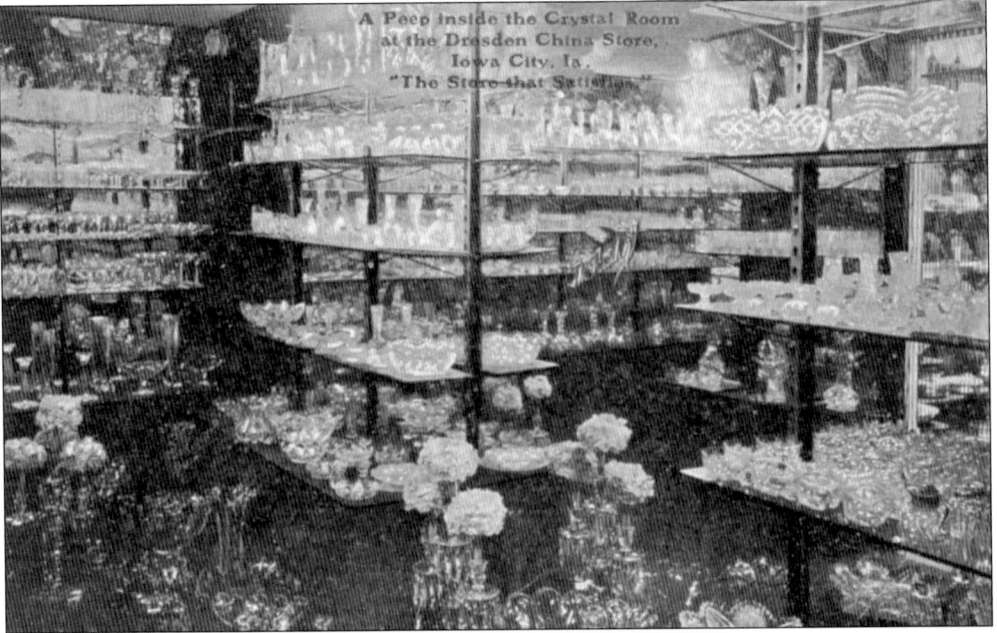

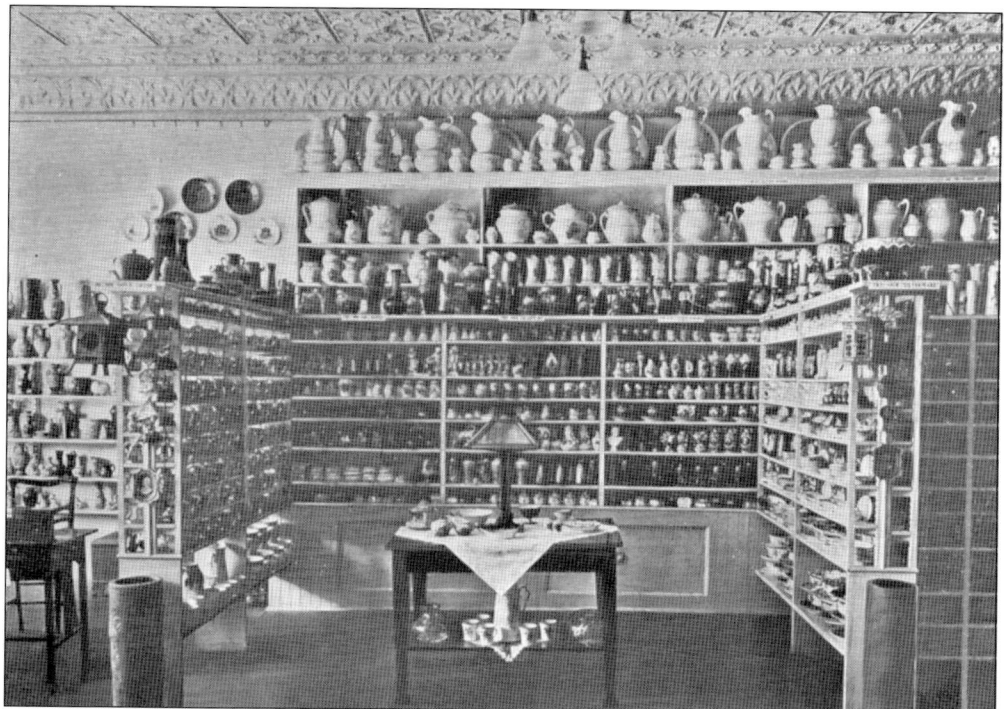

Uniquely designed, clearly marked, and now highly collectible local souvenirs were designed and sold at the Dresden, which occupied space now home to Prairie Lights books. Owner Willard Welch provided important 1908–1928 library board service.

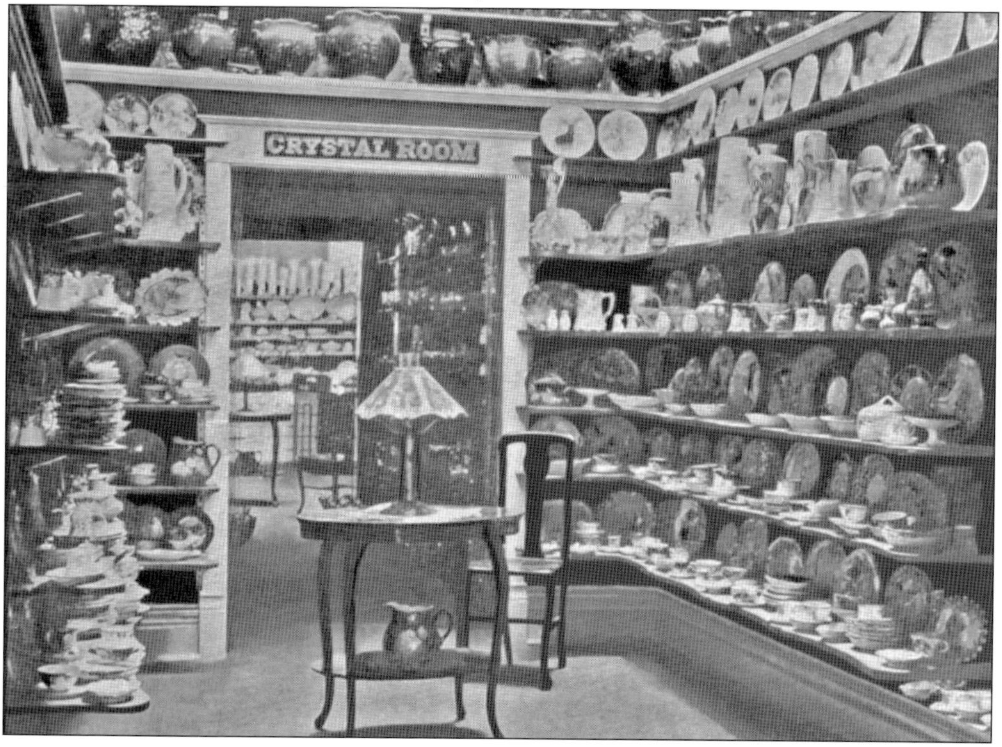

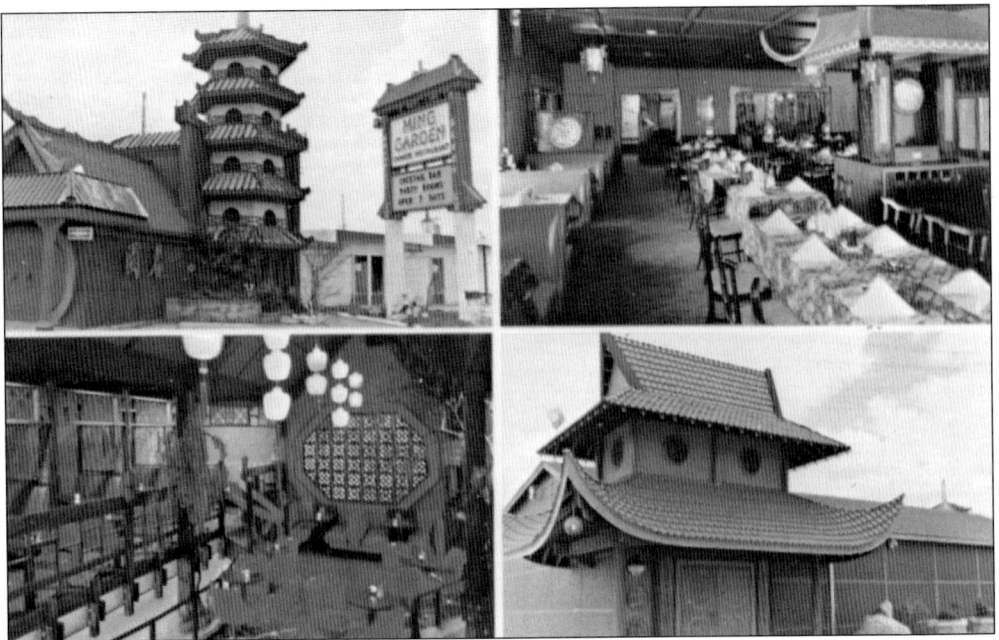

Ming Garden hailed from "The Coralville Strip" during the third quarter of the 20th century. Its Hung Far Lounge in the lower left of the 1960-era image above included a water feature complete with goldfish. It succumbed to "progress" about 1983.

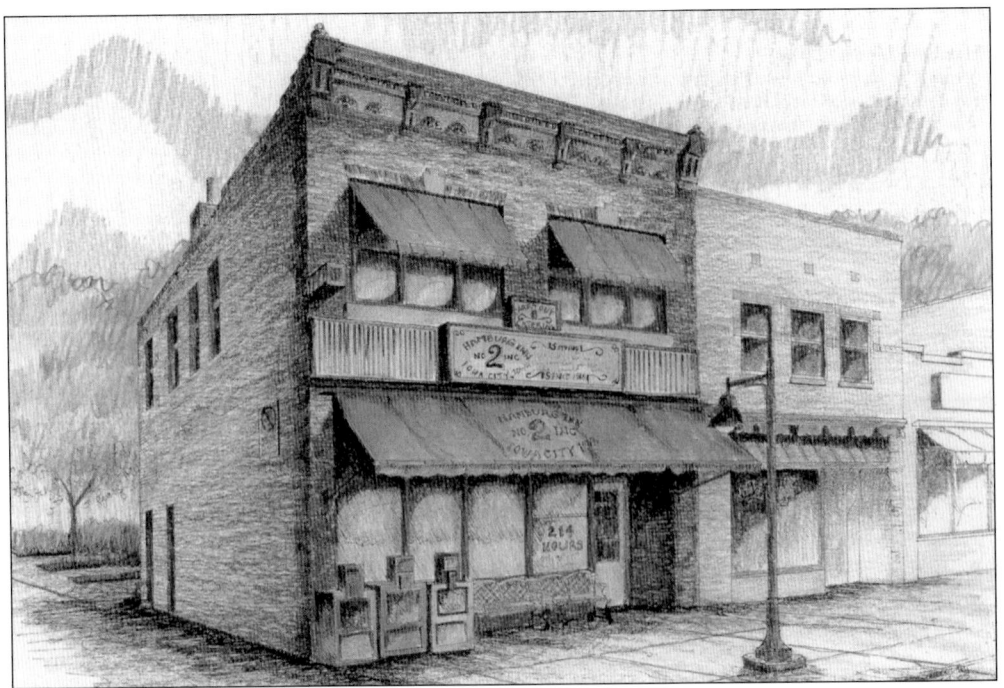

Above, a survivor is the Hamburg Inn, which began life during the 1950s and carries on today. It has a reputation of serving presidents Reagan and Clinton, plus scores of wannabees each political season, which now seems to extend year round every year!

Three

FUN AND FROLICS
CHAUTAUQUA, THEATERS, AND SPORTS

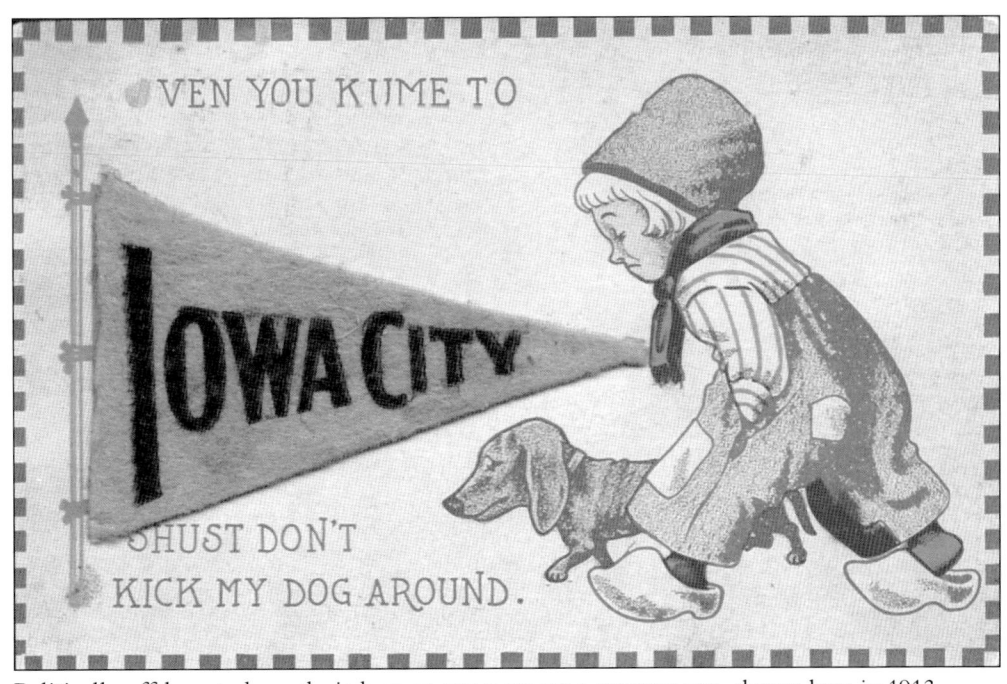

Politically off-base today, ethnic humor was rampant a century ago, shown here in 1913.

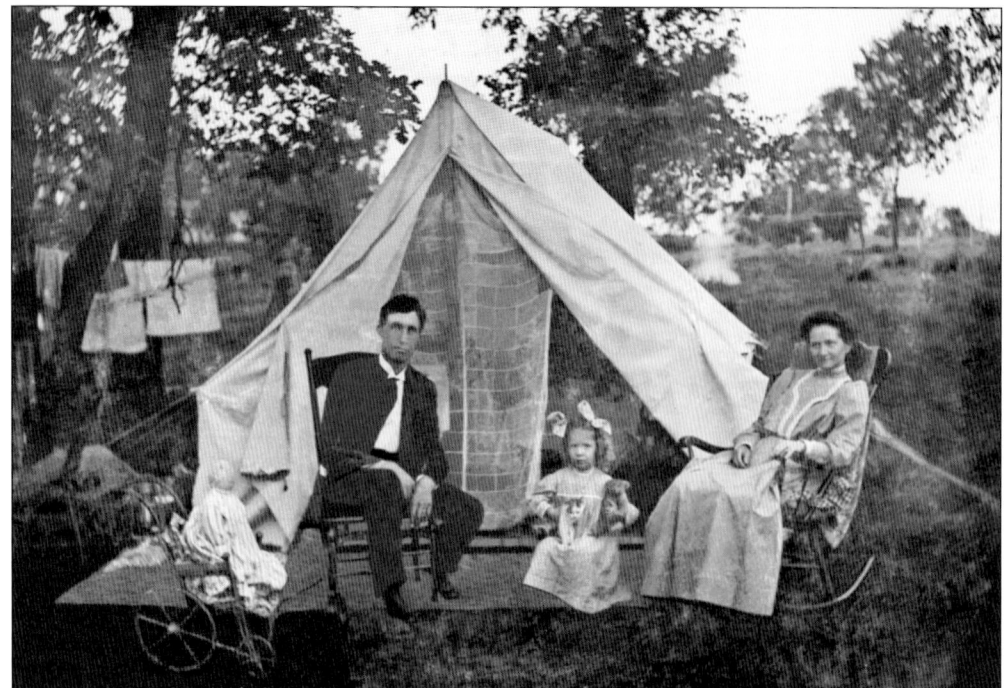

Iowa City Chautauqua offered relief from summer heat in the breezy bluffs above the river in what now is the Manville Heights neighborhood from 1906 into the 1920s. In August 1907, a card signed, "Eleanor, Mary, and Walter" show them posed outside their motor home.

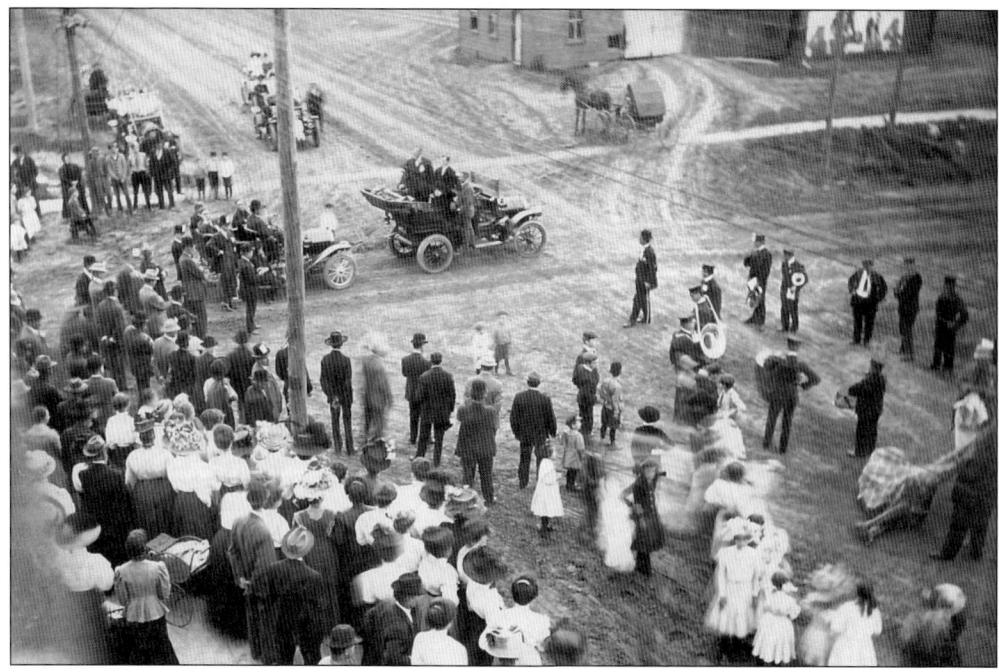

Ambassador business groups organized parade units to visit town celebrations, as with these "Iowa City Boosters" rolling along a Lone Tree street during April 1910.

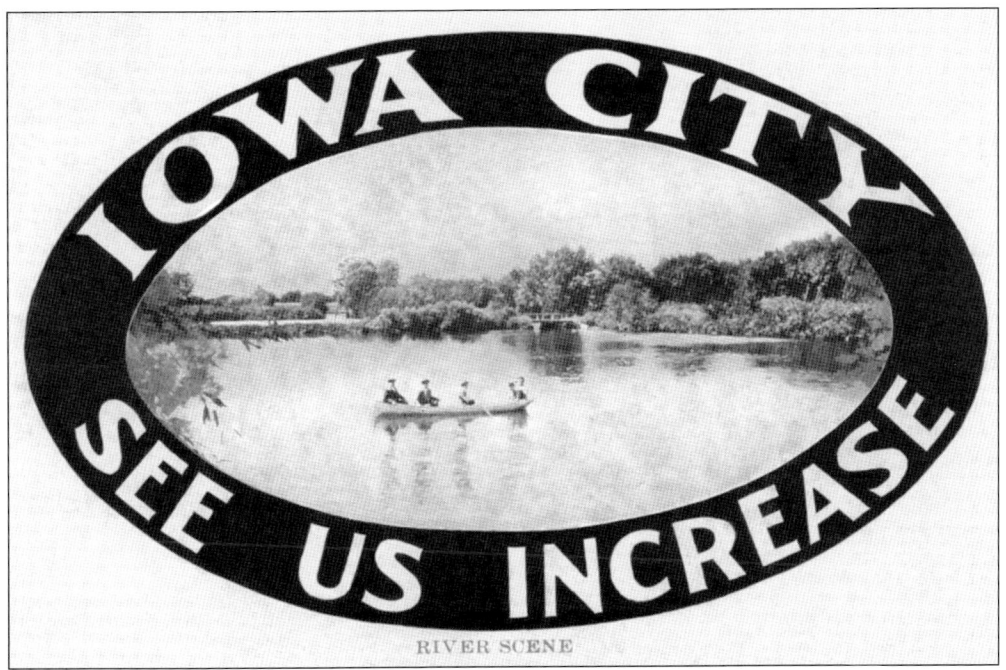
RIVER SCENE

The university in Iowa City has experienced an evolution in its name, beginning in the 1847 constitution as "State University"; later "Iowa State," which now serves its sister in Ames; then "State University of Iowa"; and now "University of Iowa." When it was working to evolve to the SUI name, a promotion during fall 1910 used those new initials to create this "See Us Increase" motto. It appeared in both university and community materials including these postcard images. The one above is perhaps a canal scene in New York, but the one below does feature Iowa City's 1881 City Hall.

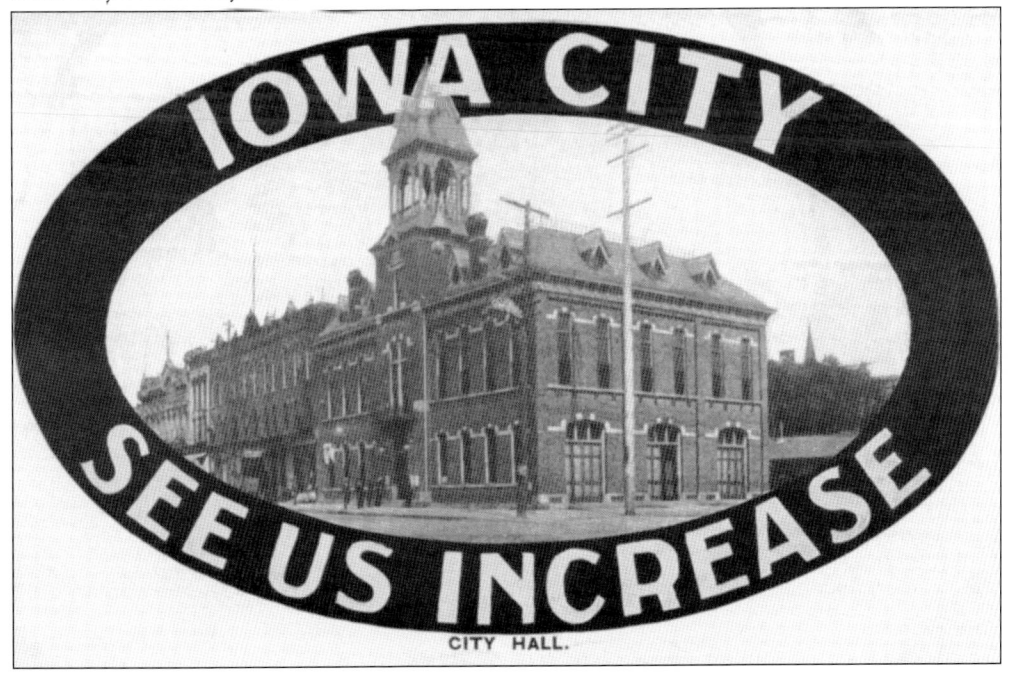
CITY HALL.

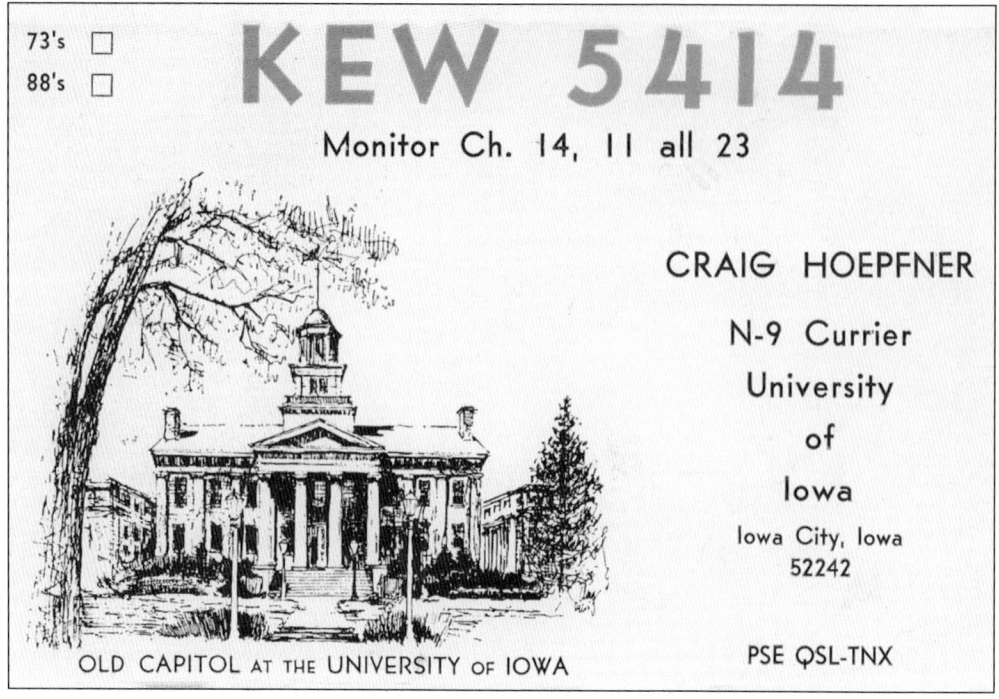

Amateur or "ham" radio hobbyists are constantly trying to reach farther with their signal, talk to someone in every state, or on every continent. Still today, they regularly rebuild the electronics and antennas of their "stations" to do so. During an initial early-20th-century explosion in participating numbers, postcards were used to confirm signal "picked up" in a specific locale, to chatter about strength and ideas, or simply to further friendly social contact. Samples include one above from the Currier dorm on the UI campus, and another below from a Washington Street residence.

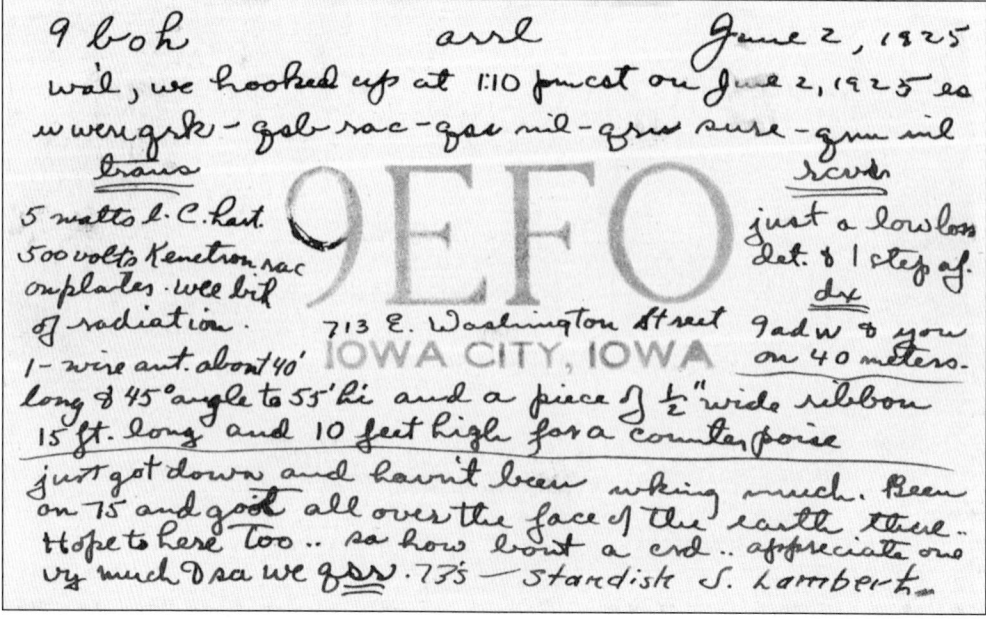

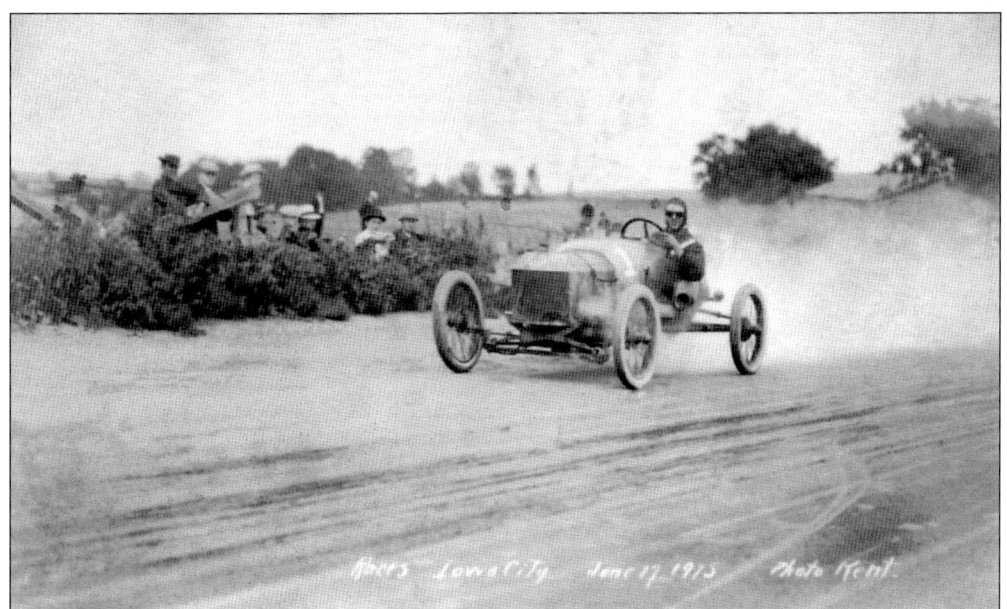

Fairgrounds in the Morningside Drive neighborhood now capped on the hill by City High provided a site for this "Races" postcard image by local photographer legend and naturalist Fred Kent, dated in his hand as June 17, 1915.

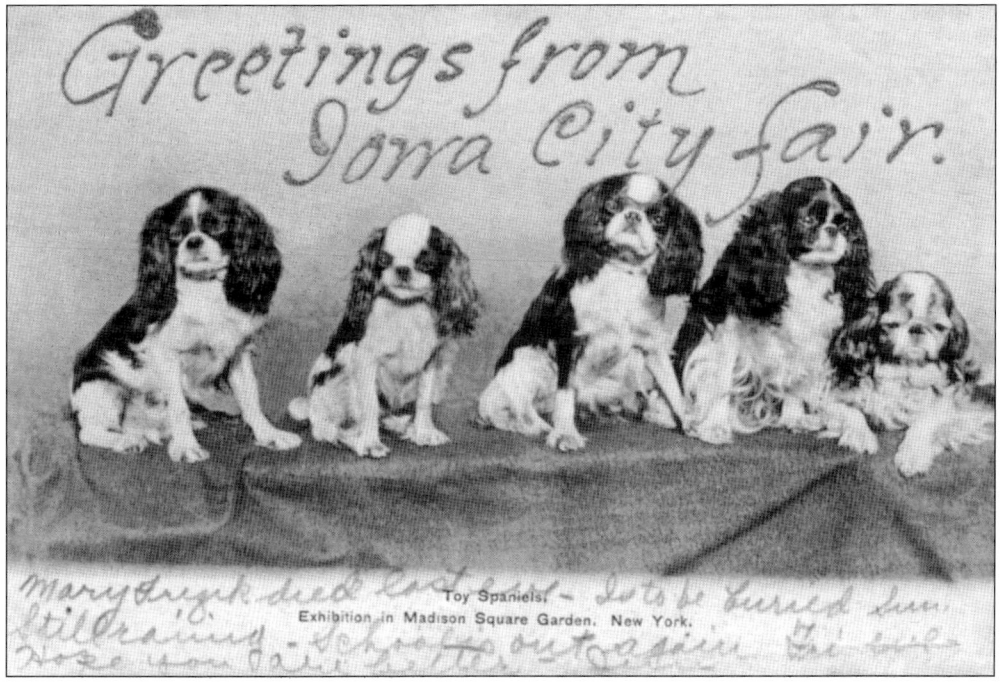

Fairs in Iowa City date from 1853, when one occurred on the statehouse grounds, now the university's Old Capitol Pentacrest campus. The card below represents one in 1907 on 40 acres, or about 19 square blocks, now the City High area. The message isn't about fairs at all but carries all sorts of absolutely depressing news and weather.

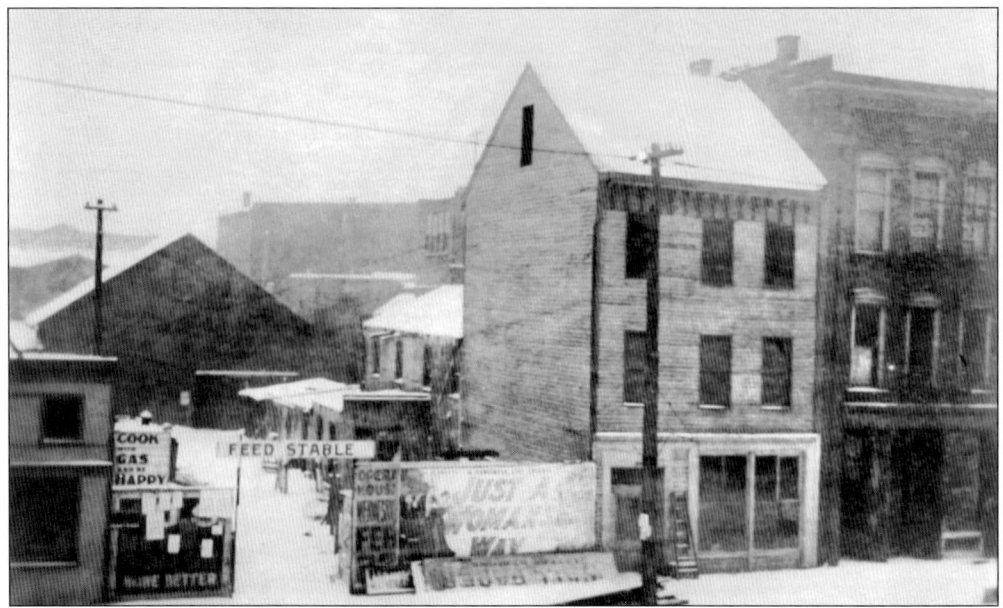

The Englert Theatre is an Iowa City institution dating to its September 26, 1912, opening on this snow-covered site, shown about 1907 or 1908, of predecessors Foster Livery and the Schuttler Hotel in the light-colored, three-story structure. The Paul-Helen building succeeded the one at right during 1911.

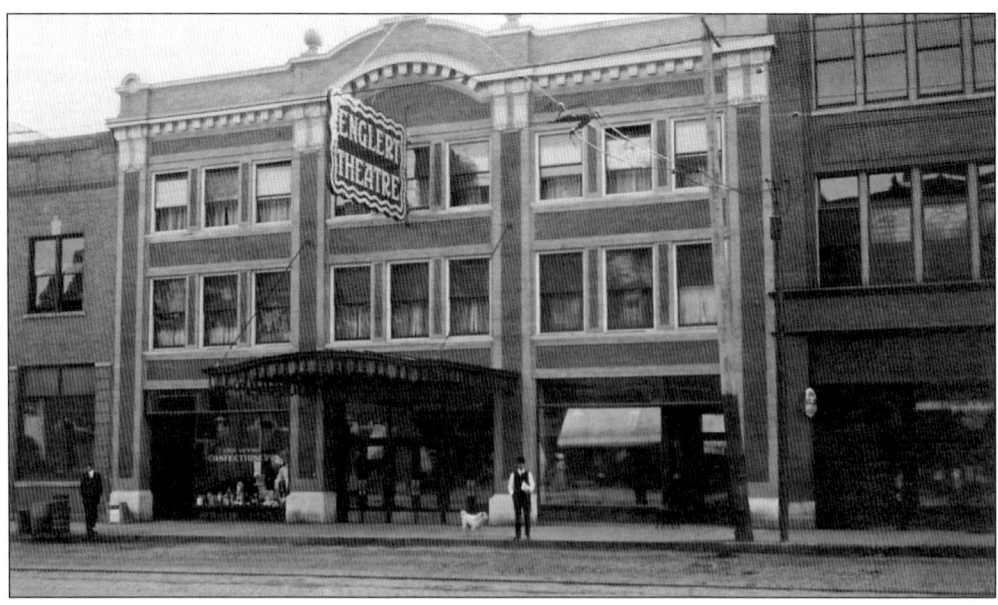

Above, on opening day as both legitimate stage and movie house, the original Englert Theatre front featured a flat mundane rectangular sign hung high above a hotel drive-under-type canopy. More garish marquees came along well after a 1926 fire burned out the original interior. The likes of Ethel Barrymore, Sarah Bernhardt, and Ed Wynn peopled its stage, and up to 60-piece orchestras accompanied such motion picture fare as Covered Wagon and All Quiet on the Western Front.

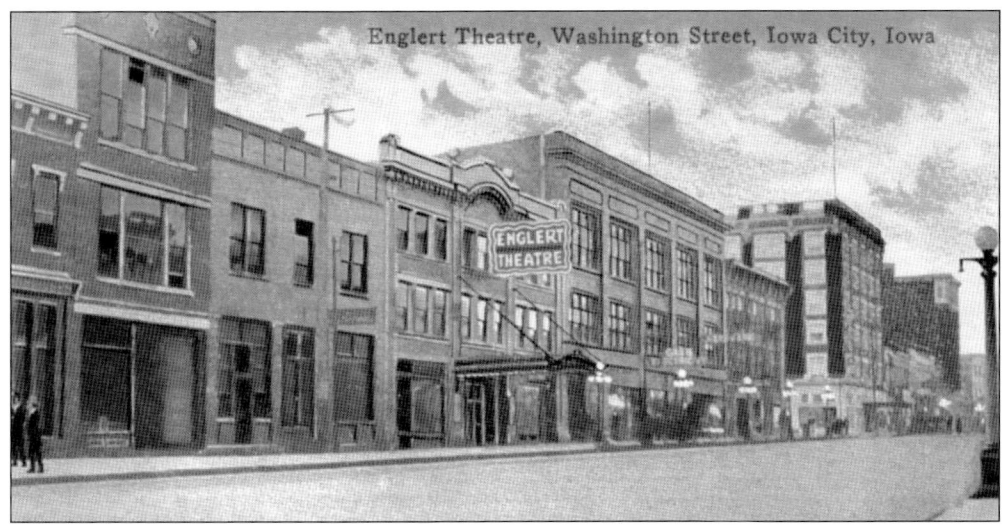

Named for the family who originally built it, the Englert Theatre occupies the center of this 1915-era image. With the Paul-Helen building adjacent, the original six floors of the 1913 Hotel Jefferson before it was extended two floors during 1928, and at far right, the six-story Johnson County Savings Bank (later Iowa State Bank) was erected in 1912. The street surfaces would have been littered with "road apples" from horses that had used the livery that the Englert replaced. Few cars were yet in use.

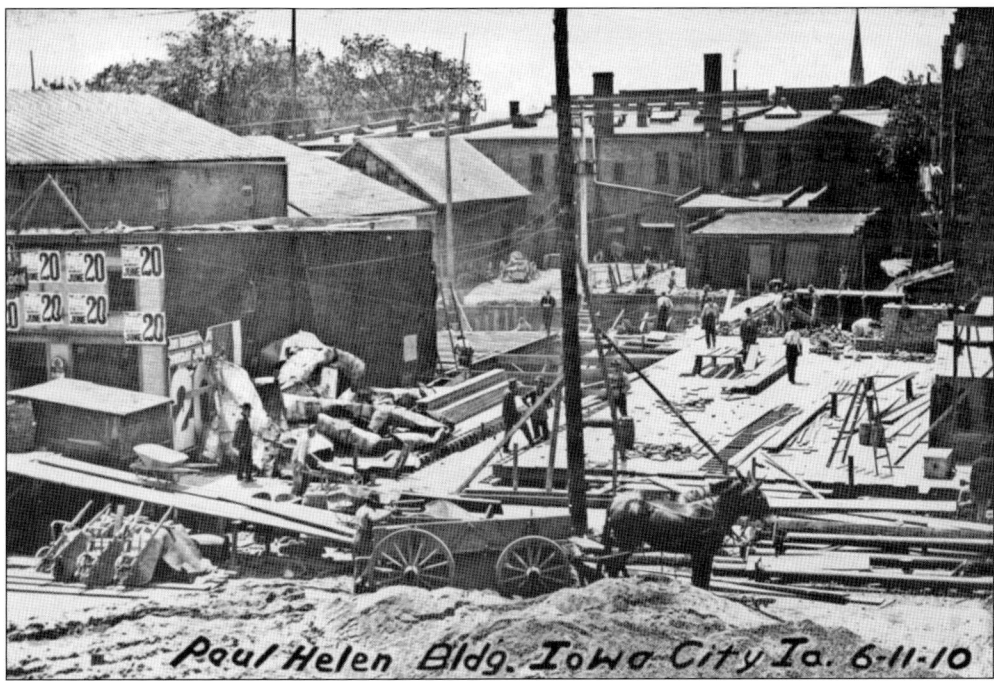

The Paul-Helen building next door to the Englert—home to the gas and electric utility for decades and later to other stores, plus offices upstairs–displays "by hand" construction in the 1910 image above. The owners named it for two of their children.

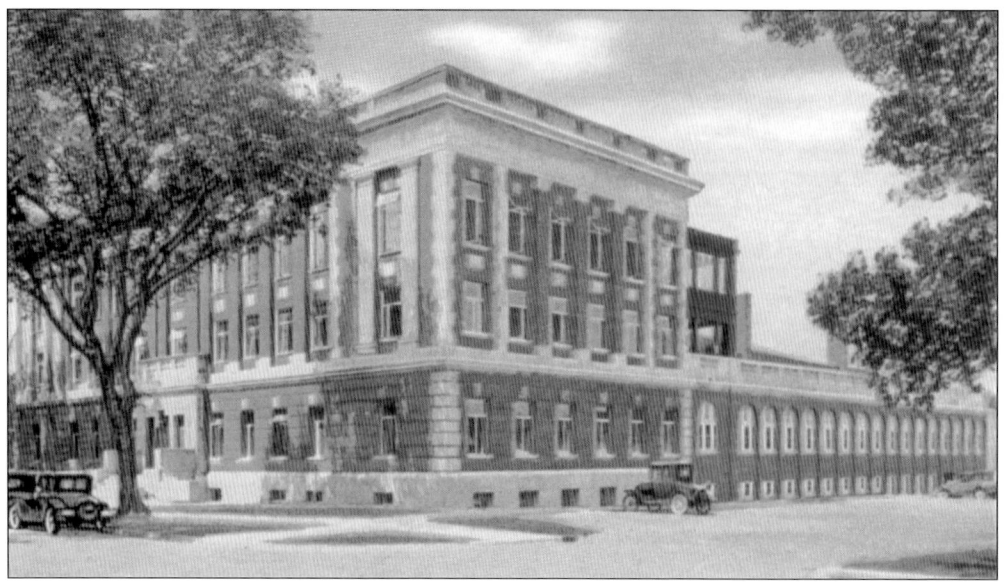

The "memorial" in Iowa Memorial Union was intended to boost fund-raising efforts by honoring World War I warriors in naming the university's first student activities facility built specifically for the purpose. Fund-raising efforts failed, only eventually to be bailed out by the faculty's Triangle Club, which offered to lease a large area for 50 years to create a commercial financing opportunity. Above, the 1925 and 1927 sections of the now much larger IMU structure are offered in this postcard image.

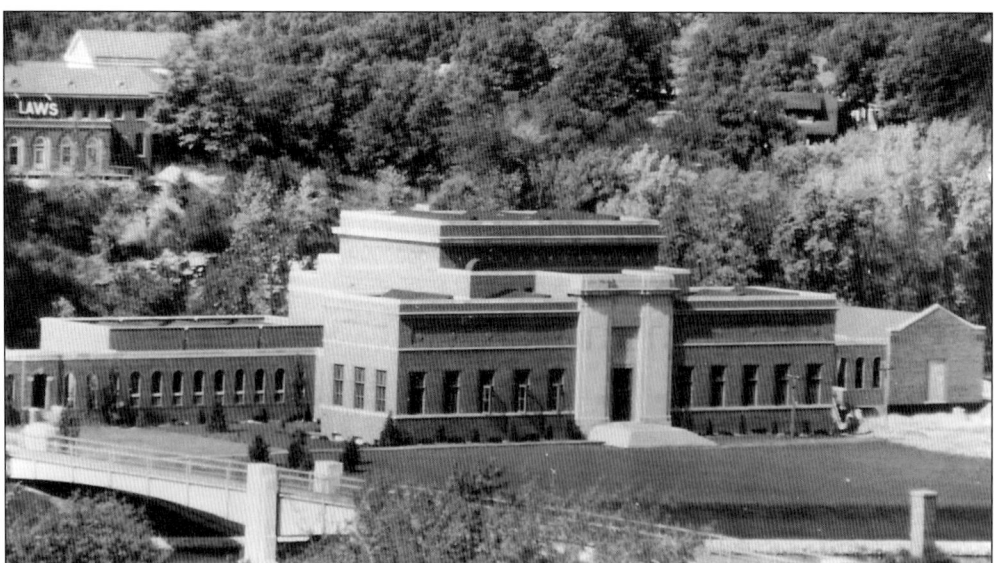

On marsh landfill dirt, wagoned to the site from the 30-foot-deep bowl dug for Kinnick Stadium during 1928, the original 1934 Art Building shines in utter newness in this postcard image. It and the Law Commons dormitory visible on the bluff above the river plain experienced shared births using WPA money. The dormitory was demolished for a new edifice, and the Art Building was simultaneously destroyed by a 2008 flood.

40

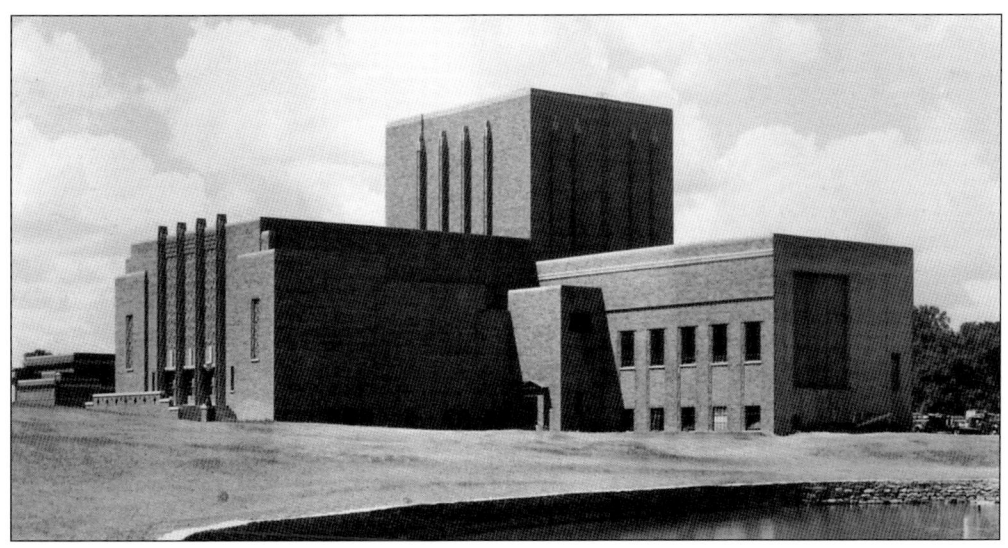

As the University of Iowa (UI) prepared for what would become a fine arts coup d'état in 1938, in addition to its new art building of two years earlier, it erected University Theatre along the same bank of the river, shown here in a 1940s image. Art and theater were the first elements of what would become an extensive fine arts complex including an art museum, music building, recital halls, and a large performing arts venue. In 1938, the university rocked academia with an announcement that it would accept paintings, plays, compositions, and other art works to fulfill composition requirements for advanced degrees. Fine arts blossomed at Iowa during subsequent decades.

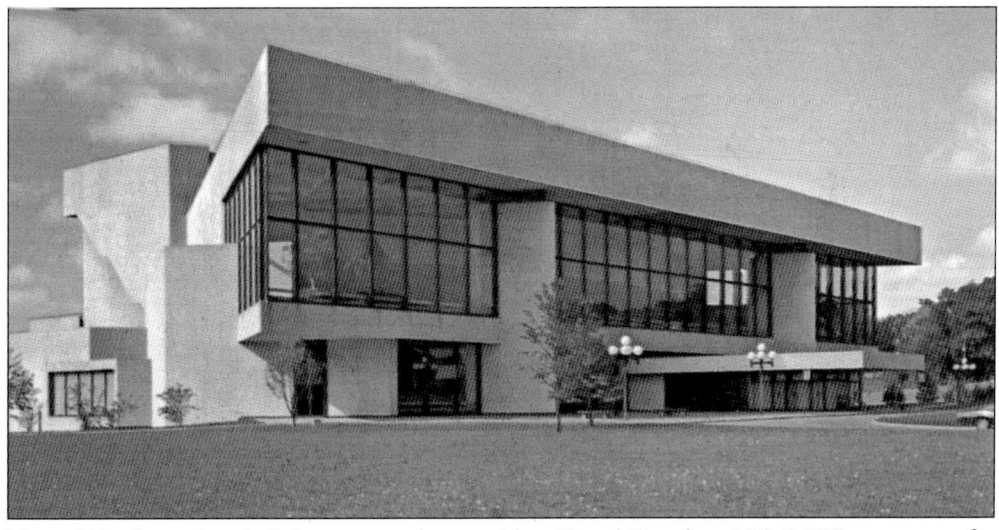

Named for the university's longest serving president Virgil Hancher, UI's 2,500-seat venue for performing arts—including graduation exercises for individual colleges, and other activities—is presented by a 1975-era image below. Hancher Auditorium and the rest of the nearly billion-dollar fine arts campus facilities were protected by a large reservoir and its associated dam upstream 10 miles on the Iowa River. The entire arts campus was lost to a 2008 flood that ensued as the river poured over the dam's spillway for weeks.

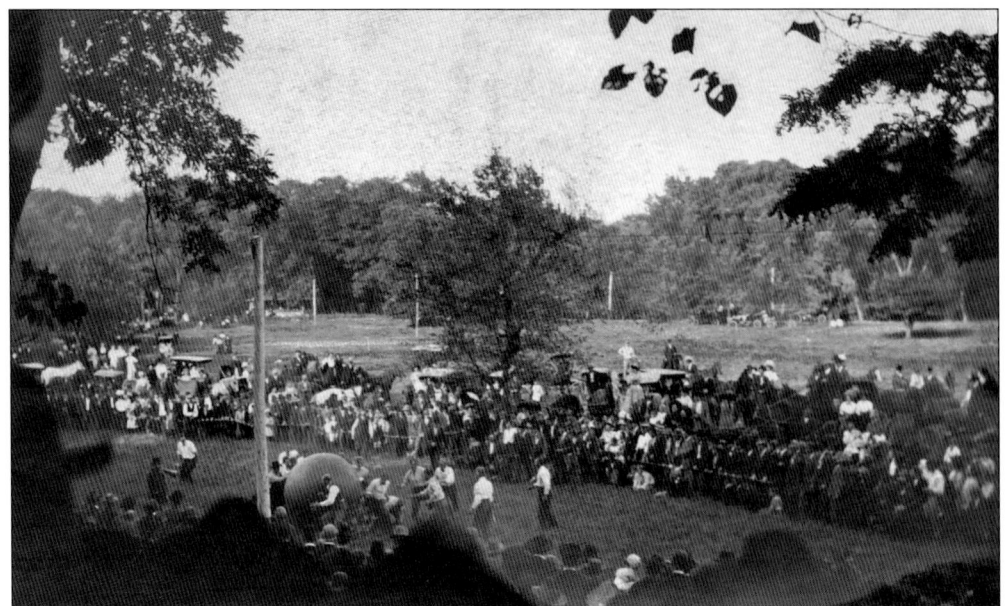

Before flag football, basketball, volleyball, tennis, soccer, and other such "modern" games came to dominate playtime among families and friends, it was baseball and pushball that took the cake. Above, "Farmers' Day" in City Park sponsored by the local commercial club (now Chamber of Commerce) provides a fall 1909 image of a pushball contest using a standard six-foot diameter ball to be rolled across goals at either end of the field. It was a gentlemanly endeavor, of course.

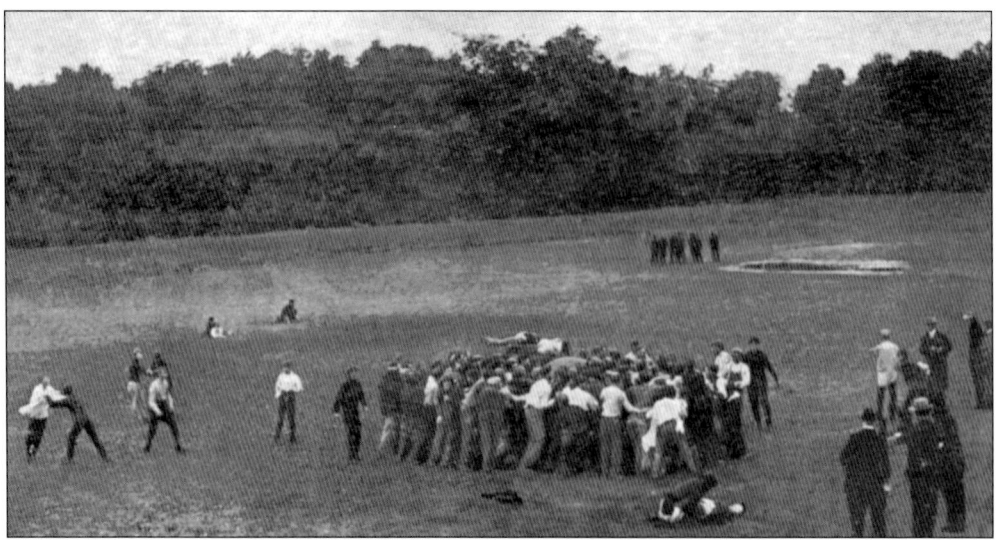

A not-so-gentlemanly contest occurs during a fall 1908 freshman-sophomore match in Athletic Park, where the baseball pitcher's mound is visible at right. Intended to put freshmen "in their place," matches often resulted in fisticuffs, with three such events occurring as the main game continues. Football was played at the far (Burlington Street) end of this field before Kinnick Stadium was built in 1929.

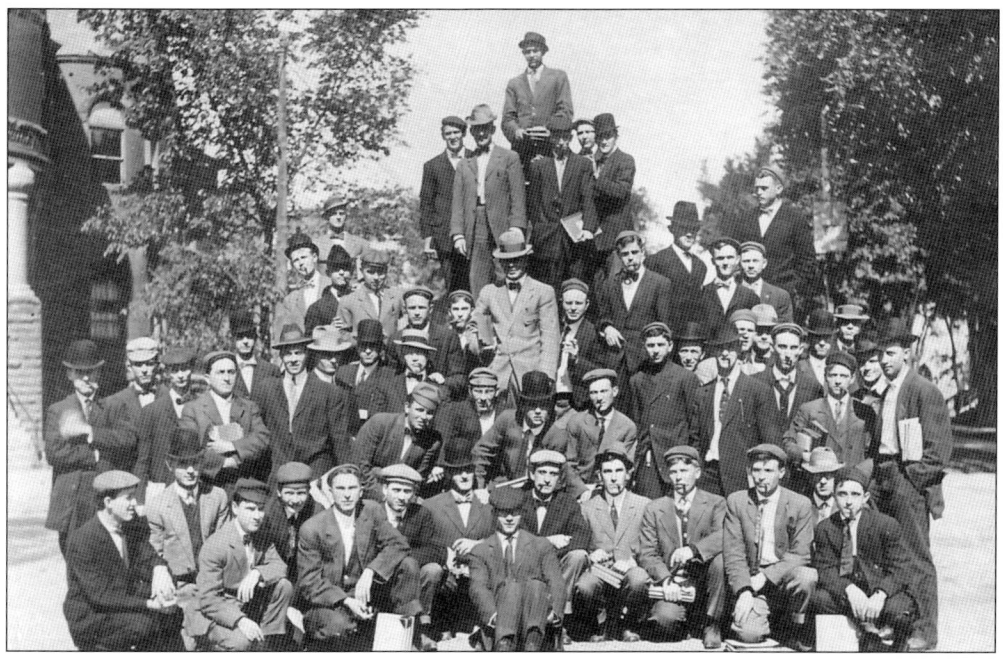

Aquatic appurtenances are both useful and fun things. Above, a fraternity or college group sits and stands on an early fountain in Iowa City centered in the Iowa Avenue and Dubuque Street intersection. Provided by the Women's Improvement League about 1905, as below, the fountain offered water to horses. Fraternities used it regularly for hazing and tarnished its reputation. A 1909 offer from a new trolley company to move it to the upper level of City Park made way for center-of-the-street tracks in its former location.

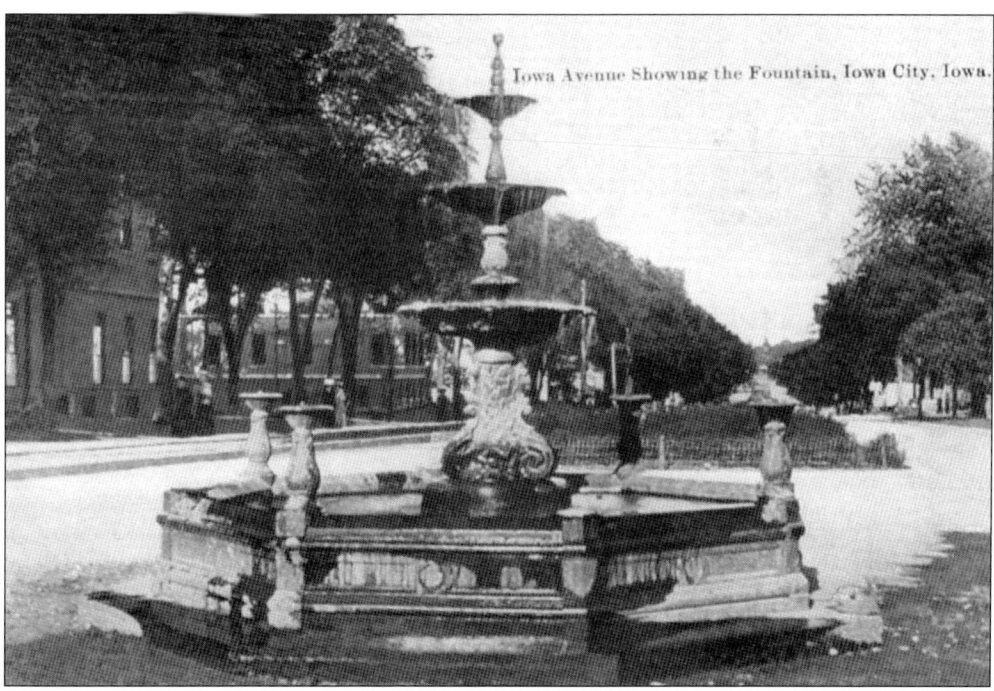

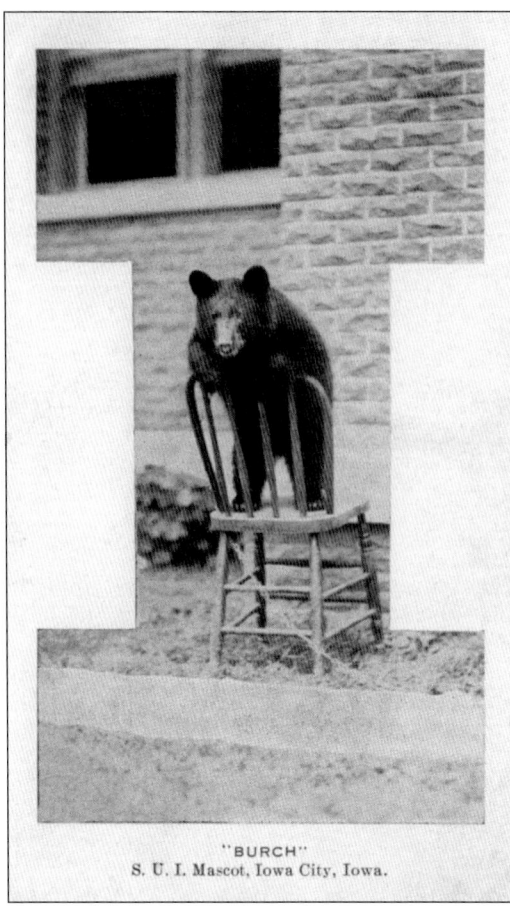

"BURCH"
S. U. I. Mascot, Iowa City, Iowa.

Herky the bear somehow does not fit, nor did the "Burch" mascot offered by students during 1909, as shown in the image at left. Burch's chain can be seen dangling below the chair seat. The poor guy drowned in the Iowa River, which ran along the west edge of Athletic Park between Iowa Avenue and Burlington Street, an area used during pre-Kinnick days for intercollegiate baseball and football games. Likewise for the Great Dane Rex, another mascot that thrilled fans before making an unsuccessful attempt to ford the river. Both short-lived mascots were kept by fraternity men, which may offer an insight to their temperaments.

University "Yell Leaders" pose for Fred Kent's camera in 1920 on Iowa Field, below Athletic Park stands and fencing. The stands were so tight they stretched out over the river on one side, and over the CRandIC tracks carrying electric cars that passed the other side of the field.

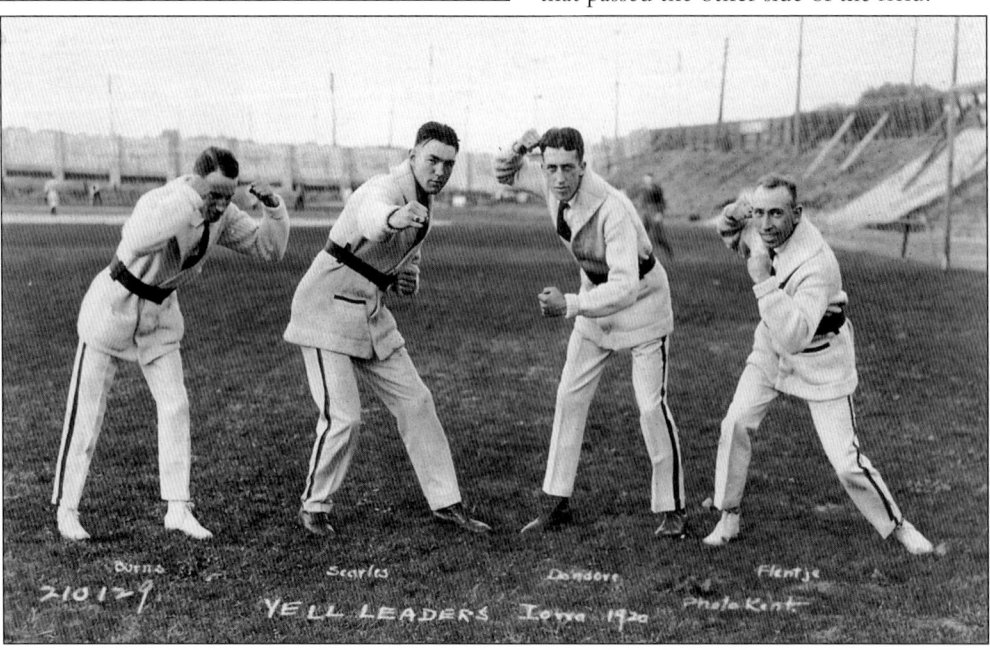

Herky the Hawk, seen at right, first surfaced on Iowa gridiron during 1948, created by the imagination of journalism instructor and 1942 UI graduate Dick Spencer. Spencer's mascot was named by John Franklin of Belle Plaine in a statewide contest. The Hawkeye name, often shortened to simply the "Hawks," comes from that of the sharp-eyed and stealthy Native American hero in James Fennimore Cooper's 1826 novel *Last of the Mohicans*.

Kinnick Stadium is packed for a football contest when it had only "knothole" seating on the grassy slope of the north end zone and a 1958-built west press box above the post–World War II student housing Stadium Park barracks complex. North end zone stands now house the student section in a rising aerie, and a new press box features a full-feature club atmosphere for high rollers.

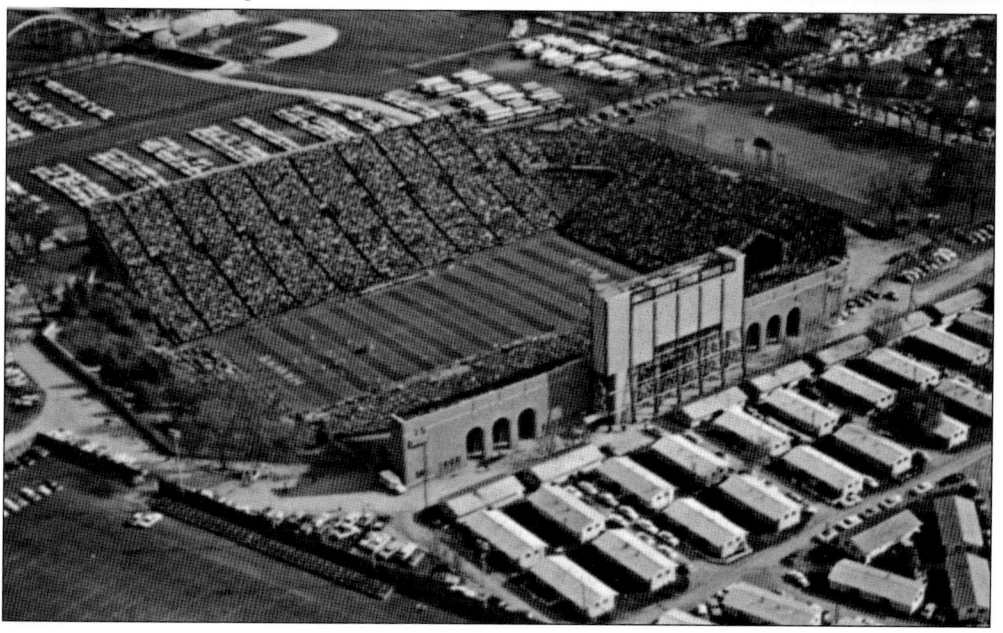

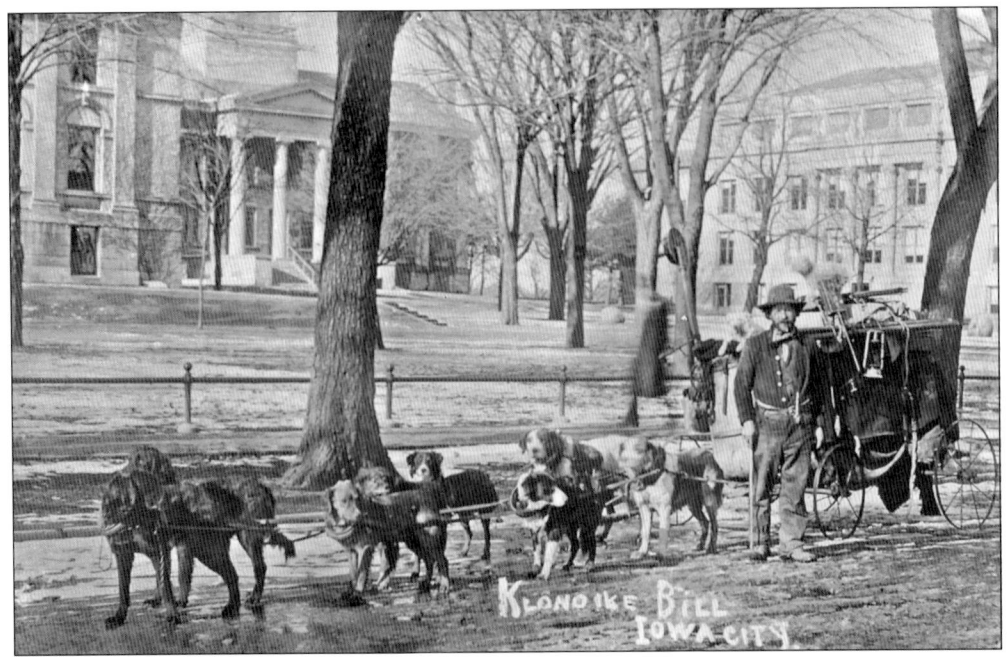

An itinerant character who the photographer identifies as "Klondike Bill" poses on Clinton Street along the Pentacrest Campus, stopping sometime soon after Macbride Hall, at right, was completed during 1908. Photographers are never satisfied with just one shot, as demonstrated here by one image with the lead dog standing and likewise the team, and a few feet farther down the street with the lead dog lying down and the team seeming ready to follow suit. Homelessness is the terminology of the modern age, but whether this gentleman fits that phenomenon or some other is unknown.

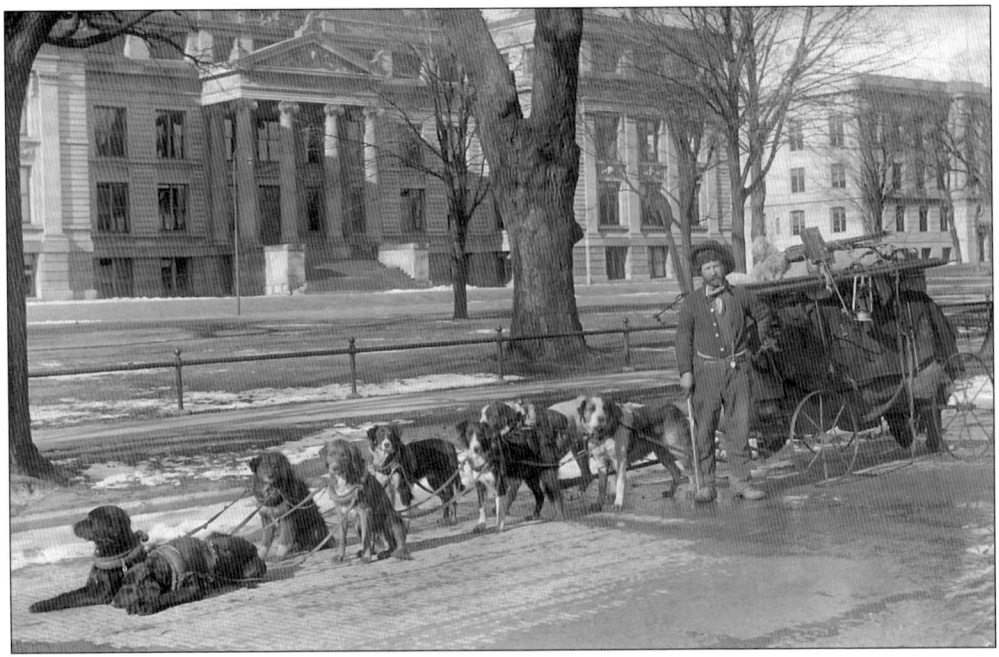

Four

BUSINESS AND WEATHER
HATCHERY, BANKS, AND WEATHER STATION

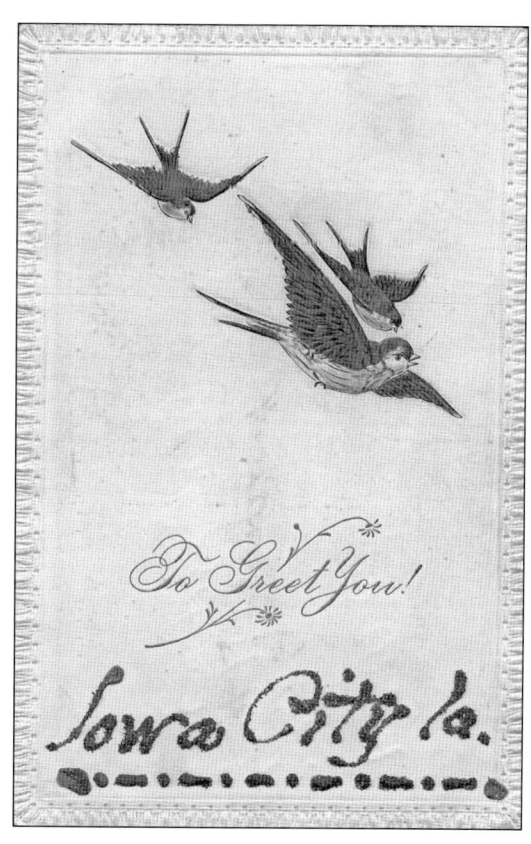

A fluted, 1910-era card printed in Germany is shown here.

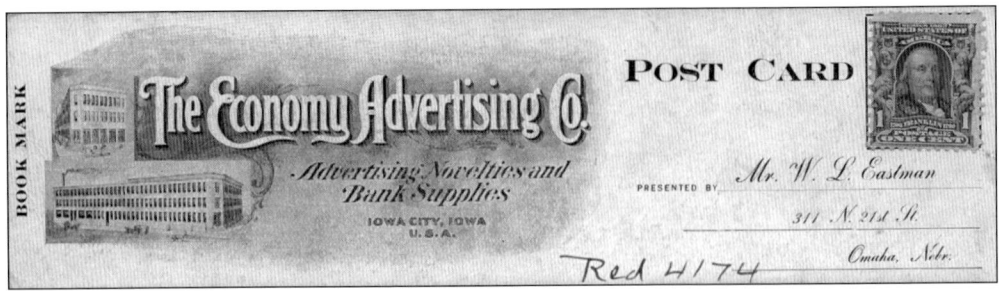

The little jewel above measures 2 inches by 7.25 inches, by far the smallest among 3,000-plus in the author's collection of Iowa City cards. Per printing on its left edge, it is intended as a bookmark, so the user would have ready access to the advertising for the services of a longtime Iowa City company still operating today, a national purveyor of calendars and novelties of all sorts. All are aimed at advertising a product or service. This one has been working for its creator for a century.

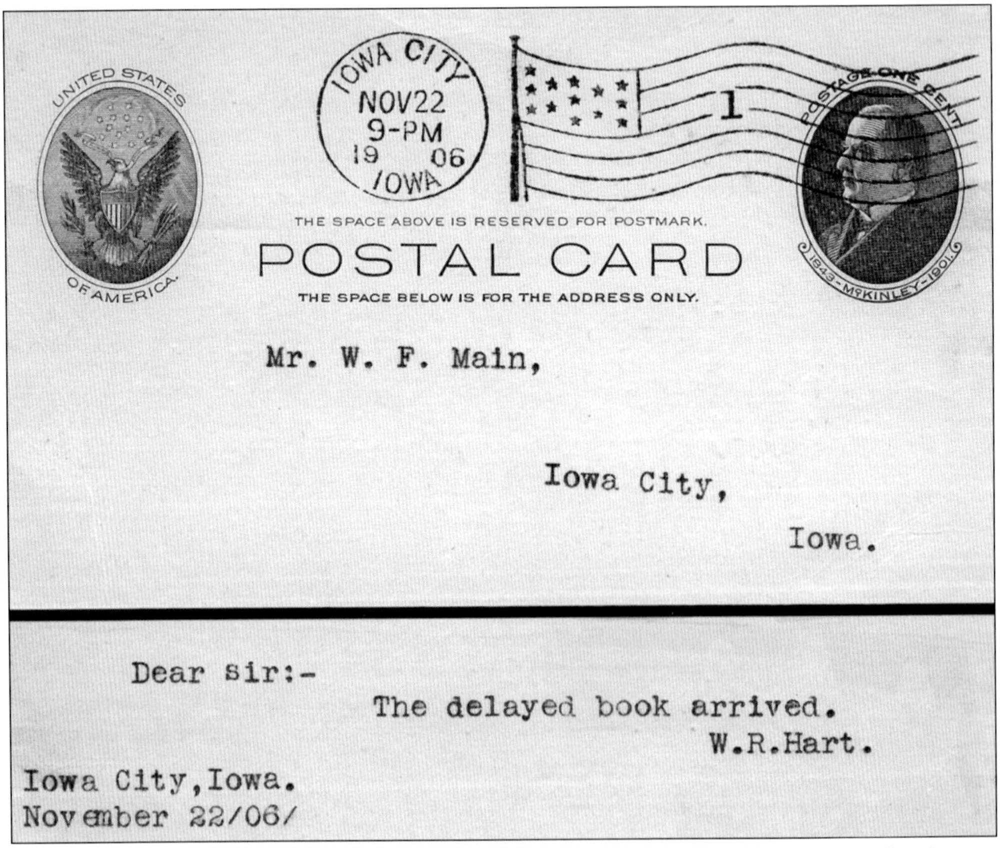

The W. F. Main Company manufactured jewelry and related items in Iowa City for about a decade, a century ago, and wholesaled hundreds of items made elsewhere. Its organization was impetus for a town—East Iowa City—which never existed as a municipality, but was subdivided using numbers and letters as street names in what now is southeast Iowa City. East Iowa City's First Avenue was platted farther from the center of Iowa City than its Seventh Avenue, making those surviving street names backwards in modern-day Iowa City from standard usage in most community layouts.

48

At right, Hall's novelties and gifts offers a Swiss movement musical mug priced on the reverse face of this 1950-era card at $6.50, or a dozen at $43.20. Hall's had a 40-year run at 127 South Dubuque Street, growing out of what had been Curtis Florists of Leonard and Hubert Curtis, who also had a greenhouse on Riverside Drive near the airport. About 1970, Hall's Gift Shop added "and Betty's Flowers" to its name, then met its demise about 1973 with demolition of its longtime home in downtown urban renewal. Below, Iowa Chick Hatchery of Ralph Littrell and Keith Wilson was a big spring business from a still existing building, now in other uses, located along Jackson Avenue west of Creekside Park in southeast Iowa City. It offered many farm services, including the supply of Wayne Feeds.

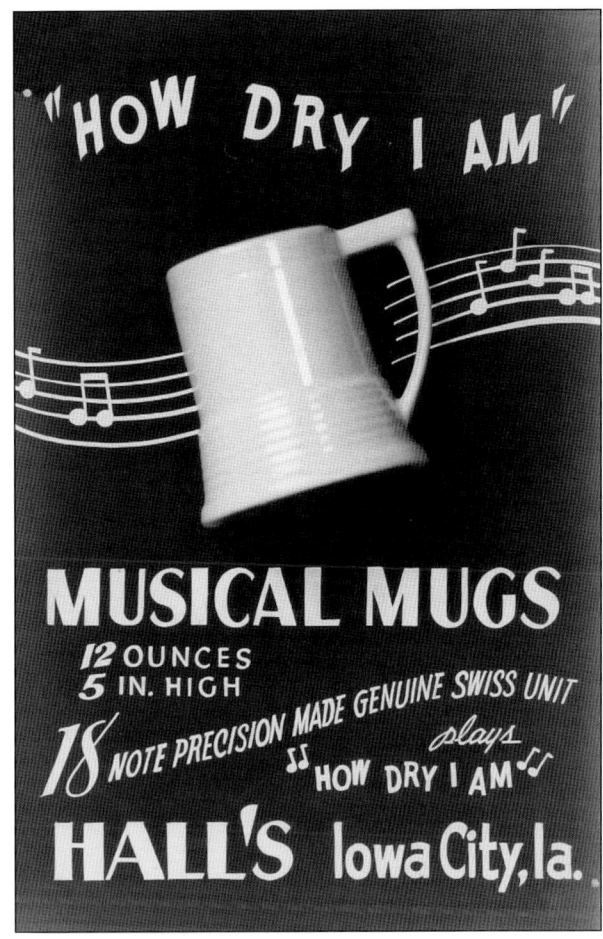

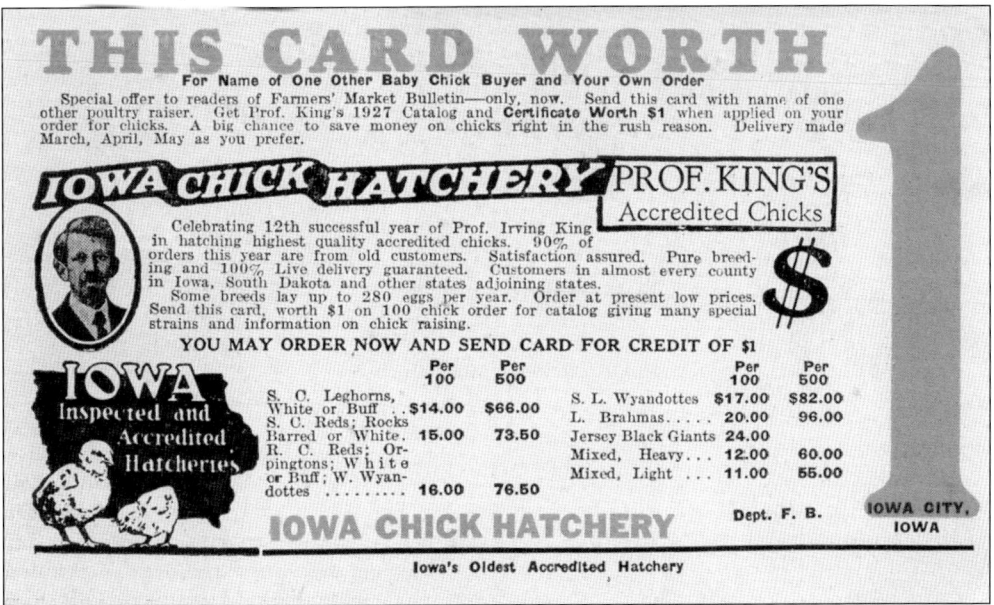

Supreme Council of the Royal Arcanum.

Office of the SUPREME SECRETARY.

Boston, Mass., *July 12* 1882

To the Officers and Members of *Athens* Council, No. *566* R. A.

Brothers:— Your remittance of $ *32.12*, on account of Assessment No. *36*, has been certified by the Supreme Treasurer as received by him on the *8* day of *July* 1882. It appears by the record of membership of your Council in this office to be the correct amount for said Assessment.

W O Robson
Supreme Secretary.

Founded in Boston just five years before, this 1882 insurance premium card was dated and addressed to Iowa City grocer J. W. (Walter) Lee, whose store was at 124 South Clinton Street. Royal Arcanum, which still operates from a Boston home base, is a fraternal beneficiary society offering life insurance and annuity products. It operates under the leadership of its "Supreme Regent."

ESTABLISHED 1849.   CAPITAL, $50,000.

OFFICE OF P. J. REGAN.

TERMS CASH.   Iowa City, Iowa, October *10* 1896.

Dear Sir;—The Nursery Stock bought of us the past season will be delivered at *Norway* on *Friday* the *23* of October, 1896. Your bill amounts to *16* DOLLARS and _____ CENTS. It will be to your interest to meet us promptly on day of delivery. Stock not called for on day of delivery will be subject to extra charge. Bring covering for roots. Please inform your neighbors. Bring this card with you on day of delivery. Call for your stock on day of delivery; do not let it lie and spoil. No countermands accepted.

The No. of your bill is *81*

Call at *Depot*

P. J. REGAN.

An 1896 card announces a railroad delivery in Norway, Iowa, by a longtime Iowa City business founded by Patrick Regan, manufacturer of barbed wire fencing, as well as a nurseryman. His farm along the north bank of the Iowa River, across from what now is City Park, was site of an early golf and country club now owned by the Elks.

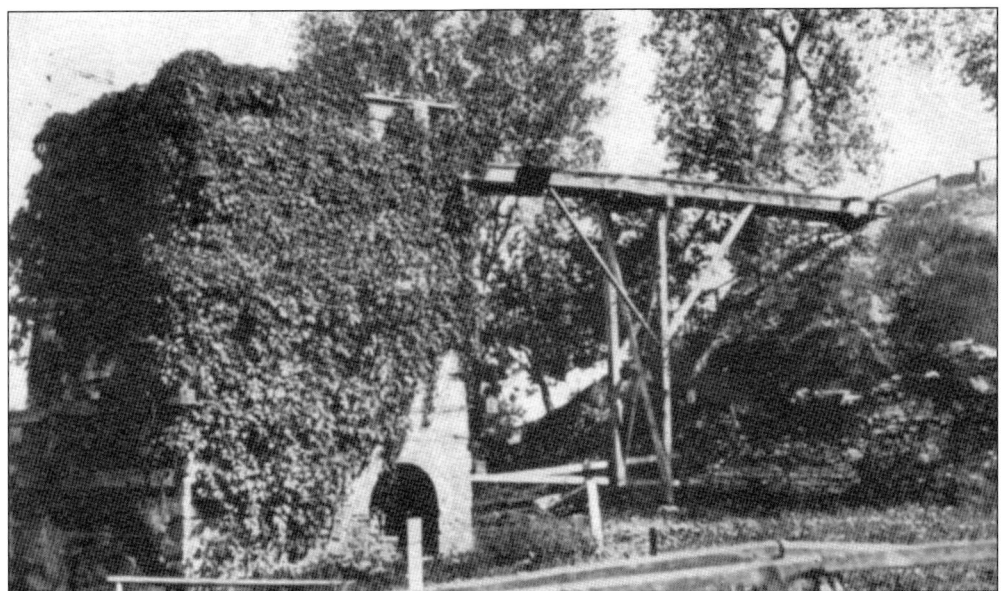

From the 1910 era, the above image records a pioneer limekiln, which shows on an 1868 birds-eye map of Iowa City. It could be fed wood from timber along the west riverbank, now site to Hillcrest Residence Hall on the University of Iowa campus. Such furnaces heated limestone to produce quicklime, an ingredient in mortars and plaster, and also it was used to stabilize mud floors. All were important uses in erecting 19th century Iowa City structures.

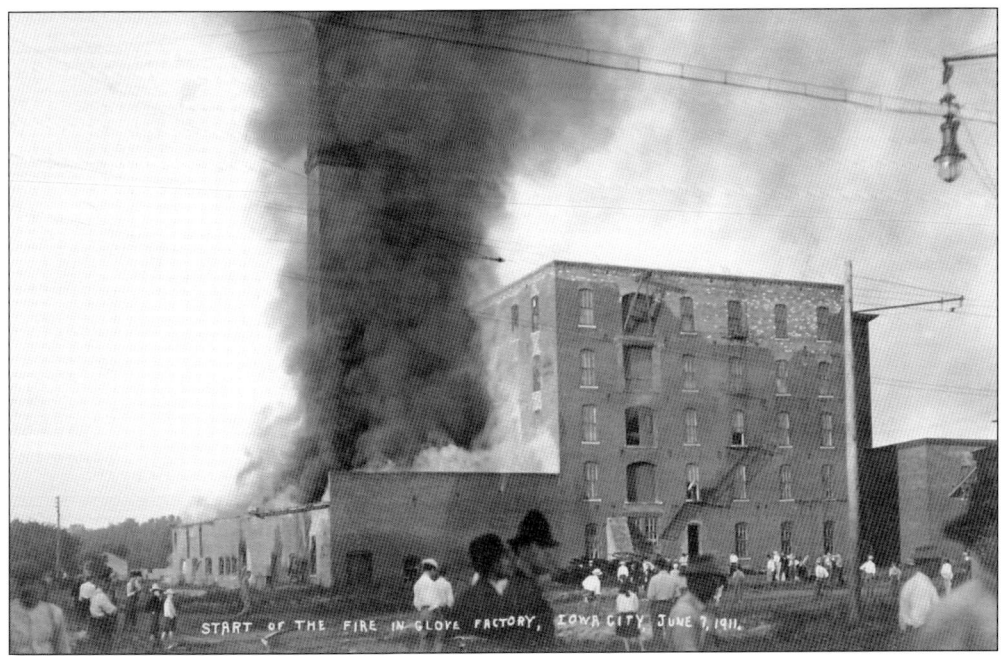

A 1911 image captures smoke and flames billowing from the town's largest employer the Rate glove factory, which occupied the square block catty-cornered northwest of the current Johnson County Administration building. It employed some 75 people, including about 50 women.

```
Nonpareil Members:
  The 1941-42 Nonpareil dancing season will open with a
party at the Varsity Ballroom the evening of Oct.14.
Dancing will be from 9:30 to 12:30.The musical program
will be presented by Len Carroll and his orchestra.
  Please be prepared to register yourselves and your
guests at the door. Dues may be deposited with the
Sec.-Treas E.T.Jolliffe as you register.

The committee in charge is:
    Mr. and Mrs. Milo Novy, Co-chairmen
    Mr. and Mrs. C.W.Faust
    Mr. and Mrs. A.M.Hora
    Mr. and Mrs. W.J.Holub
    Mr. and Mrs. Lawton Petrick
```

A Goosetown neighborhood social engagement is announced in the above fall 1941 card sent to bank cashier Milo Novy and his wife, Libby, who show as committee cochairs. The Nonpareil (peerless) Dance Club was about to start its season in the Varsity Ballroom, located on the third floor of the Paul-Helen Building at 209 East Washington Street, to the music of the Len Carroll orchestra. Treasurer Elwin Jolliffe was UI comptroller.

Iowa City, March 5th, 1883.

Dear Sir and Brother:

Yourself and Lady are cordially invited to a

RECEPTION and BANQUET,

tendered the

Grand Lodge Iowa Legion of Honor.

AT HAM'S HALL, ON

Wednesday Evening, March 7th, at Nine o'clock P. M.

COMMITTEE.

| E. E. BRAINERD. | A. E. COMSTOCK. | N. R. PARVIN. | T. W. TOWNSEND. |
| M. R. LUSE. | E. O. SWAIN. | R. H. ALLIN. | D. E. COOVER. |

TICKETS, 35 CENTS EACH PERSON.

An 1883 invitation of Masonic fraternity dignitaries invited recipient and Iowa City pioneer James McCollister and his lady to Ham's Hall, located upstairs along Iowa Avenue just east of Dubuque Street for dinner, and a reception at a cost of 35¢ each. The Masons were in rented quarters at that time prior to erecting their 1914 temple at 312 College Court, now considered the spiffiest of local fraternal halls.

> **FIRST NATIONAL BANK**
> Iowa City, Iowa, Feb 7th 1883
>
> Jas McCollister, Esq
> Dear Sir:
>
> A. Lachrau has paid the balance due on Johnson $500. Note & wants all papers including release.
>
> Yours truly, J. B. HADDOCK, Cashier.

An 1883 card addressed to Iowa City pioneer farmer and entrepreneur James McCollister announces that the bank has the money paying off a loan and now wants "all papers including release." Notes like this one passing through the mail gave the postmaster and carriers considerable news to pass on to whomever they pleased. The bank, which was not related to later institutions chartered in the same name, no doubt was following standard practice of its day.

> **EMIL L. BOERNER**
> PHARMACIST
> 113 E. Washington St   IOWA CITY, IOWA, MAR 26 1929
>
> Dr. Mr. Young —
> A check for 2.50 rebate in Mr. Bodenheimer's steamship passage came this morning. This you can get at any time. We have no reply yet about the R. R. fare.
>
> Yours truly,
> Emil L. Boerner

Likewise, above, with a 1929 note from century-long Boerner Drug owner Emil Boerner addressed to a Kalona man. Clearly, business practices are now much more confidential than those of 8 and 12 decades ago. During 1929, Boerner's and its delightful soda fountain was located downtown, but later operated west of Kinnick Stadium in a building now used as University Heights Town Hall.

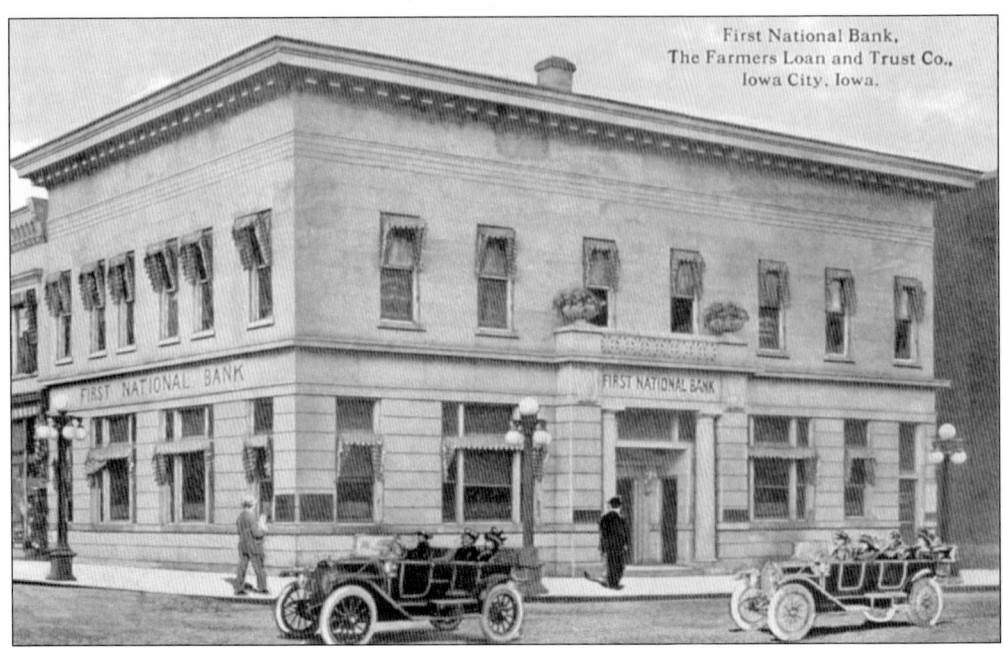

The First National Bank, seen in a 1910-era image above, offers an early view of its renovated facility facing south onto Washington Street. Its original orientation had been west toward Dubuque Street, seen as the side of this building. In an era when farm loans were another ball game, the owners had another company, the Farmers Loan and Trust Company, to do business in that league. This, as well as all other banks in Iowa City, were bankrupted overnight during February 1932, victims of the Great Depression. A contemporary postcard displays the lobby of First National Bank below.

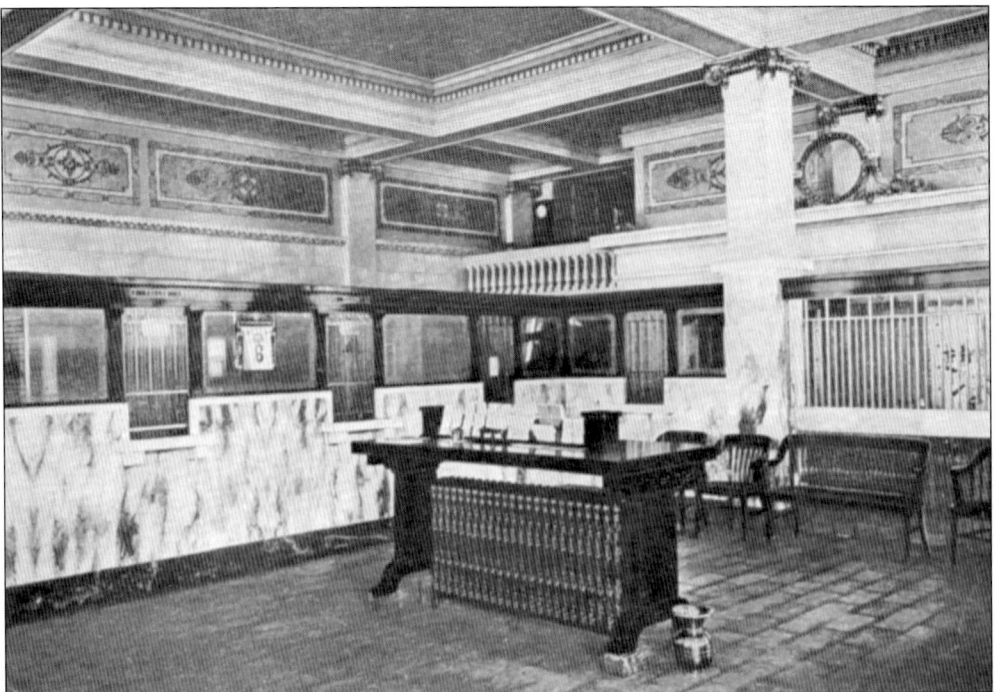

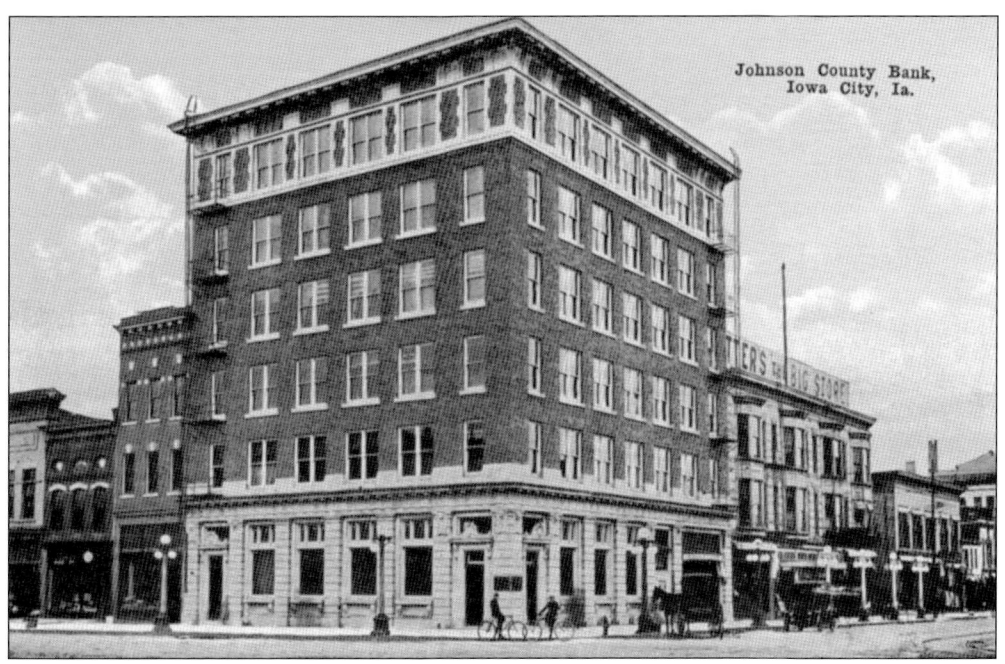

This 1912 postcard image shows a brand spanking new Johnson County Bank facility on the bank corner at the Clinton and Washington Streets intersection across from the Old Capitol Pentacrest. It was the first modern multi-floored structure in Iowa City, followed the next year by Hotel Jefferson, built on the other end of the same block. After its loss during 1932 to the Great Depression, a bank was reopened here in its place by Ben S. Summerwill, a South Dakota rancher and lumberman who, by 1932, was serving in the federal reconstruction office in Des Moines, as Iowa State Bank, which recently joined the MidWestOne banking institution. This was after Ben's children and grandchildren followed their patriarch in owning and operating the ISB. A postcard contemporary to the image above displays the Johnson County Bank lobby below.

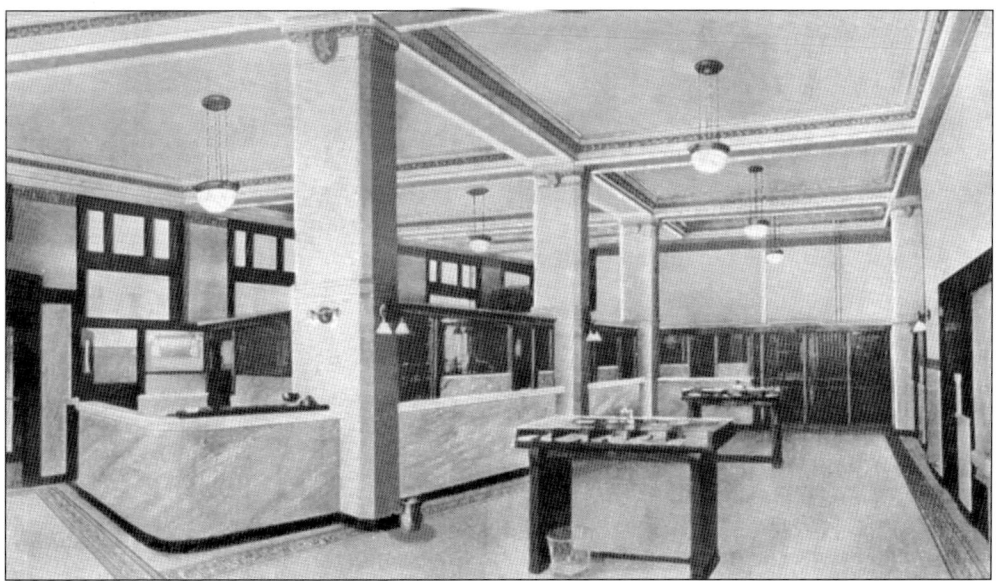

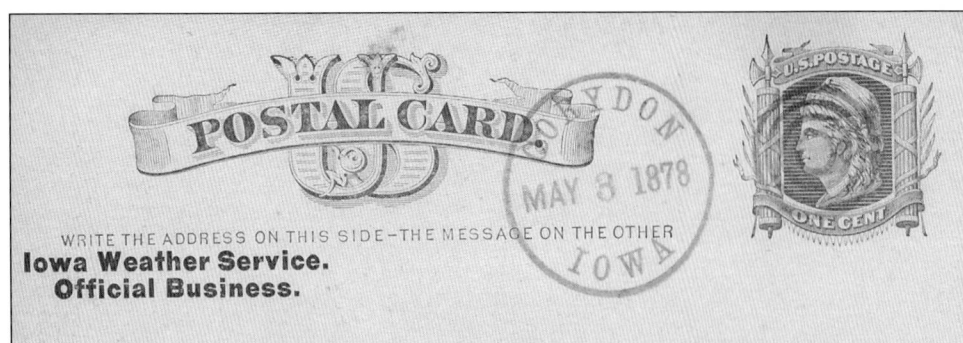

Above are front and back views of an 1878 weather report from Corydon, Iowa. The 966-page 1883 *History of Johnson County Iowa*, written by Hiram A. Reid—although his name doesn't appear in the volume—states on page 537: "Dr. Gustavus Hinrichs of Iowa City was father and founder and master-builder of the Iowa weather service . . . and already (has) given Iowa a rank second to no other state or country in the scientific repute of her meteorological work." The rooftop at his home a block north of Old Capitol bristled with weather instruments. European trained, he came to an infant University of Iowa, and by using a laboratory method of teaching science in a lectures-only era, he put the university on the map to a snobby eastern seaboard, and in Europe as well. A rural-dominated Iowa legislature even agreed, as the Civil War ended, to pay for a building for him—called North Hall—next door to Old Capitol.

Five

ON THE AVENUES
STREETSCAPES, INCLUDING A DOUBLE-PAGE SPREAD

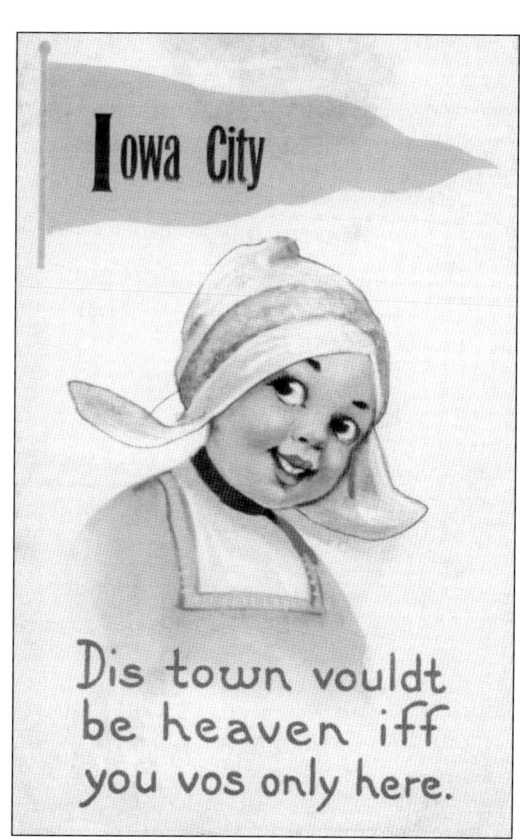

Iowa City's ethnic flavor shines in this 1915 card.

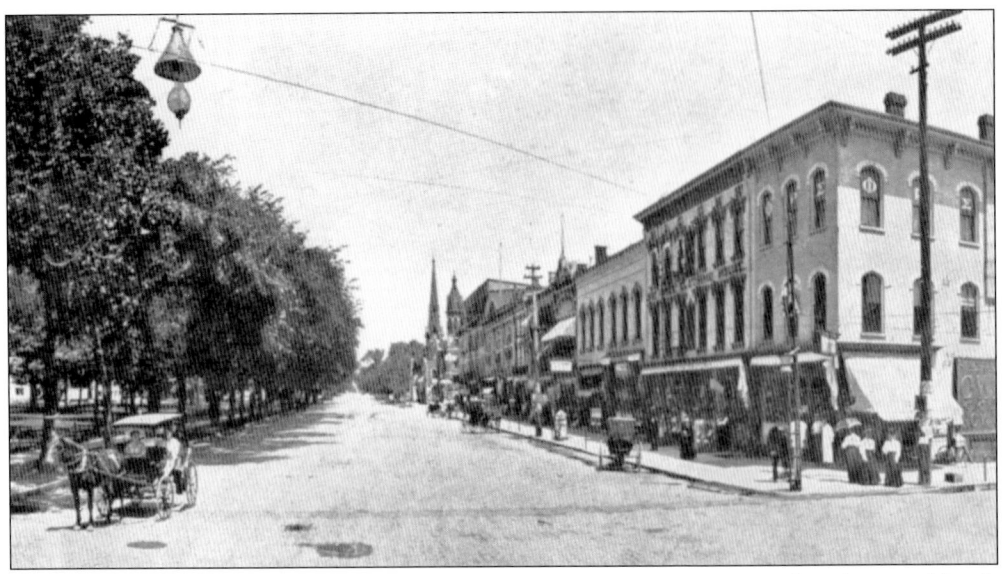

The Clinton and Washington Streets intersection, known to generations of students and locals as the "Whetstone Corner," observes the clippity-clop of a surrey with fringe on top passing leisurely along about 1910. Whetstone Drug, with its popular soda fountain and postal substation directly across from the central Pentacrest Campus, kept the corner busy. It was a local landmark for a century, which began in 1874 with druggist John Whetstone.

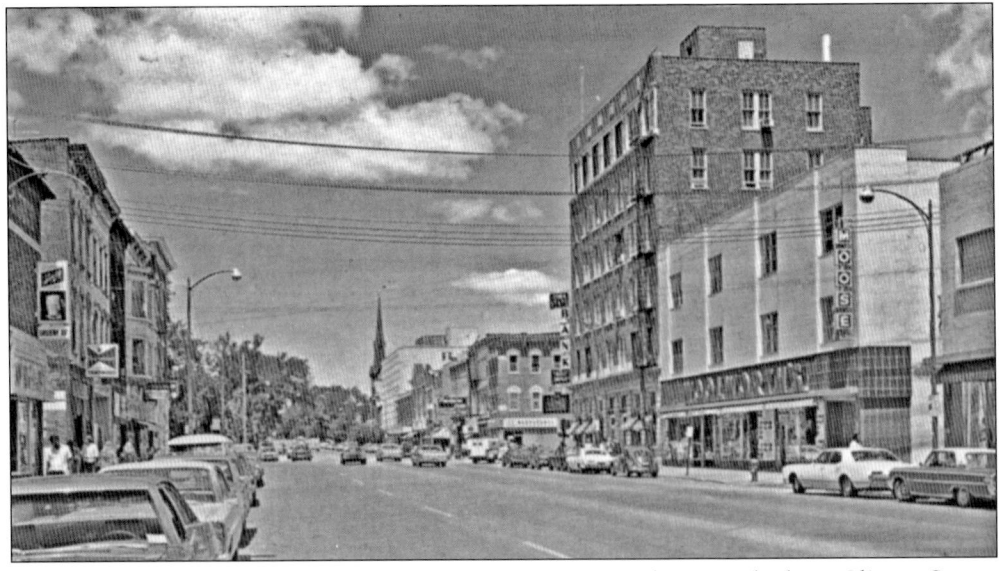

Whetstone's still inhabited its corner in this 1972 image. Looking north along Clinton Street, it features Woolworth's five-and-dime next to the six-floor Iowa State Bank building, adjacent to the Whetstone Corner on the right face of this image. The Congregational United Church of Christ spire shows at the far end of that streetscape. The other face, which included such venerable downtown stalwarts as Burger Chef, Ewers Shoes, Epstein's Books, and Deadwood Tavern, was lost to urban renewal the following year.

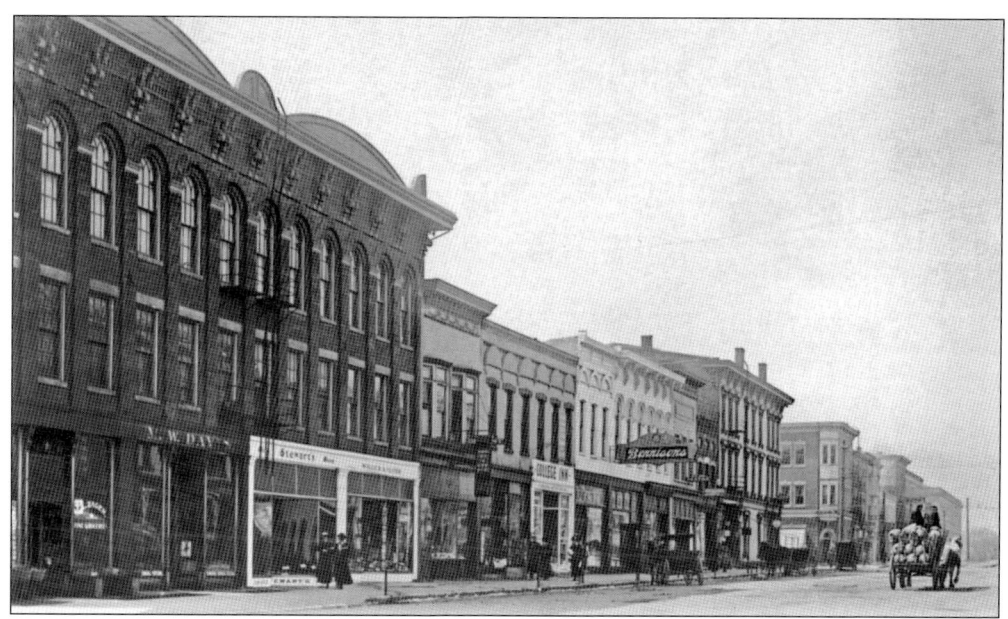

The Washington streetscape above offers a 1910 view of two Civil War–era standouts in Metropolitan Hall, at left, and the large three-floor Cooke, Sargent, and Downey bank building at the other end of the block. Both were gone two years later. Fire razed the hall where Civil War soldiers mustered for ceremonies in departing for the war front, opening a site for Hotel Jefferson. The bank building was succeeded by the six-story Johnson County Savings Bank building—which later became the home of Iowa State Bank for seven decades. Below, the 1881 City Hall building dominates the skyline looking west two blocks to tree-covered Pentacrest.

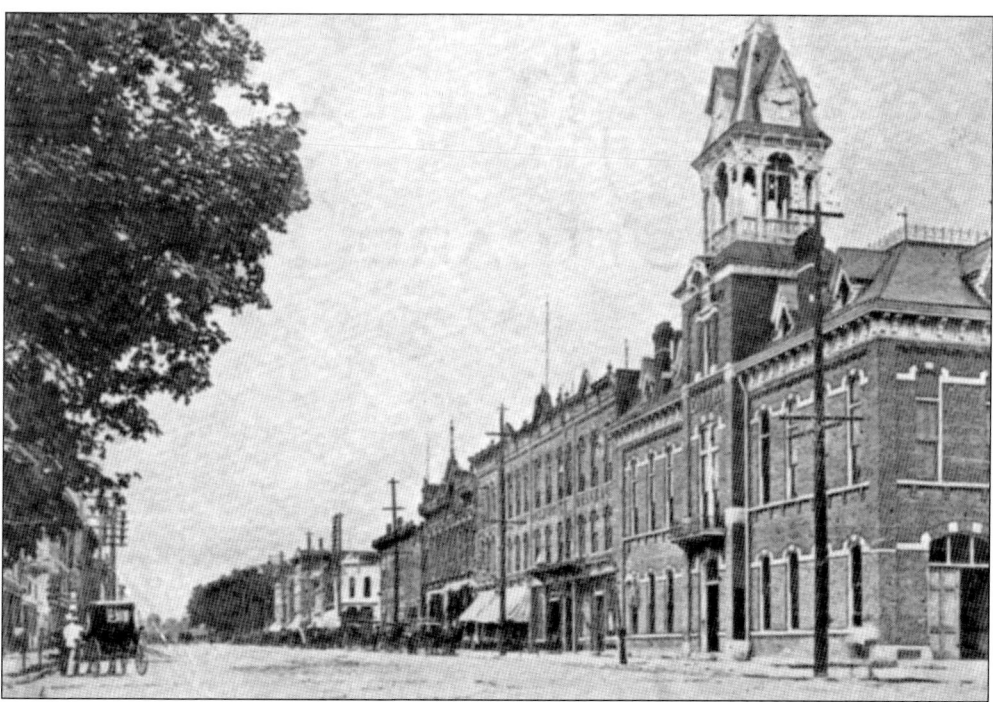

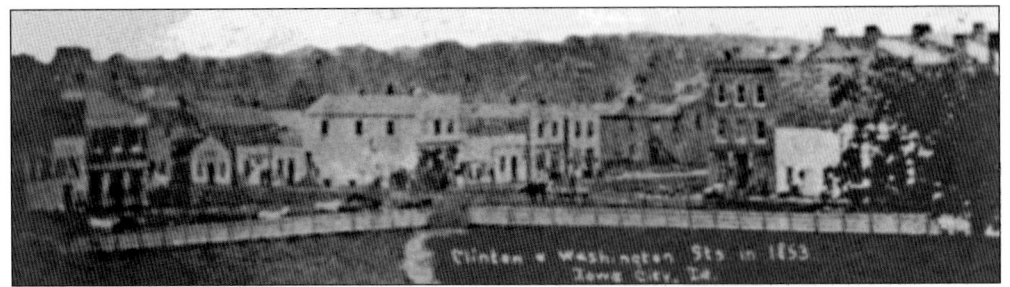

Like the 1853 image of Old Cap and local fair shown on page 10, this pioneer image taken the same year looks from Pentacrest at the Whetstone-Iowa State Bank corner.

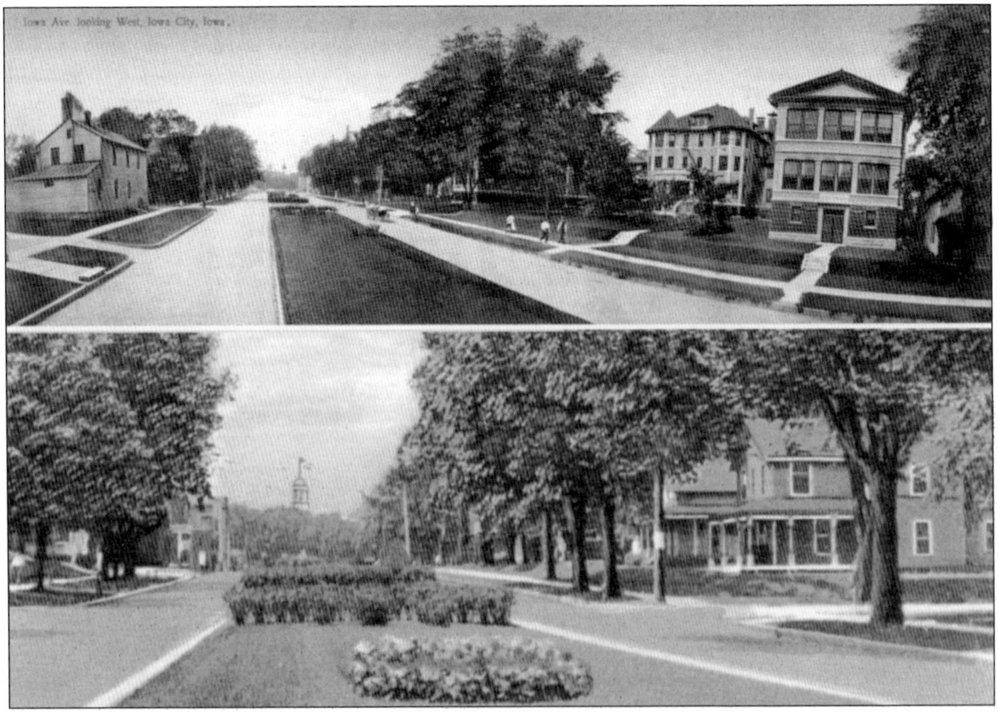

Iowa Avenue was laid out in 1839 as a grand 100-foot-wide route from the statehouse grounds to the governor's mansion, just like in the nation's capitol city, where the White House sets off to one side of the Mall. The statehouse became Old Cap, but an executive's mansion was never built on the Governor Street bluff as intended. The top 1910-era view includes early University Hospital at right and a residence at left. The lower image displays Iowa Avenue about 1910 looking west from near Gilbert Street.

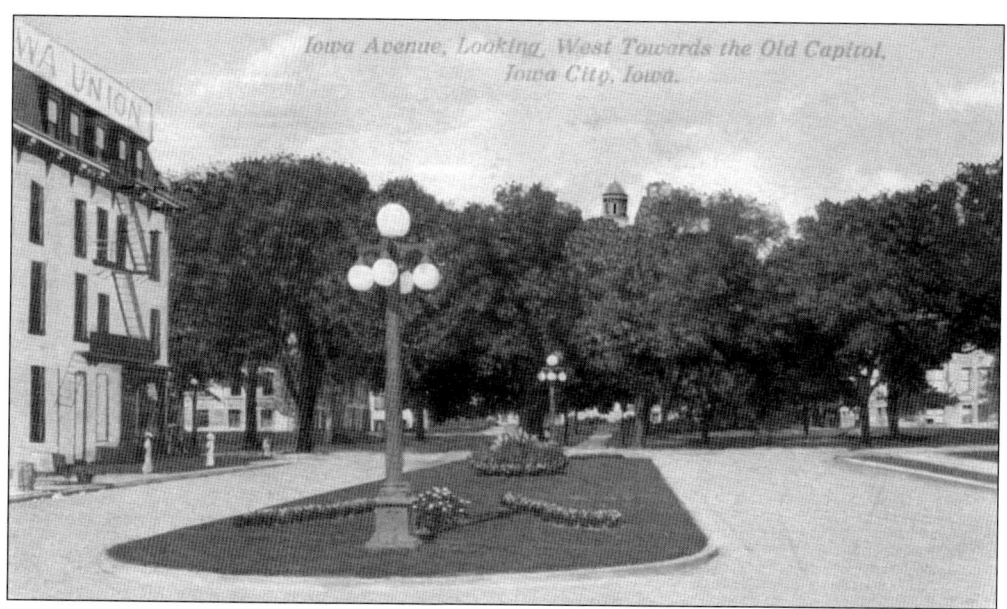

The St. James Hotel is shown with an "Iowa Union" sign on its mansard in this 1915-era view of Iowa Avenue from a half block east of Pentacrest. The upper floor of the 1872 hotel structure was used as one of the predecessor student activity sites prior to the Iowa Memorial Union's 1925 opening. The hotel burned during 1916, forcing union uses across the intersection into the old Universalist Church, renamed Unity Hall. Below, a 1907 image presents Iowa Avenue from near Linn Street with the stinky old chemistry building setting at right. Down that block, the Byzantine-type spire of the Universalist Church marks where the university's Phillips Hall stands today. The horse and carriage at left passes in front of First Christian Church. In both these images, like those on the prior page, the Old Cap dome appears to have been added for artistic effect; it would have been hidden by an elm canopy reaching up a block in front of it.

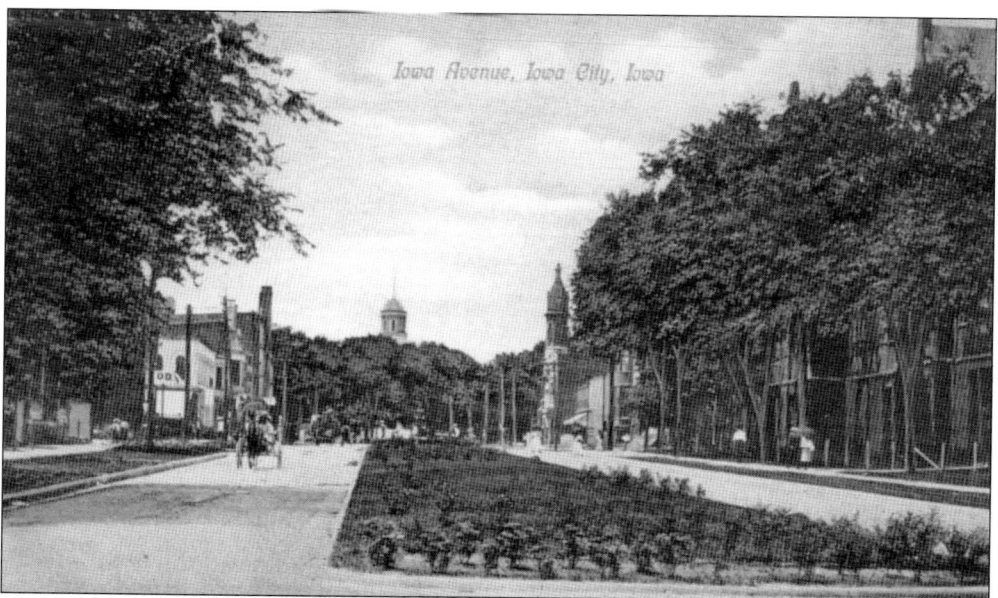

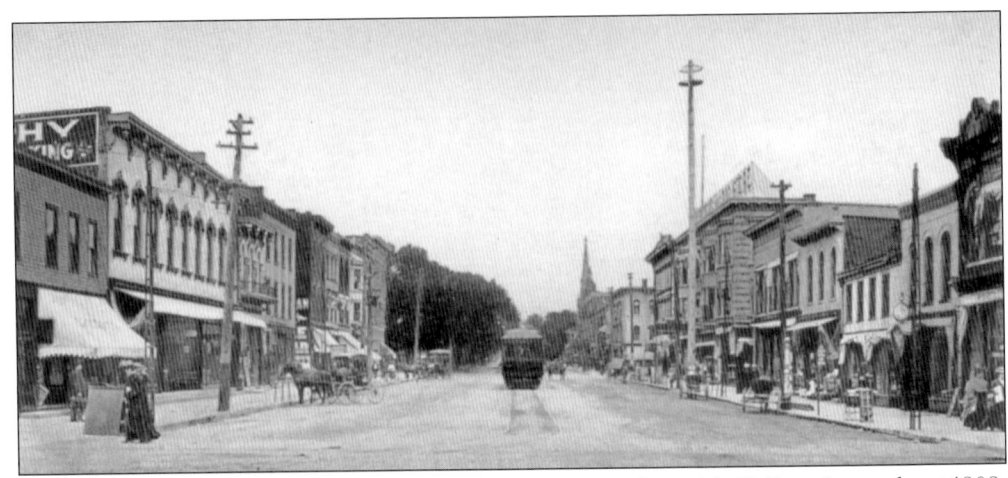

Clinton Street is shown here looking north from its intersection with College Street about 1908, just four years after interurban rail service was initiated between downtown Iowa City and central Cedar Rapids. A year after this image was taken tracks were added for the first of what became five local trolley car routes. The first ran east along College, using Johnson Street to access Burlington Street and Muscatine Avenue, and turning south at Rundell Street to a storage and maintenance shed. Later routes took Dubuque Street north to both a crossing at Park Road into Manville Heights and out Church and Dodge Streets to Conklin Lane. Yet another jogged out Iowa Avenue, Jefferson Street, and Bloomington Street to Center Street to access Oakland Cemetery, plus a short route ran south to the Rock Island depot. Buying a monthly pass could cut the cost of twice-daily rides to a few pennies, and you needn't drop your horse at a livery all day while you worked.

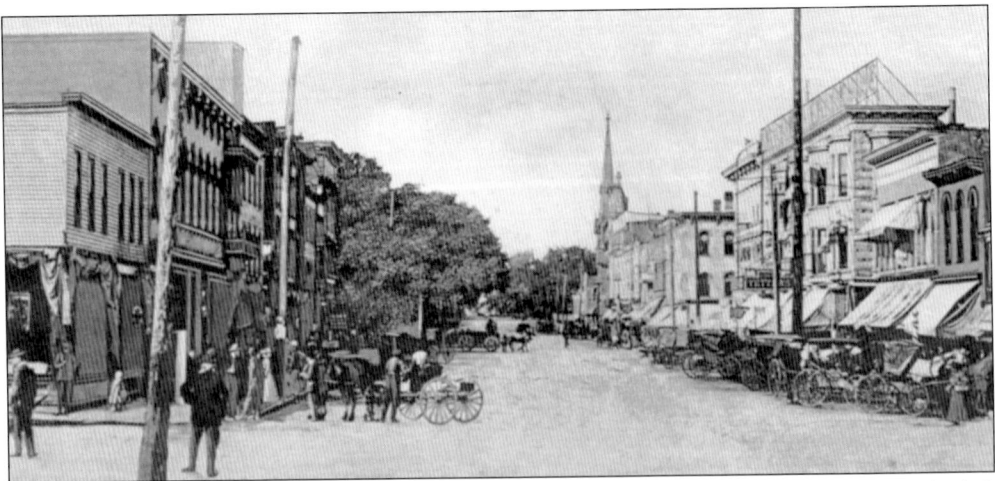

A similar section of Clinton Street is abuzz with activity, a surrey jam on shopping day. The left street face now is filled by a downtown enclosed mall, and the right is dominated by the six-story Iowa State Bank at mid-face. The far Congregational spire still exists, but the intervening one of Universalist Church, later Unitarian, is replaced by Phillips Hall. The dirt street surface, topped by fragrant road apples dropped by horses, has been replaced by concrete littered with people's trash.

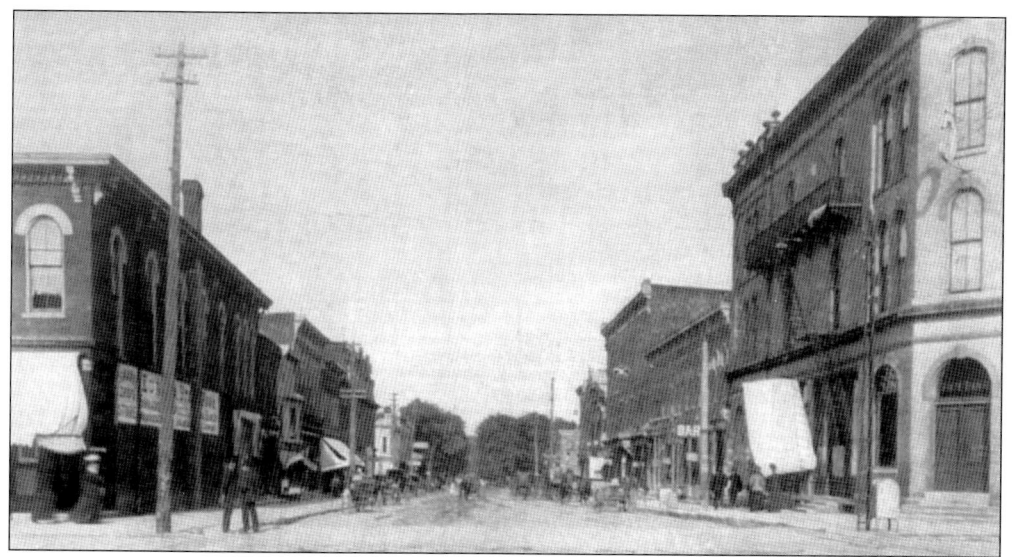

A 1909 College Street view east from Clinton Street is shown above. The Coldren Opera House is at right above Iowa City State Bank. This was a low traffic block that became a powerhouse when Sears, Wards, and JC Penney lined it during post–Great Depression years. They abandoned the downtown during the 1960s for newly built edge-of-town shopping centers, which now have yielded to a regional mall and two Wal-Marts. One isn't certain whether the canopy at right is being erected, under repair, or intended to shade a function on the sidewalk. The Opera House Bar occupied the storefront.

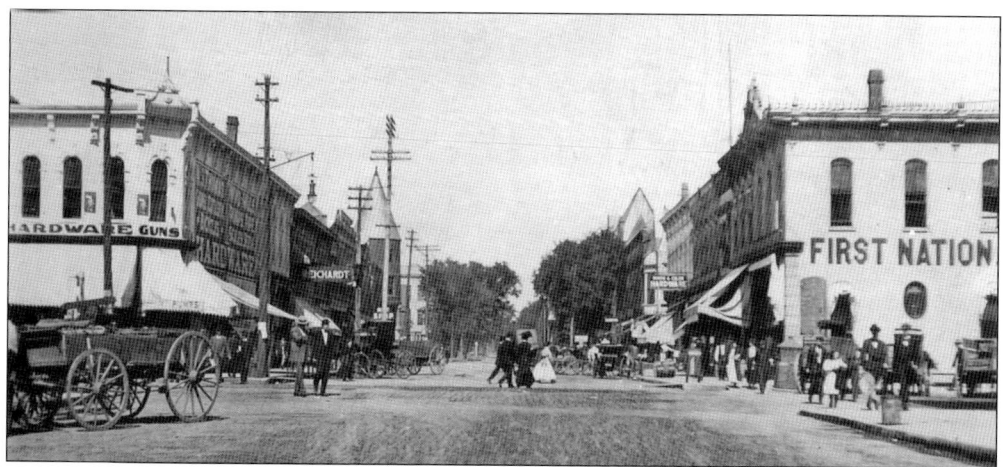

Dubuque Street is shown about 1910. The First National Bank faces Dubuque before its 1911 reorientation to face Washington Street with a new limestone veneer exterior to make it look solid. This intense commercial block was second only to Clinton Street during this era, before College Street shone a half-century later. The left streetscape begins with W. S. (Will) Thomas Hardware with the "GUNS" sign on its corner frontage and also shows the sign for Reichardt Confectionery Shop, which later added a cafe with soda fountain. Also in view is the dunce cap corner turret of the YM-YWCA, campus central for TV's first regularly offered broadcast show anywhere and site of UI's first ever basketball game.

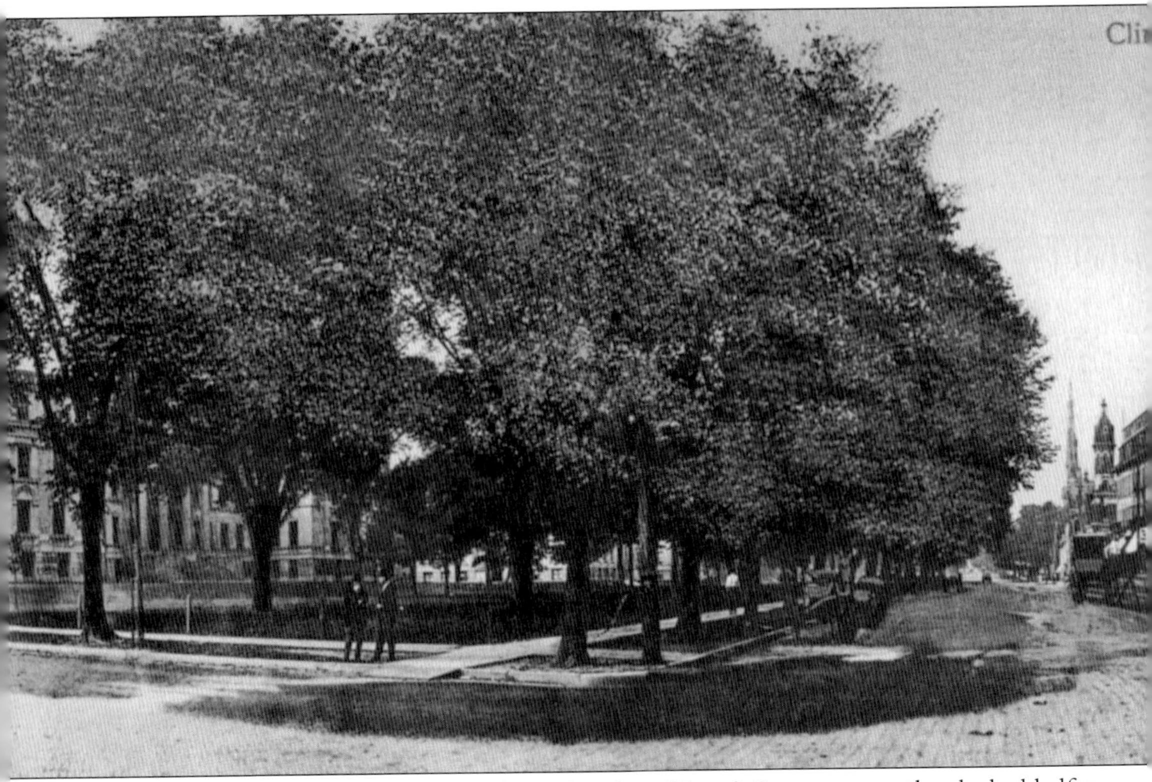

From a shady grove of elm trees on the University of Iowa's Pentacrest, to the clocked belfry tower of old City Hall at extreme right, this delightful 1903 double-sized "Mail Card" spans Clinton and Washington Streets in central Iowa City. Horses reigned a full decade before limited

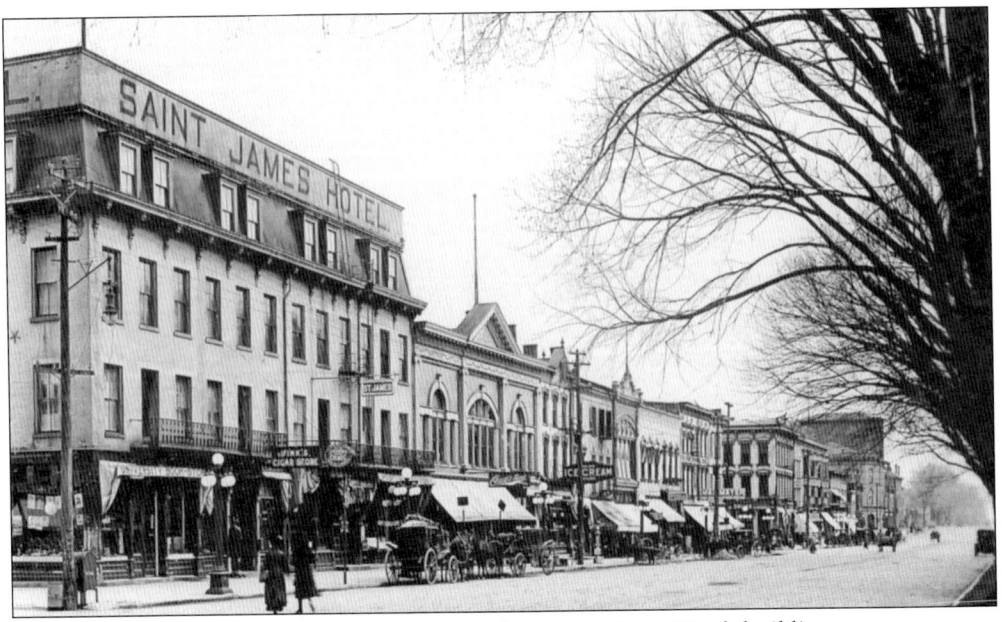

The 1911 St. James Hotel corner now serves a three-story Iowa Book building.

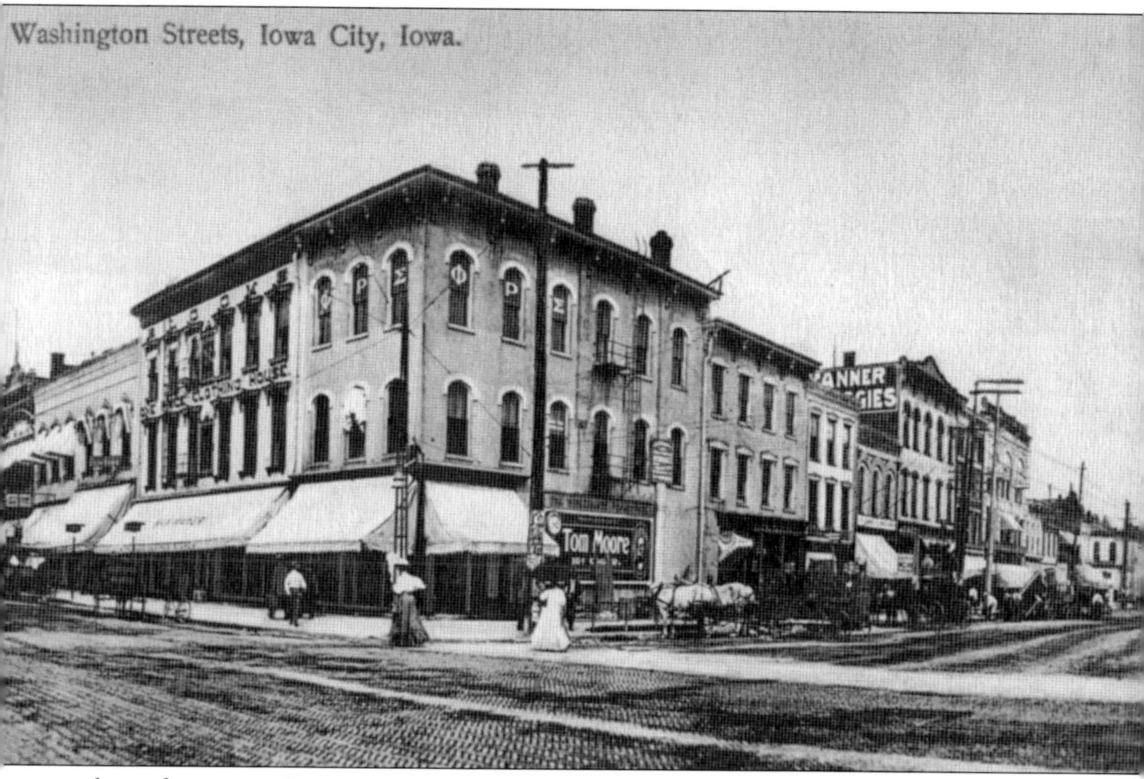

Washington Streets, Iowa City, Iowa.

numbers of motorcars began regularly plying local streets. A 1917 exhibition of new horseless carriages in tents on Clinton Street drew crowds paying an exorbitant 25¢—the price of a movie ticket—for entry.

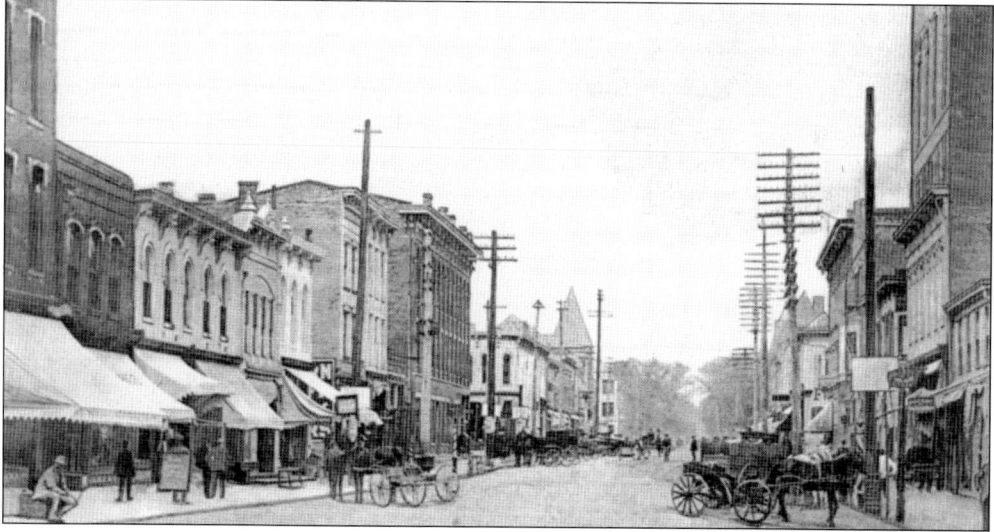

Above, a bustling Dubuque Street scene, north from Washington about 1906, displays the plague of that and later eras—aerial utility lines. Now underground downtown and in new residential areas, the visible jumble resulted from competing telephone systems both running all private lines from customers to "central" downtown. With no interconnection, businesses had to have both, until they were consolidated during 1909–1911.

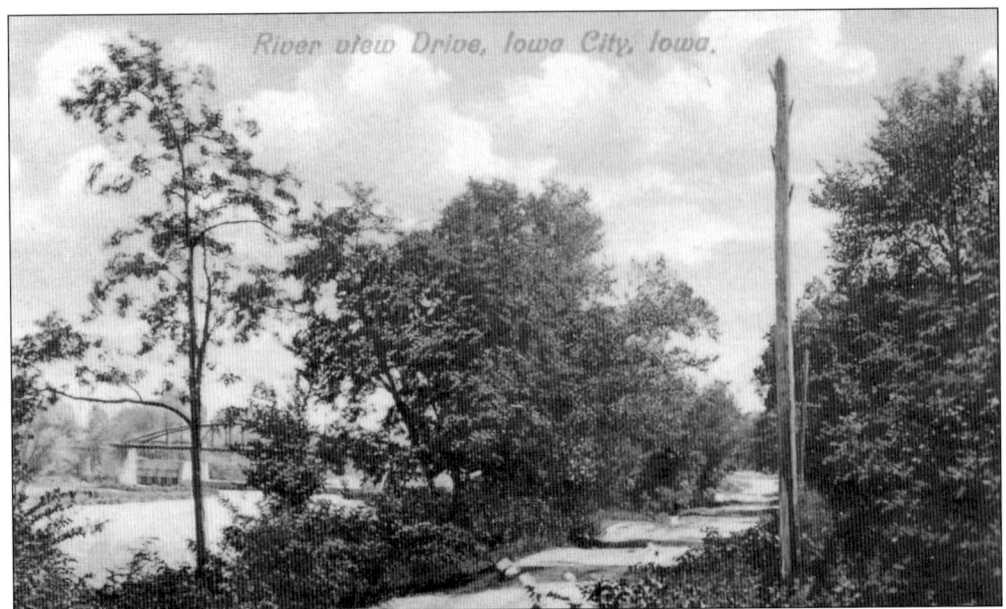

A lovely country lane scene greets us in this 1913 view south on Riverside Drive from near today's River Street. Centennial Bridge, named for construction during the nation's 1876 centennial year, shows at left carrying Iowa Avenue across the river. Now think again of this "lovely country lane" with a dirt surface during rainy season.

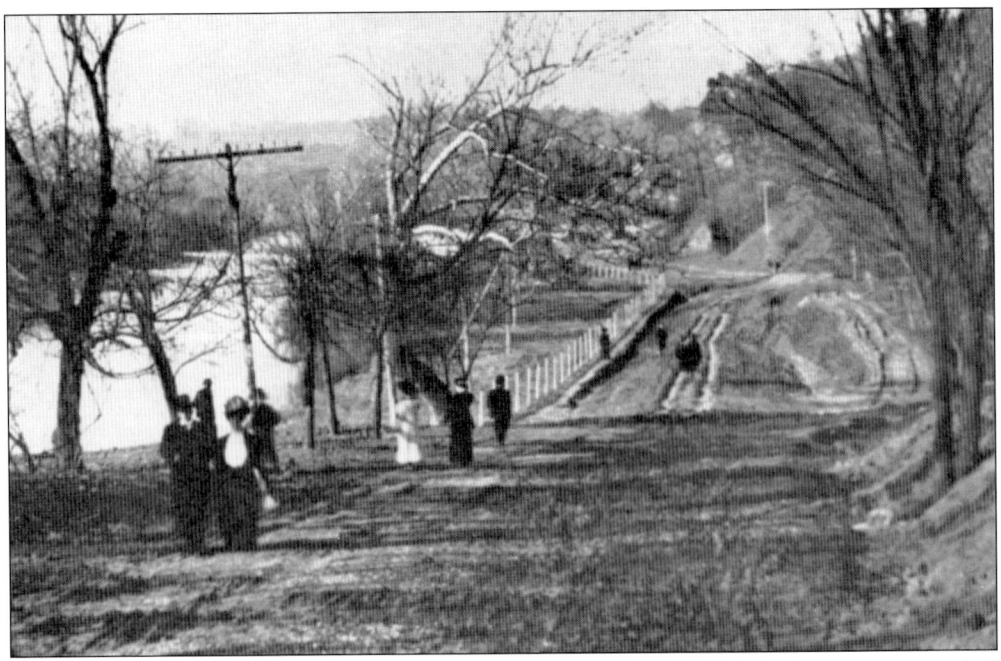

Above, just such an event greets the eye in a 1909 view north down the Dubuque Street hill toward where Park Road bridge now joins this street. Sunday strollers on the sun-dried, but deeply rutted, street were probably viewing high water beyond this scene, up where Terrill gristmill had a 5-foot-high dam. City Park had just been purchased.

Six

FRIENDS AND NEIGHBORS
CORALVILLE, RIVER, CITY PARK, AND LOVER'S LEAP

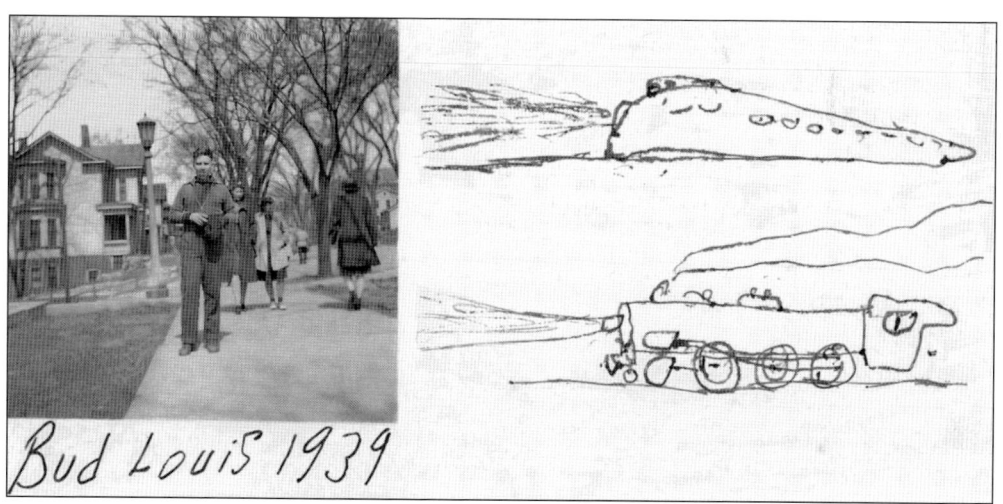

The late Bud Louis, Rexall druggist, history columnist, and railroad enthusiast, sent this 1939 postcard as a token of friendship. A young Bud hikes North Capitol Street on a card he autographed and drew sketches on from a railroad era he witnessed.

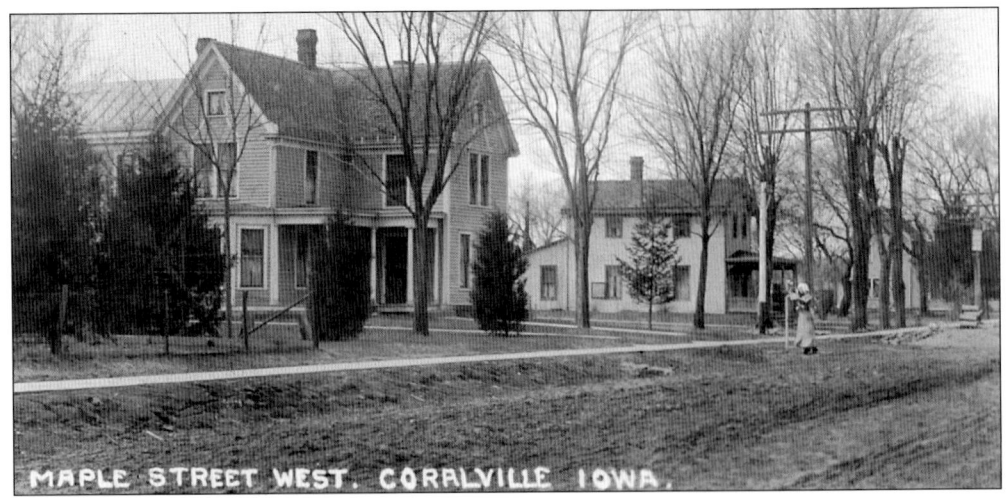

This 1910 Coralville neighborhood is now a commercial zone. Schizophrenic Iowa City seems to view neighboring Coralville in contradictory terms: a good place to eat, shop, and send overnight guests, but without the proper snobby sophistication and intellect necessary to find the restroom. But Coralville has taken advantage of this attitude. It is now the commercial hub of the area, where fortunes are being made regularly in retail and service activities that were disdained as beneath the dignity of proper Iowa City folks.

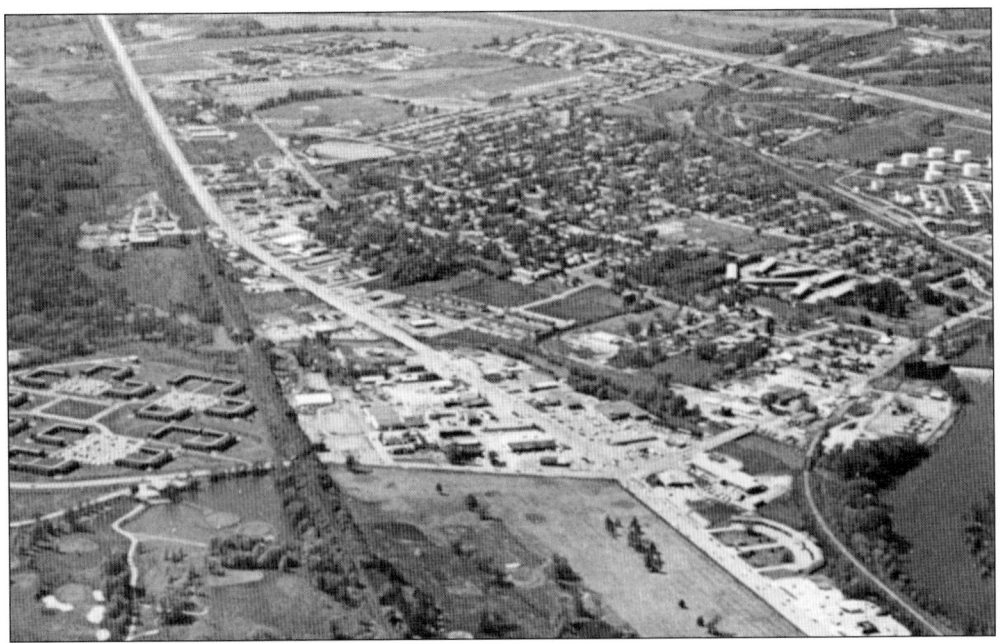

A 1960-era aerial image shows the "Coralville Strip" running from lower right to upper left, plus the town's tiny residential area and Interstate 80 in the upper right. Settled contemporarily with Iowa City during the 1840s for its superior river site for a dam, Coralville populations remained small, until large retail and development space was zoned out of Iowa City during the 1960s. From 2,400 in 1960, it now tops 18,000 people.

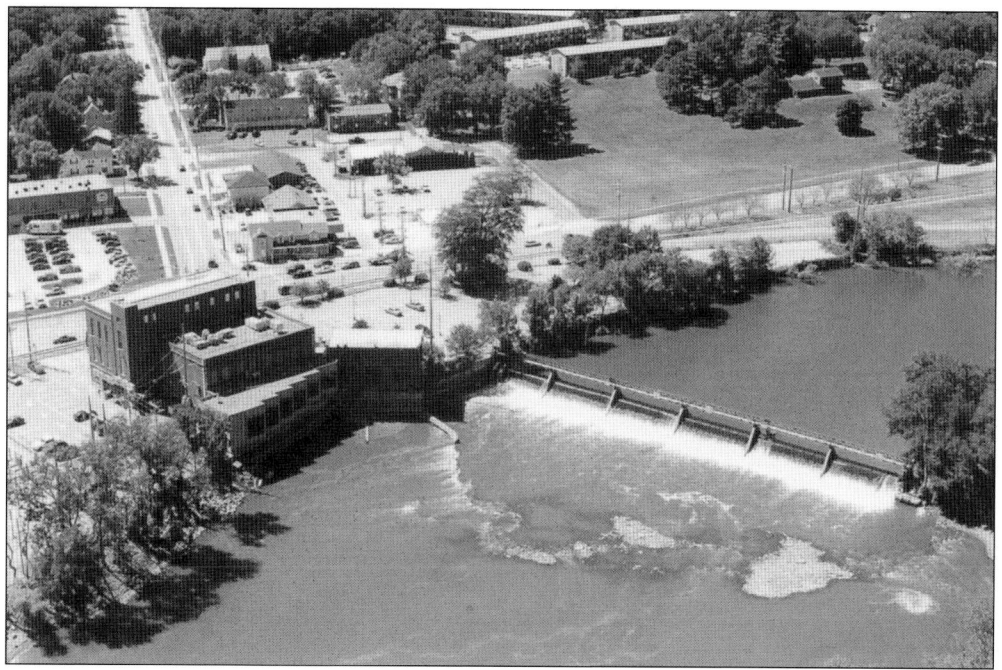

Coralville boasts the best site along the Iowa River for a dam, with "Coralville formation" bedrock exposed for easy footings, plus an ability to impound a large pool within narrow confines, providing high waterwheel strengths. A mill was first opened in 1844, just ahead of a similar one called Terrill Mill at City Park in Iowa City. Later, as seen above, a utility constructed a large generating facility, now in use as a restaurant with a public walkway crossing the dam. Below, a 1915 dam reconstruction is in progress.

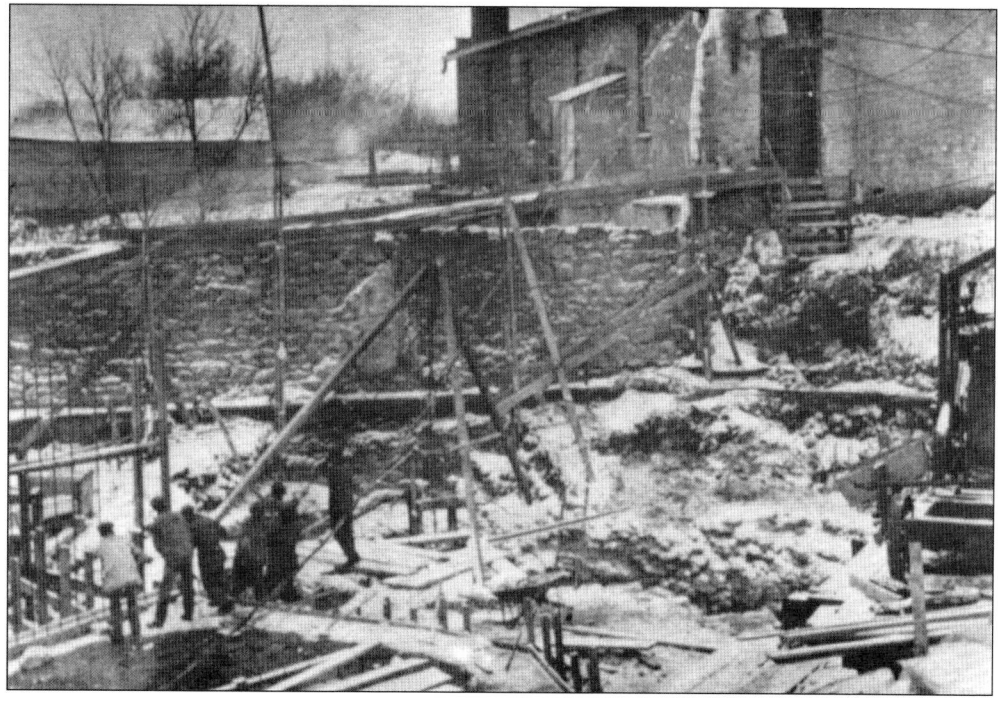

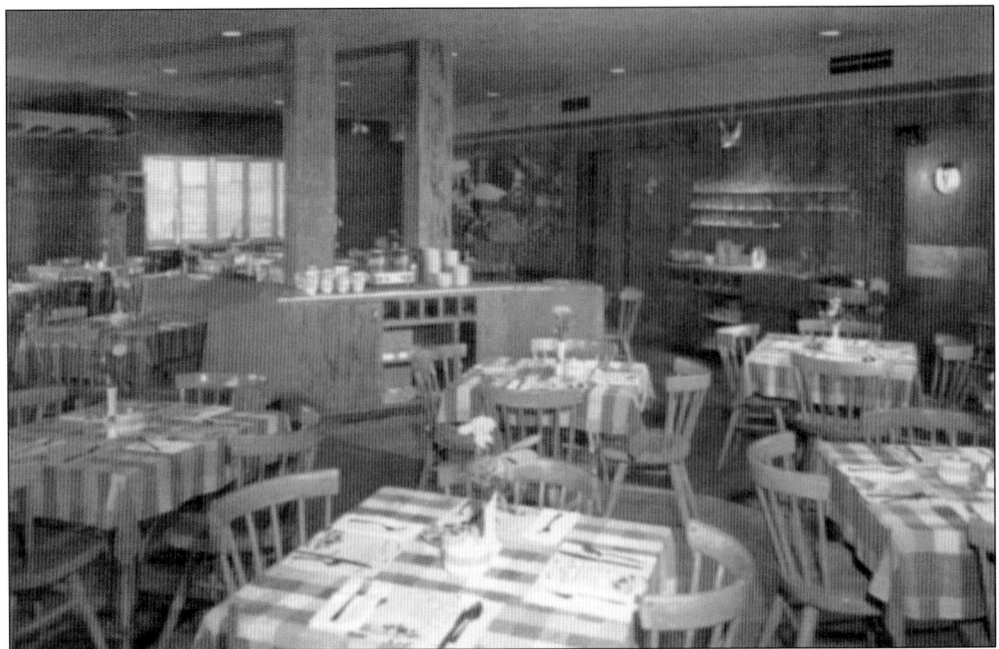

Above, Curt Yocum served beef and farm products from his own south-central Iowa farm at his Coralville strip restaurant, which carried his name from the 1950s into the 1970s. Sandwiches from Yocum's were sold aboard "Hawkeye Special" trains parked on the railroad siding at Kinnick Stadium, as football tailgating was done "train style."

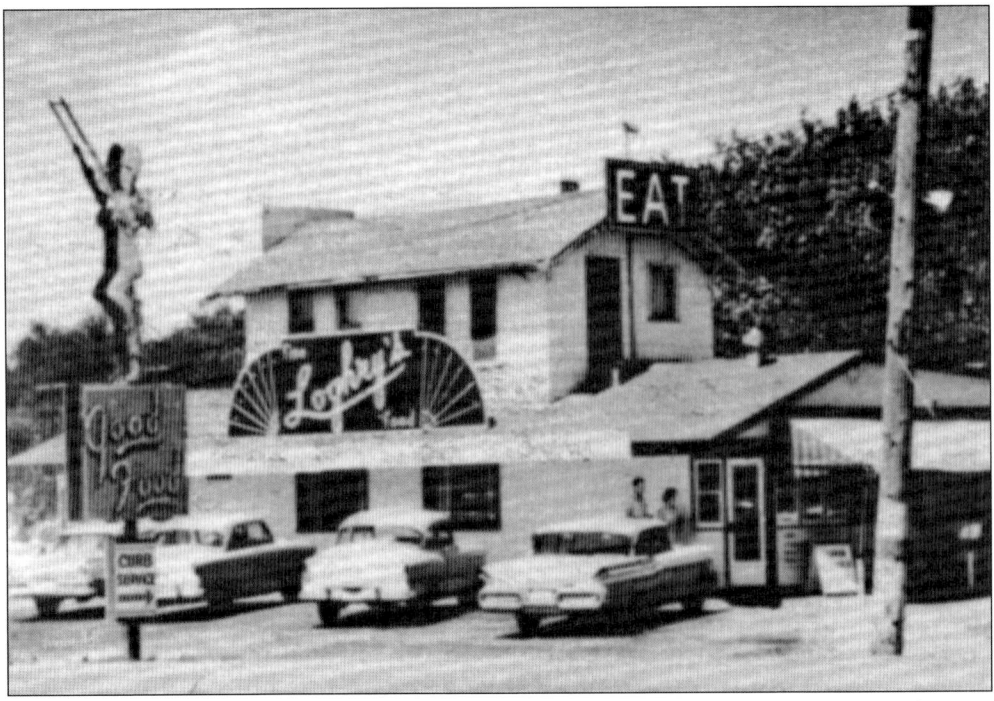

Loghry's Drive-In, on the busy Highway 6 and First Avenue intersection, was popular from its 1949 opening. After fire razed it in 1958, it reopened as Carousel Restaurant.

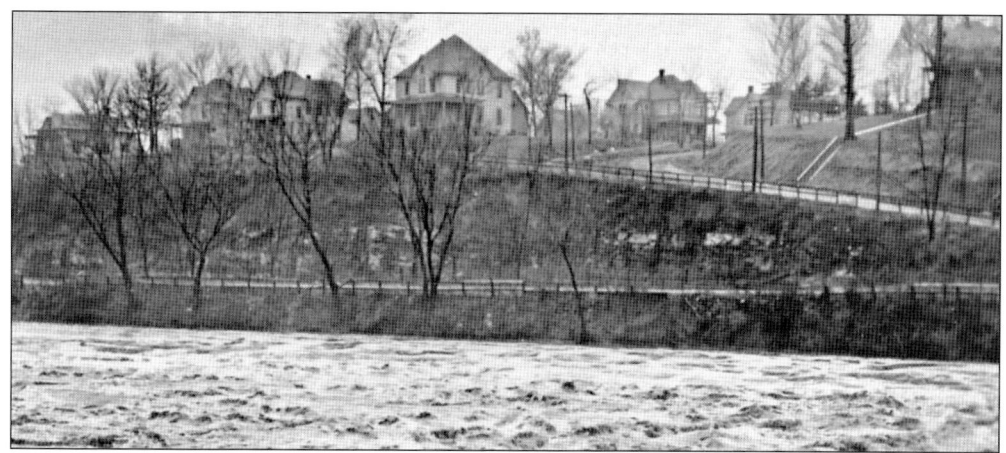

In 1911, the Varsity Heights neighborhood stands on a west river bluff site now occupied by the university's law school building. The steep access road was closed and replaced by the current Grand Avenue route during a widening of Riverside Drive, the road visible paralleling the river.

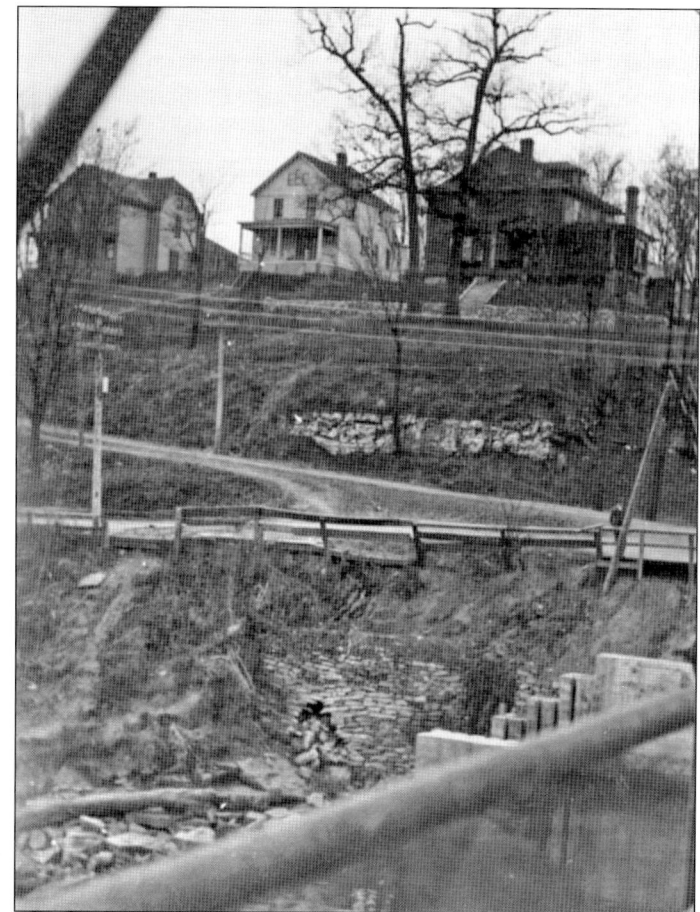

At right, an image recorded about 1908 shows more of Varsity Heights. West-bank neighborhoods were popular a century ago for views of central Iowa City, for their proximity to Pentacrest jobs, and for cool summer breezes. Homes stretched from what now is the College of Nursing site to the Rock Island high river crossing, as well as being scattered elsewhere. When the university opened its Children's Hospital in 1919, its first structure west of the river, these neighborhoods proved doomed. Hillcrest Residence Hall takes the largest chunk of riverfront space, accompanied by the law and nursing buildings. The Koser brothers saw potential.

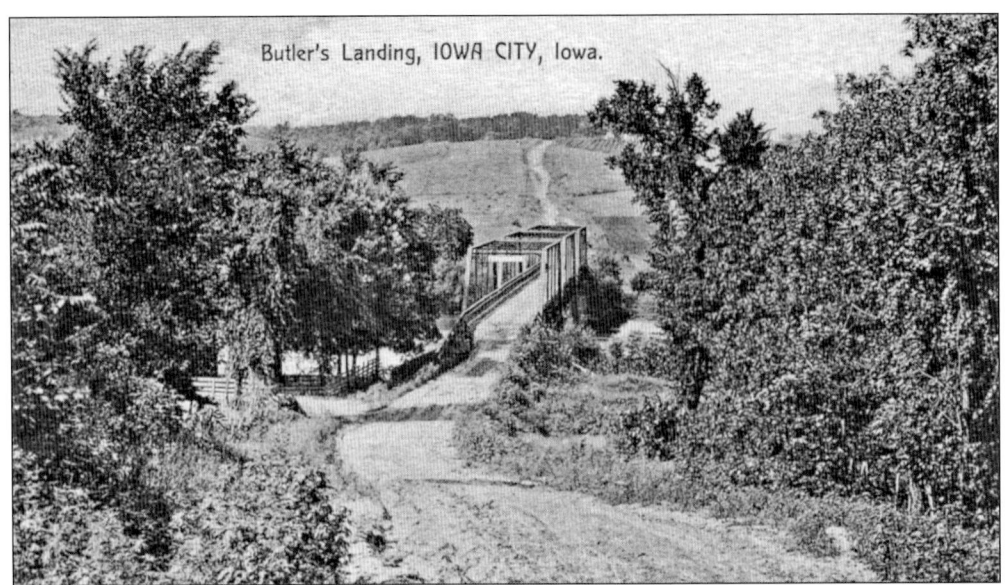

The name Butler's Landing, seen on the 1906 card above, speaks to early Iowa River history and elicits the story of Walter Butler and his capitol. His landing served as a pioneer marina where sportsmen stored craft, and where rentals were available. The scene is north of Iowa City on a road now serving the River Heights neighborhood subsequently built on the image's horizon. Butler erected what wags called "Butler's Capitol." It was a wooden shanty next to his hotel and across Clinton Street from Pentacrest. It housed Iowa territorial legislators and governor in 1841 before Old Cap was ready. Moved elsewhere, it became the City Hotel brothel.

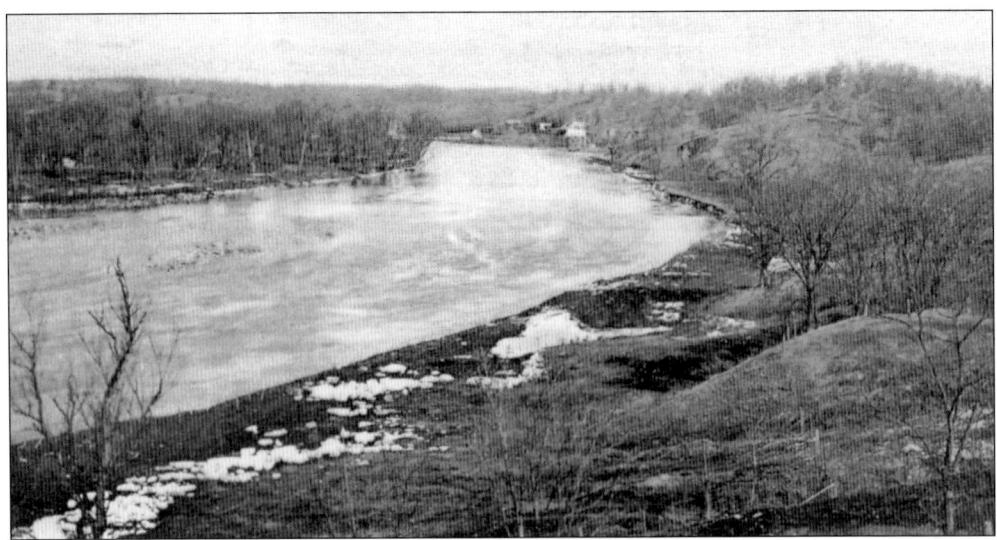

Above, the stunning 1907 view from Observatory Hill can be seen—now the site of the university president's house—north toward Terrell's Mill. The mill is visible along the river. It is the larger white-roofed structure near the center of the image, just below the horizon. Its dam is obscured by high water. Snow is visible, as is timber on the bank at left, which would become City Park in 1909. Park Road Bridge crosses at the image's center today.

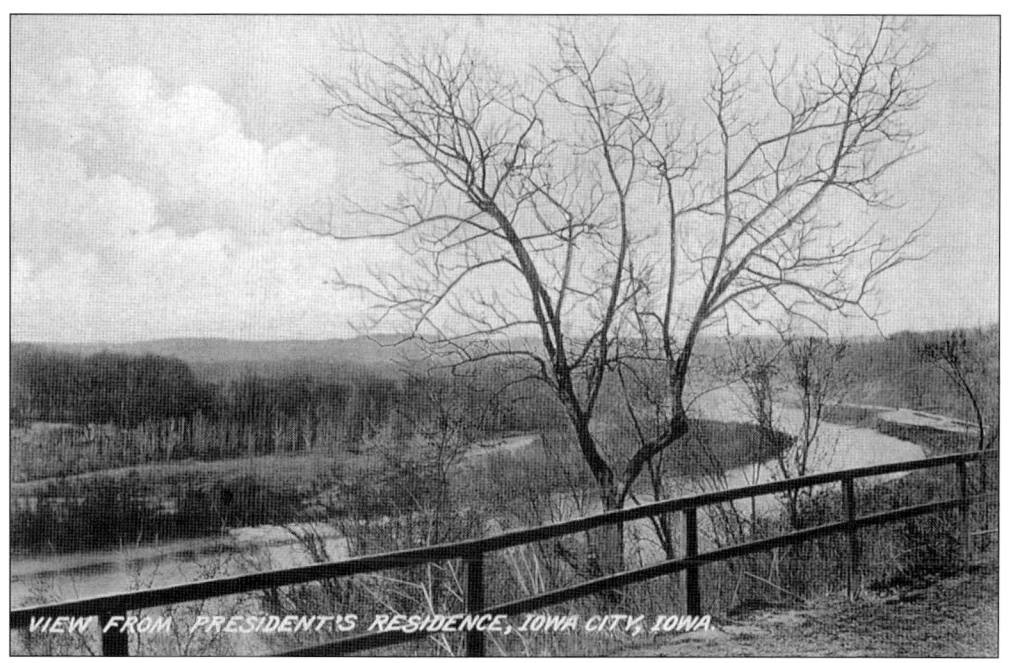

The City Park name in Iowa City devolved to current use from an earlier square-block site across from St. Mary's and First Methodist churches. This earlier site had been given to the university by the city in 1890 during political bickering about moving the university to central Iowa. The current park, seen above in a 1905-era view from Observatory Hill, began with a 78-acre purchase in 1906 from Euclid and Mary Terrill Sanders for $10,000. Below, a 1909 three-span Parker high truss, imaged soon thereafter, provided direct access to City Park and a new route to the Manville Heights neighborhood beyond.

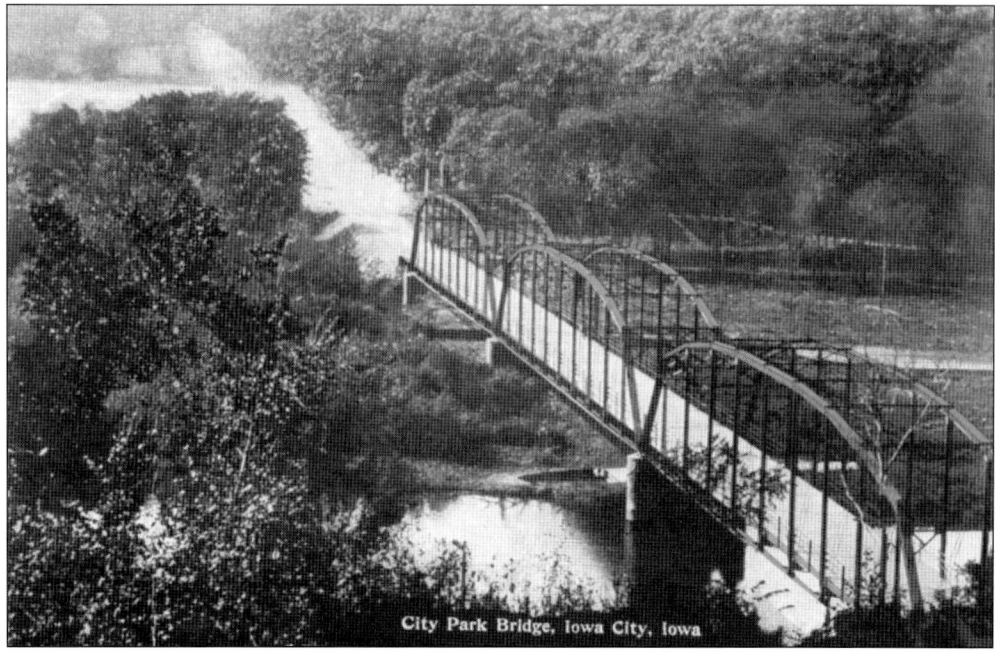

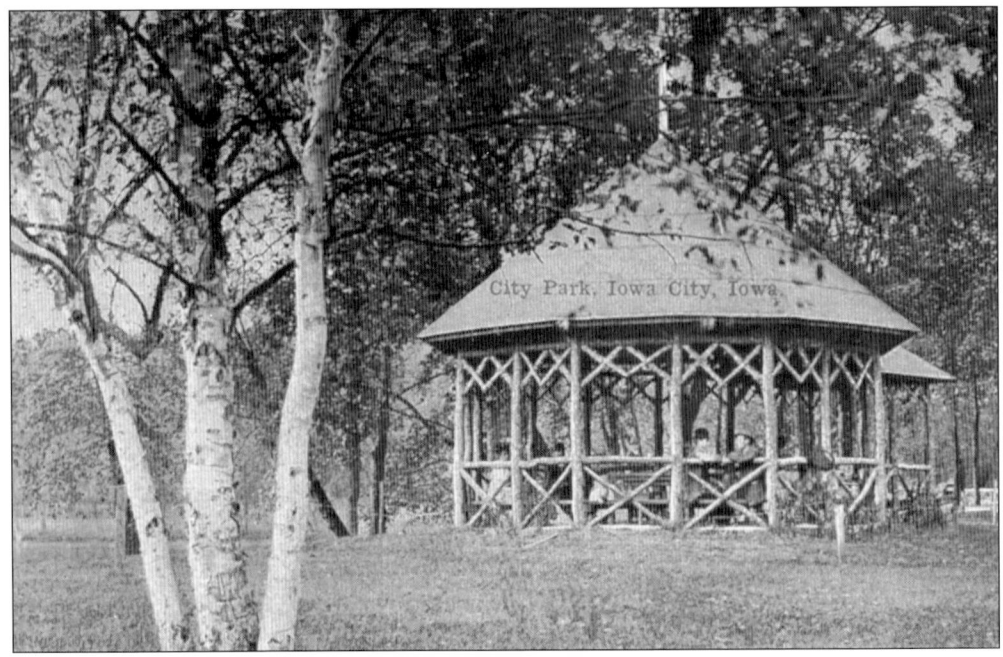

Early facilities at City Park included several birch structures, including the shelter imaged above about 1910, and a pedestrian bridge seen below and imaged a few years earlier. The bridge passed above a narrow neck of water between ponds. Other bygone facilities include buffalo pens, a prairie dog village, outdoor potties, bear cages, and a bocce court. Today's lower park facilities include a Shakespeare Festival stage, tennis courts, ball diamonds, children's play equipment, shelters galore, horseshoe courts, river access for boats, plus seasonal kids amusements that include a model train ride on a tenth-mile track. There are also indoor toilets.

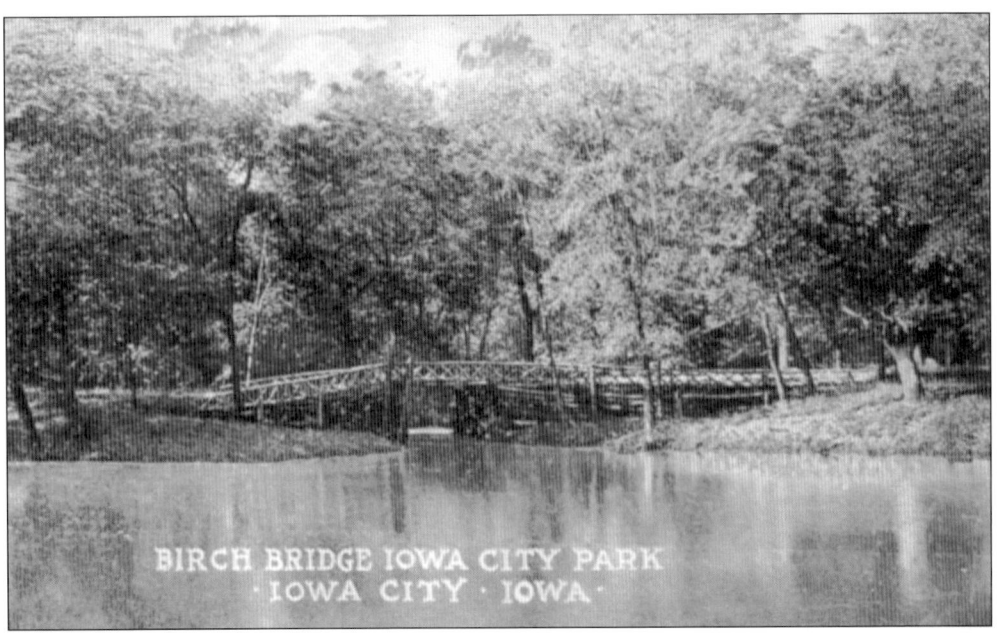

At right is a night scene of a rowboat docked in a pond in City Park. This image is from about a century ago, during an era when such proffered dark images were the fad. This one sold from 1911 into 1913 in at least five unique printings.

Below, a wooden dock, complete with a setting area, on the eastern edge of City Park provided river access, which apparently included entry for both boating and swimming, although only boating is noted in the 1910 card overprint. Swimming in the river was ubiquitous from any bank anywhere, but gentle sloping ones (with natural deposits of sand) were preferred.

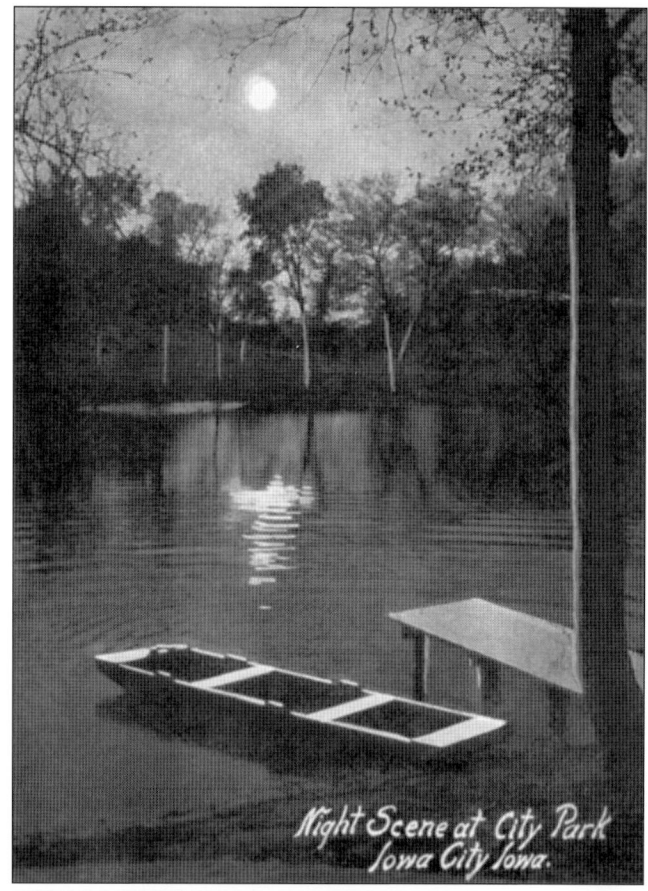

Night Scene at City Park, Iowa City, Iowa.

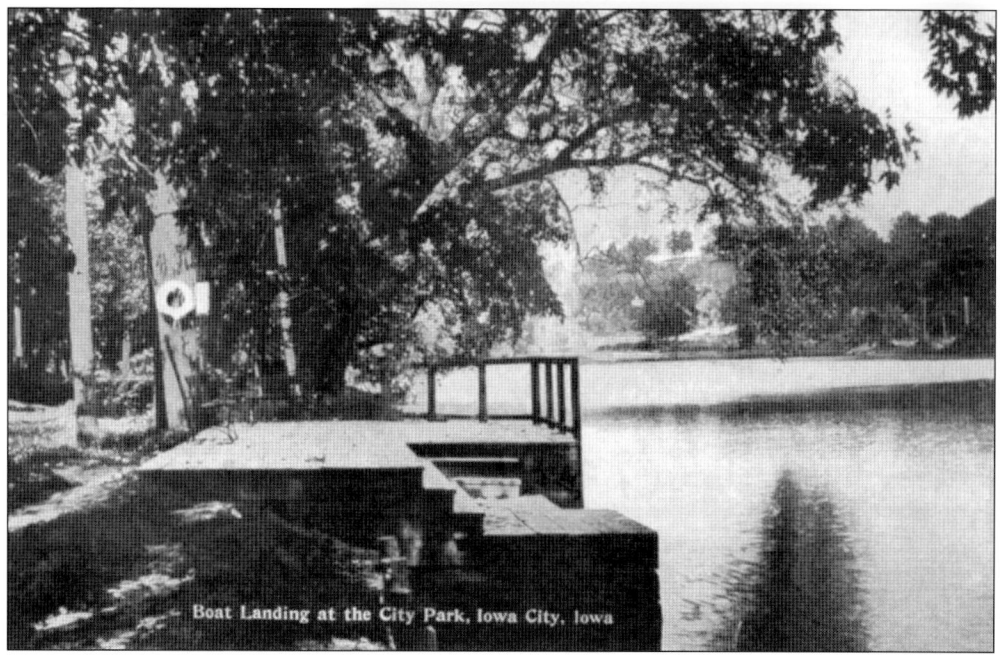

Boat Landing at the City Park, Iowa City, Iowa

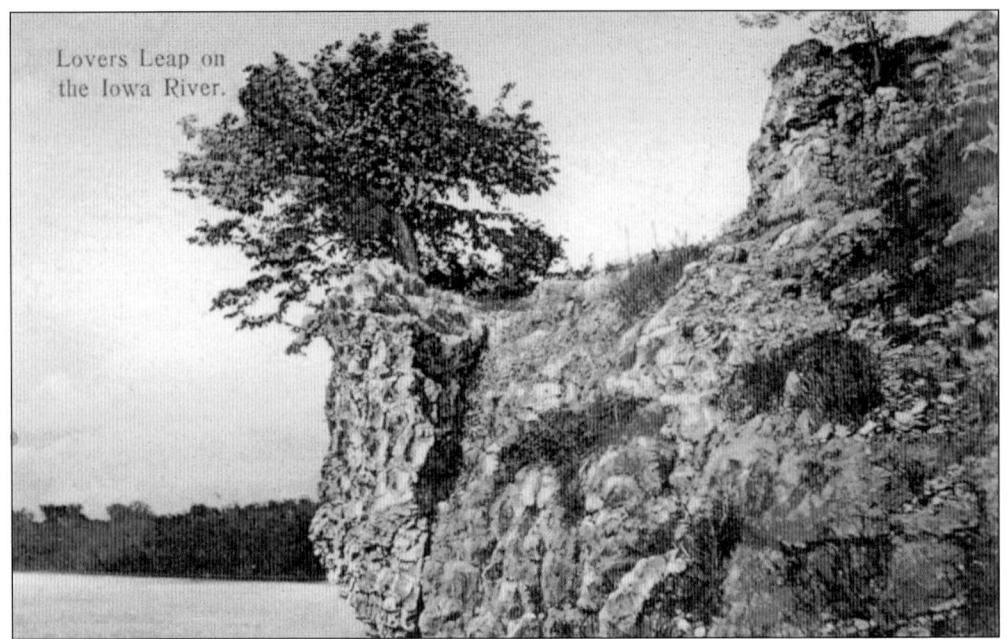

Other than a historic, heartsick Native American maiden, probably few others used a lover's leap to induce drowning. Site names like this one, imaged about 1908, mostly speak of a high rock bank topped by a plateau above the Iowa River's east bank, opposite today's Marriott Hotel in Coralville. Its access from Elk's Golf Club without crossing water would intrude on private lands. It is now heavily overgrown with trees and shrubs, but the limestone outcrop remains.

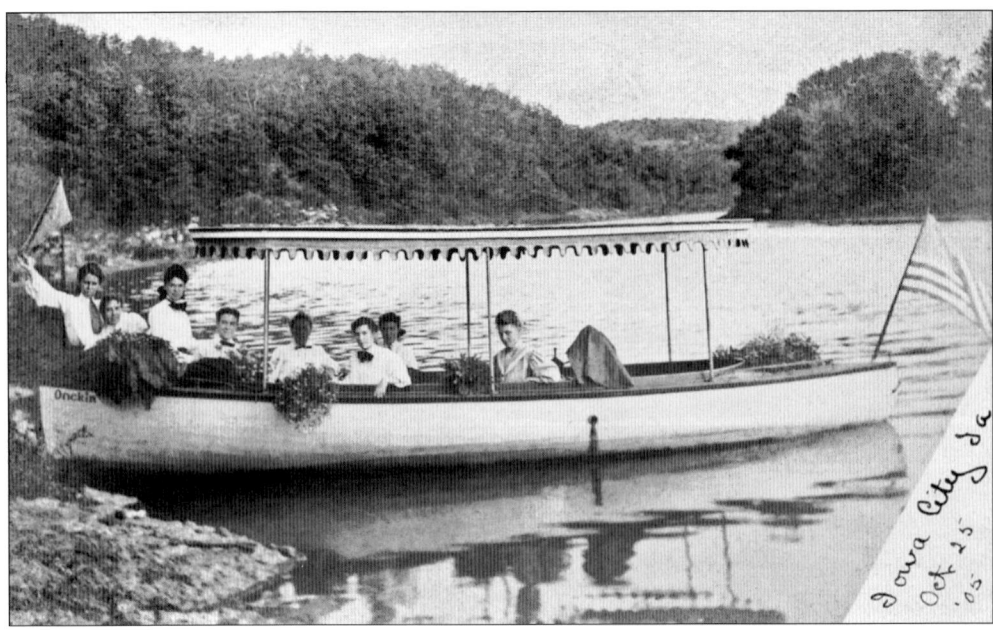

Sorority women, probably on a Sunday afternoon excursion, pose during 1905 for an image near Butler's Landing, a pioneer facility near what is called Butler Bridge today.

Seven

One-Night Stands
Motels and Hotels

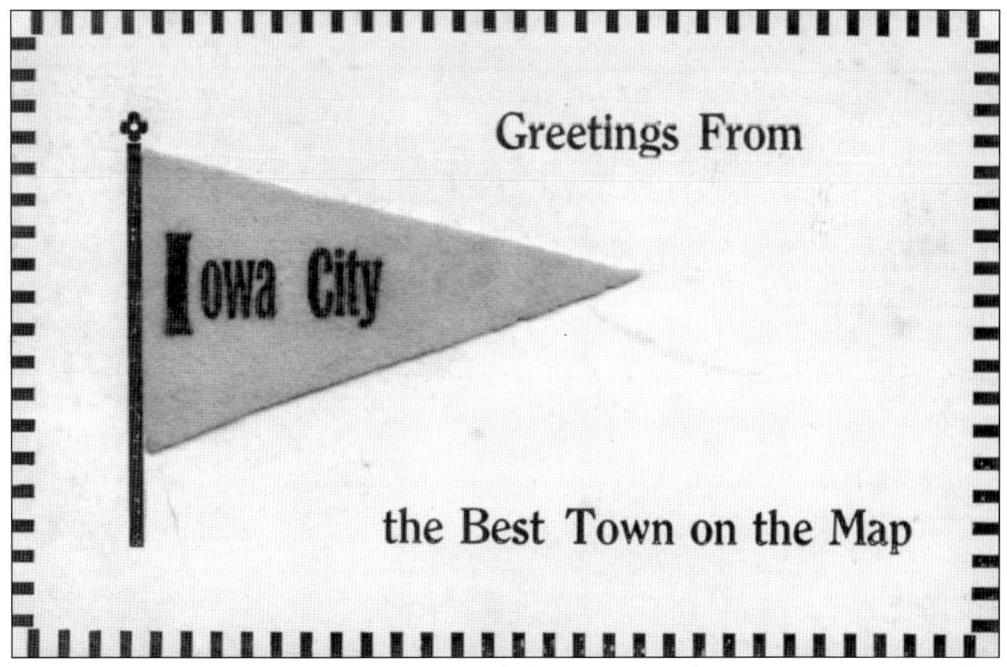

This generically boastful card, with a glued-on felt banner adding the town's name, was cancelled during 1913.

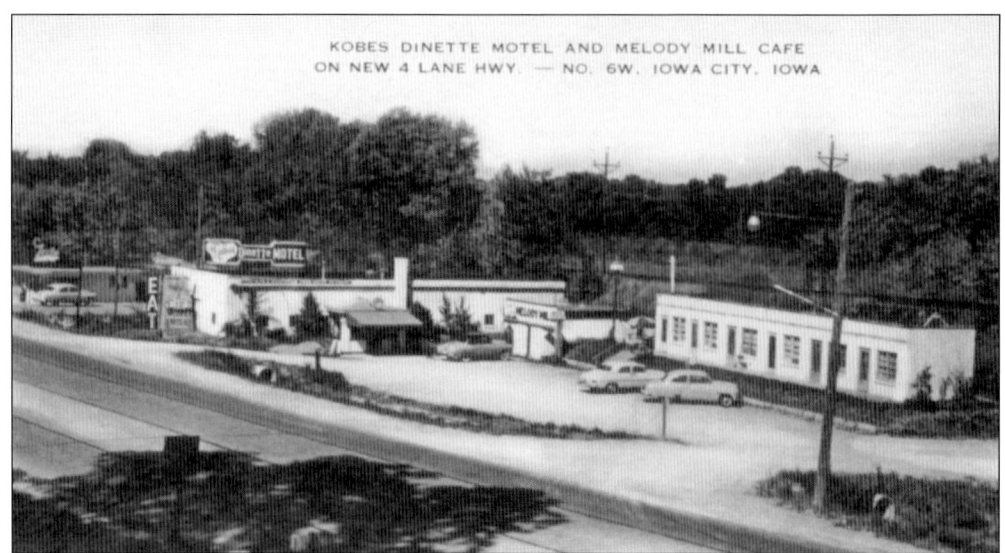

In Iowa City, one of the early strip motels bursts forth from this 1950-era card as the six-unit building at right, operated by John and Ethel Kobes. The area adjoined Rocky Shore Drive, at right, where "the Coralville Strip" along U.S. Highway 6 begins. Their larger structure at left first functioned as the Melody Mill Cafe. It included the motel office and several occasional sleeping rooms rented on nights when demand was high and the bar was not too noisy. "The Mill" was a popular 1940s hangout for young local couples, where music was occasionally live, but mostly came from a big, fancy garishly lit Wurlitzer jukebox. The cafe offered "pheasant, chicken and ham."

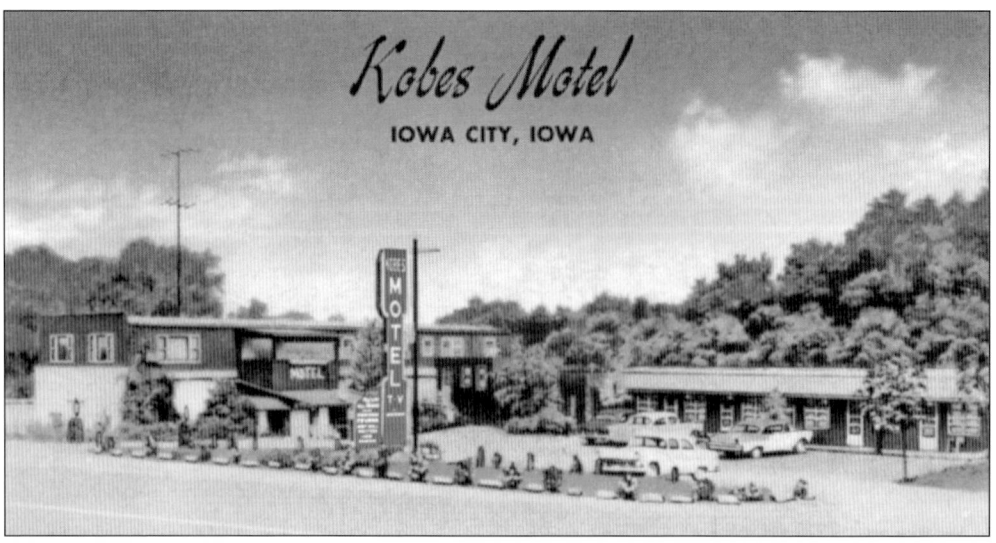

University of Iowa Hospitals and Clinics patient loads grew and added demand for more motel accommodations for patients' families. The cafe space, only a half-mile from the hospital, became more valuable in motel use than food service. The 1959 card above presents the updated Kobes, which is advertised as "Iowa City's finest and largest motel" with "all rooms air conditioned" and "free evening papers."

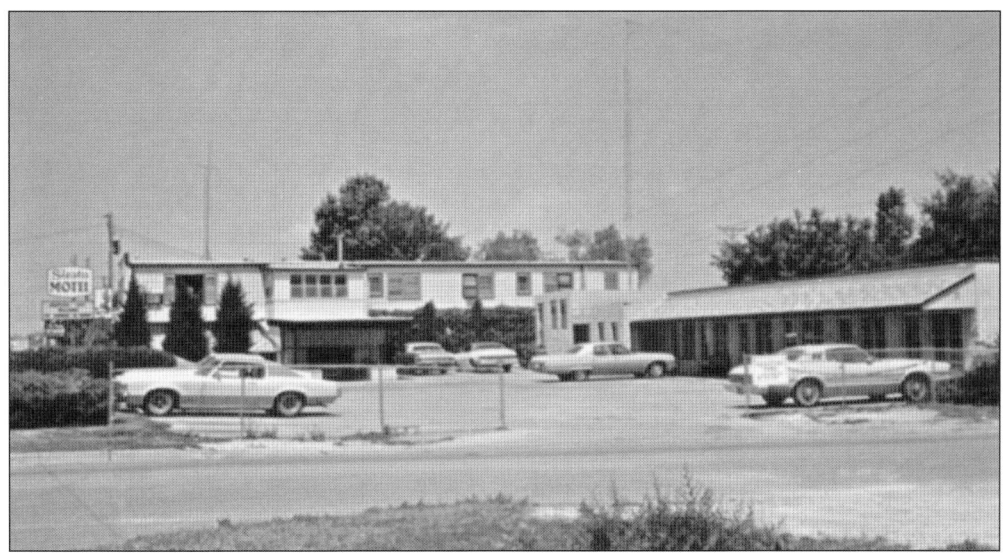

As the Kobes years waned, their operation morphed into the Siesta, advertised on the 1965 card that presents this image as offering "20 modern units" with "T.V., ice, phones, air conditioning," and offering "free transportation to and from hospitals." It was operated by Ralph and Ruby Wildman, although Ruby probably headed motel responsibility, since Ralph also functioned as a general contractor. They apparently lived at the site, at least for a time, which now serves a 1990 vintage office building.

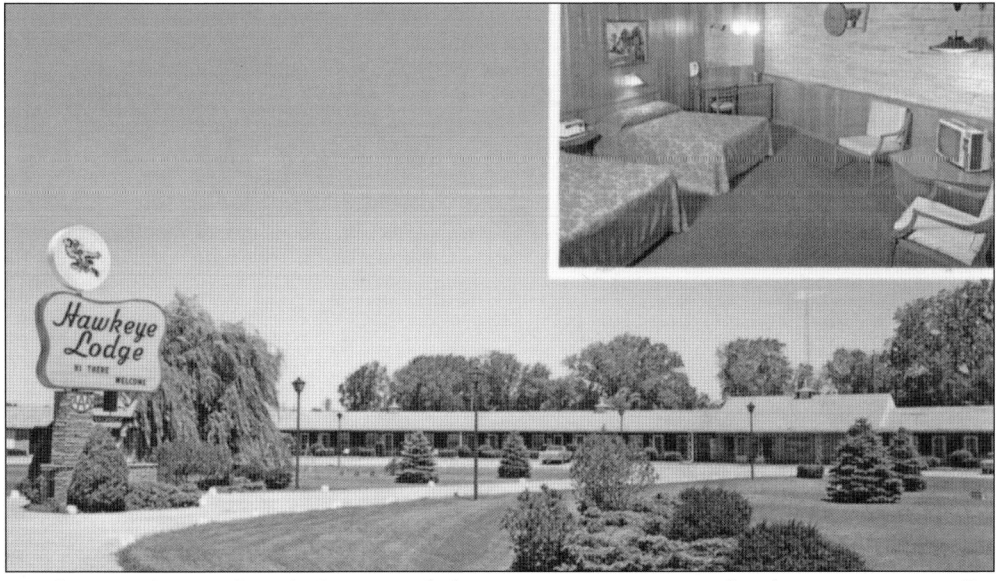

Hawkeye Lodge, a relatively late arrival about 1960, was a partnership between Russ Miller and Larry Smith. Smith had ties to the Blue Top Cabins operation a mile away, which gave him invaluable experience in the market and desired amenities. But the motel is now gone. The problem proved to be skyrocketing land values along this strip just outside Iowa City. The motel occupied a huge chunk of land that, with the 1990s, came to serve a variety of other businesses, including a multi-floor chain motel.

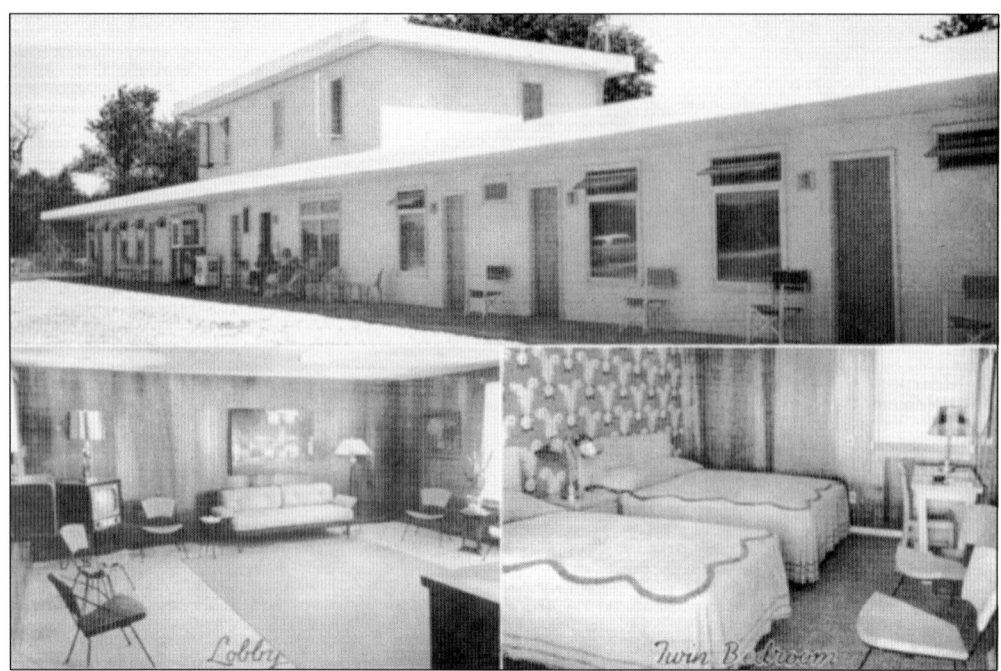

Health care services and Big 10 sports events produced growing demand for lodging space from the 1920s onward. Mom-and-pop facilities, which often provided a dozen or fewer units close to principal destinations, were first-generation offerings, two of which appear on this page. A 1950-era card above offers Motel Iowa, located "2½ miles west of Iowa City" near where Hills Bank now has a Coralville facility, with "air conditioned, central heat thermostat in each room, wall to wall carpeting," and "television available in large lobby" as shown. It was a "AAA approved motel," too. Below, neighboring Pine Edge, about 1955, included owner Isensee's residence at left.

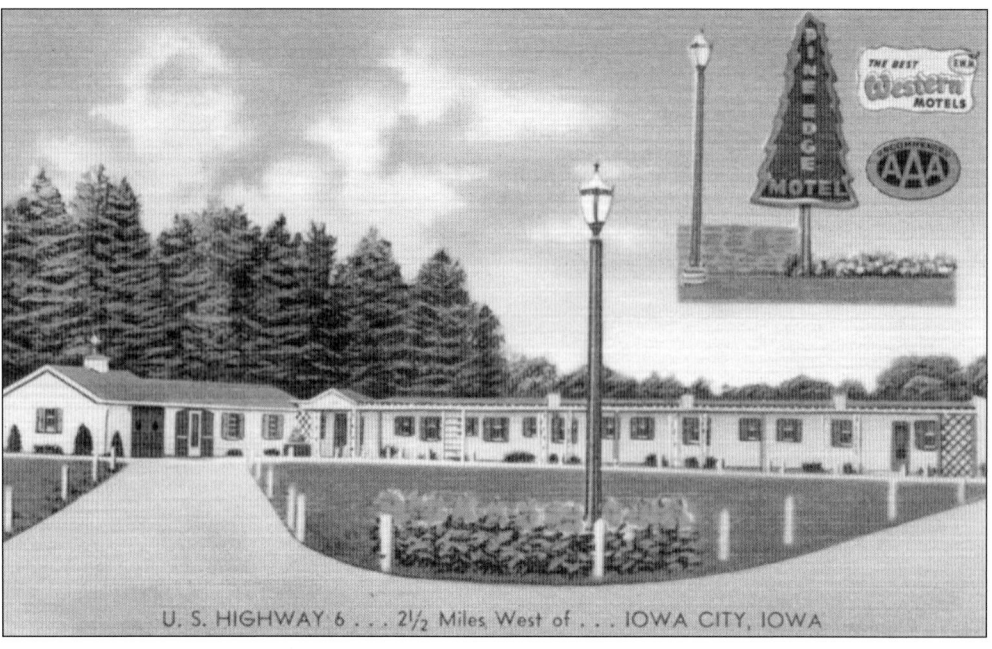

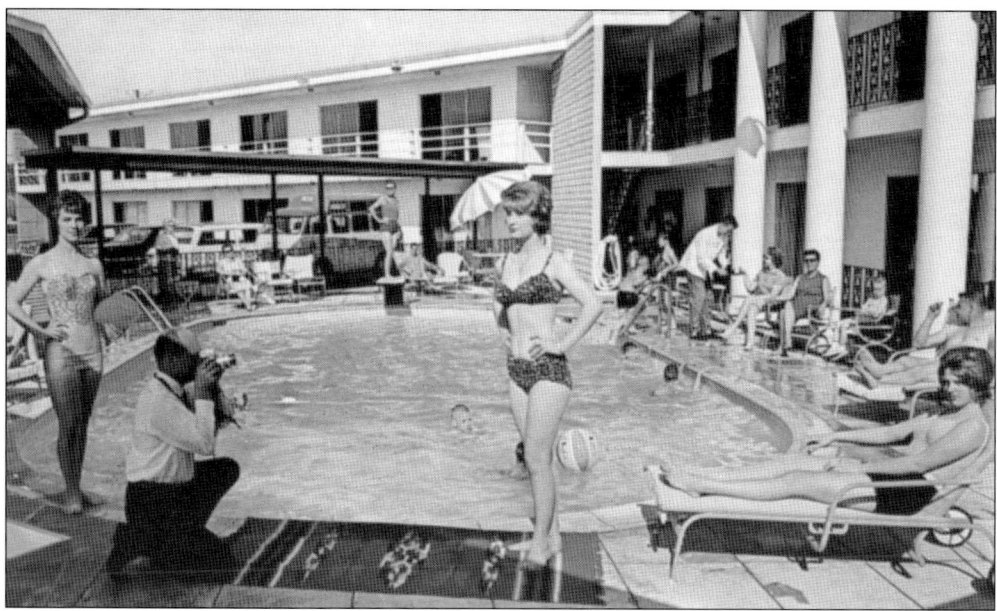

Photographers have all the fun. Above in a mid-1960s Congress Inn view, three young beauties pose in the foreground as a "photog"—to use professional slang—goggles through his zoom lens. This motel, located along the Coralville Strip next to Rapid Creek, also had incarnations as a Travel Lodge and Best Western Old Capitol Inn.

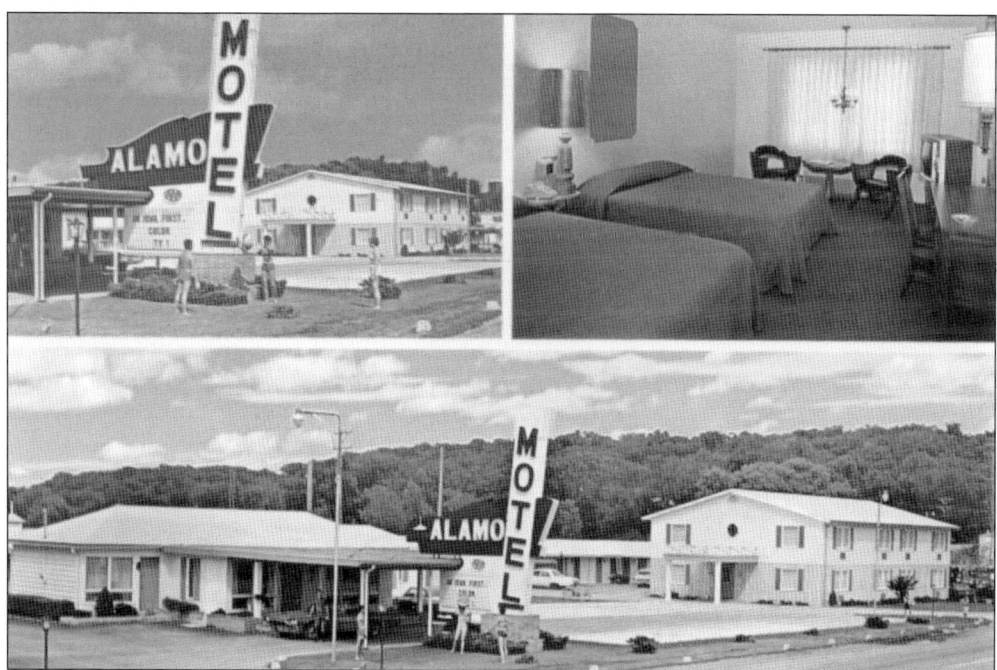

A 1950-era view presents a local version of The Alamo, which sprouted on the Iowa City and Coralville municipal boundary not far from the Kobes Dinette Motel. It offered "30 attractively appointed units with TV, phones, air conditioning, coffee-in-rooms, playground, near hospitals." Two restaurant-bars now occupy the site.

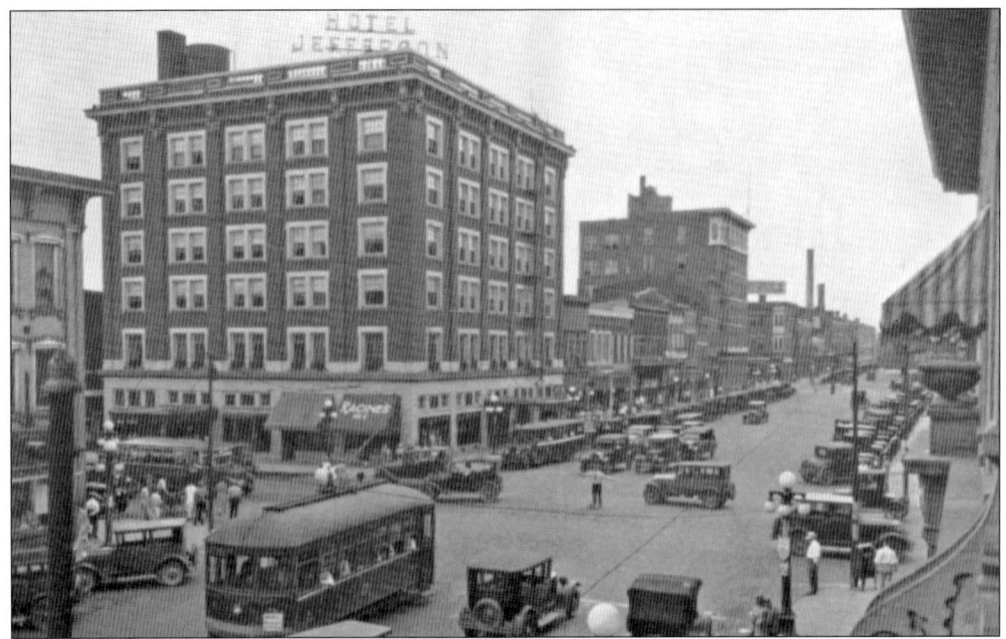

Above, the original six-floor Hotel Jefferson guards a busy Dubuque-Washington intersection about 1925. Passing vehicles that include both a trolley, or streetcar, and a go-anywhere city bus (at left), are policed by a lone cop in the center. This and the intersection a block south (left) were the first to get local traffic lights on a post replacing a policeman in the middle of each intersection. Sidewalks proved safer for the signals.

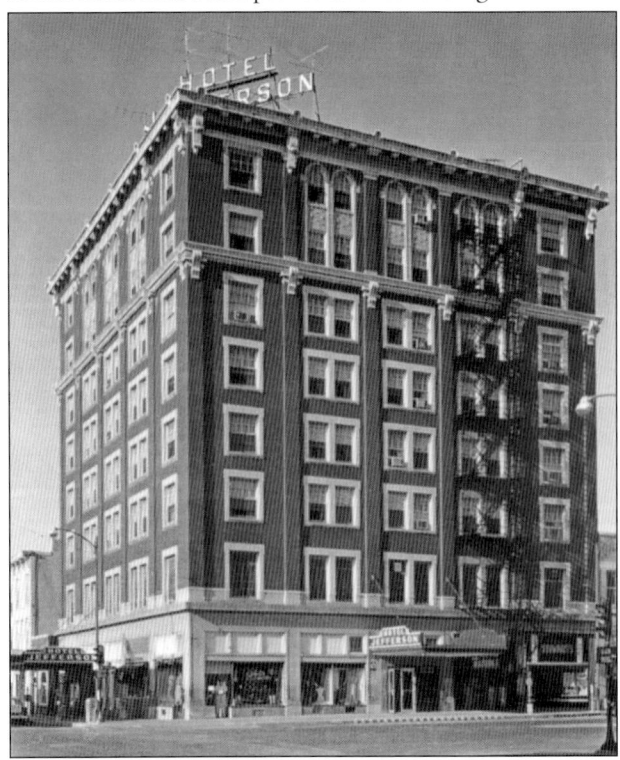

Constructed in 1913 to a towering six floors—with two additional stories piled on during the Roaring Twenties—the full-height Hotel Jefferson shown at left was the tallest commercial structure in town, until it was topped four decades later by the successor Hilton (now Sheraton) Hotel. Plaza Towers is now taller, as are several university dorms and other structures. Construction of the Jefferson effectively moved the commercial and shopping hub of the downtown a block east away from Clinton Street with its orientation to campus needs. The hotel became a listed tourist attraction with the 1934 unveiling of eight large historic murals painted in oil by then-prominent local artist Mildred Pelzer.

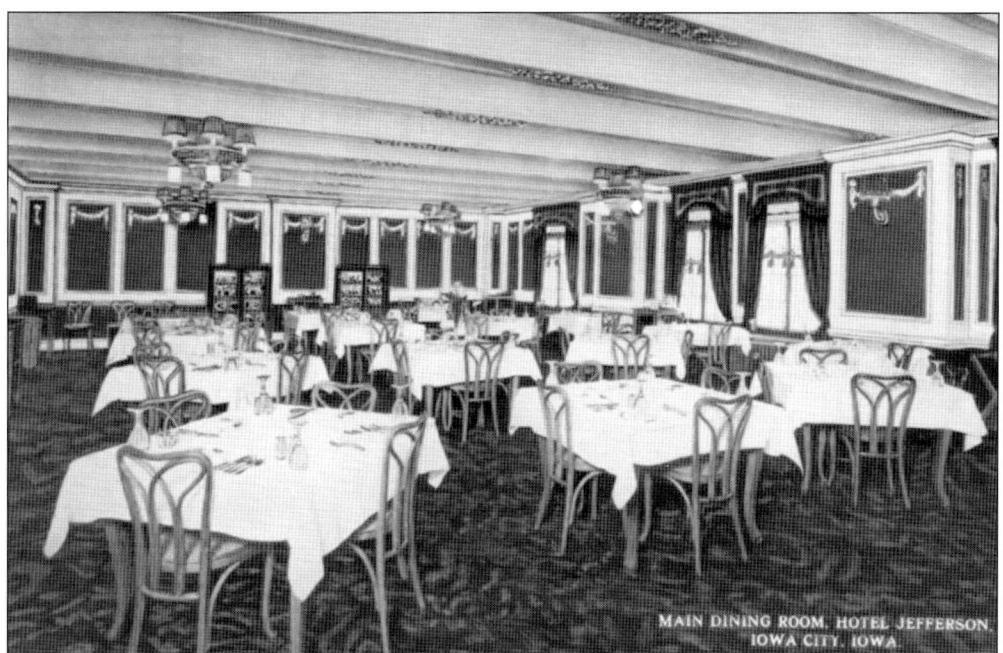

To arrive in Hotel Jefferson's main dining room one had to take the elevator or climb the stairs, then walk the mezzanine. This was another option to its popular street-level coffee shop The Huddle. Shown about 1913, service clubs, other groups, and the public lunched here regularly.

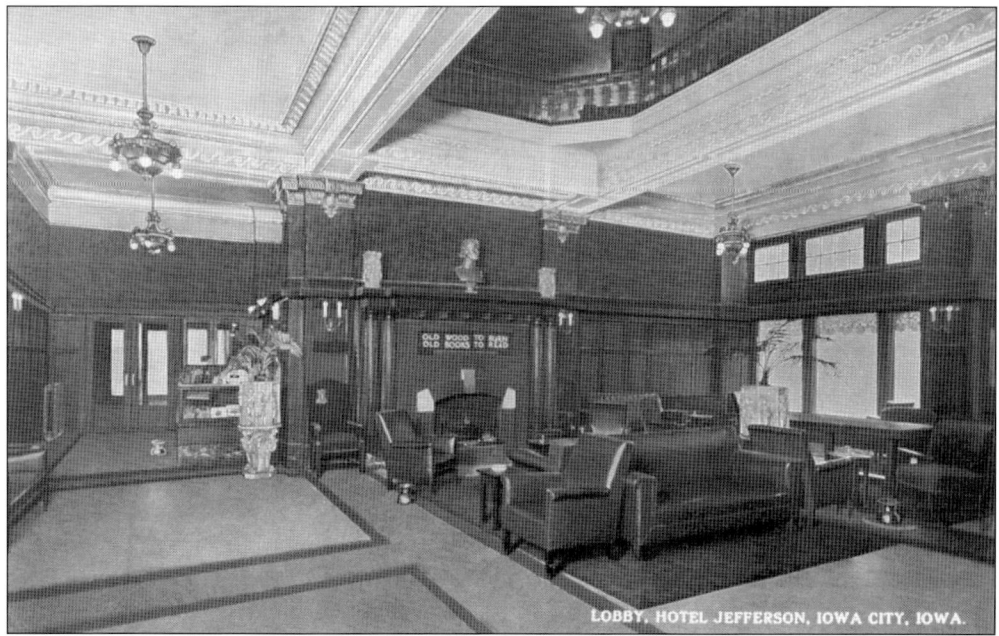

Eight Pelzer murals—each measuring about 4 feet high by 12 feet wide—hung in this Hotel Jefferson lobby, just below the ceiling in spaces between pilasters. Smaller by a width of 16 inches, the controversial We Build Our Capitol 1841 hung above the fireplace succeeding the artsy everyman bust at center of this hotel opening-day image.

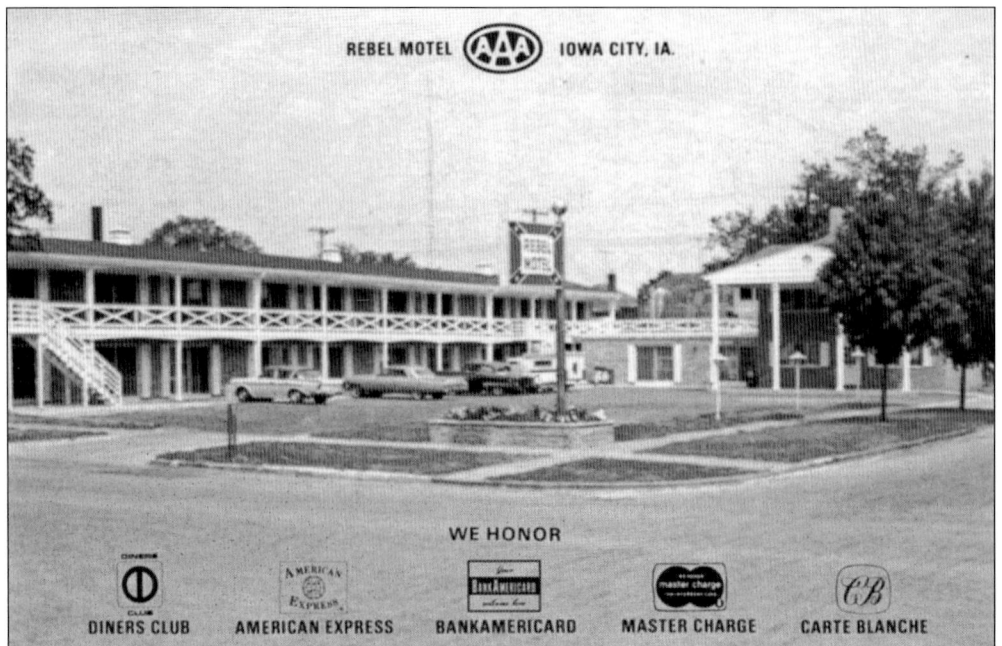

Sprouting during 1963–1964, the Rebel Motel was one of few actually located in Iowa City, since 1960s zoning was used to prevent another Coralville Strip along the three principal highways that cross the town. This one resulted on the fringe of downtown when fire razed the Oathout Funeral Home (see page 28) opening the site. It later served offices, barbershop, and light retail before being lost to the 2006 tornado.

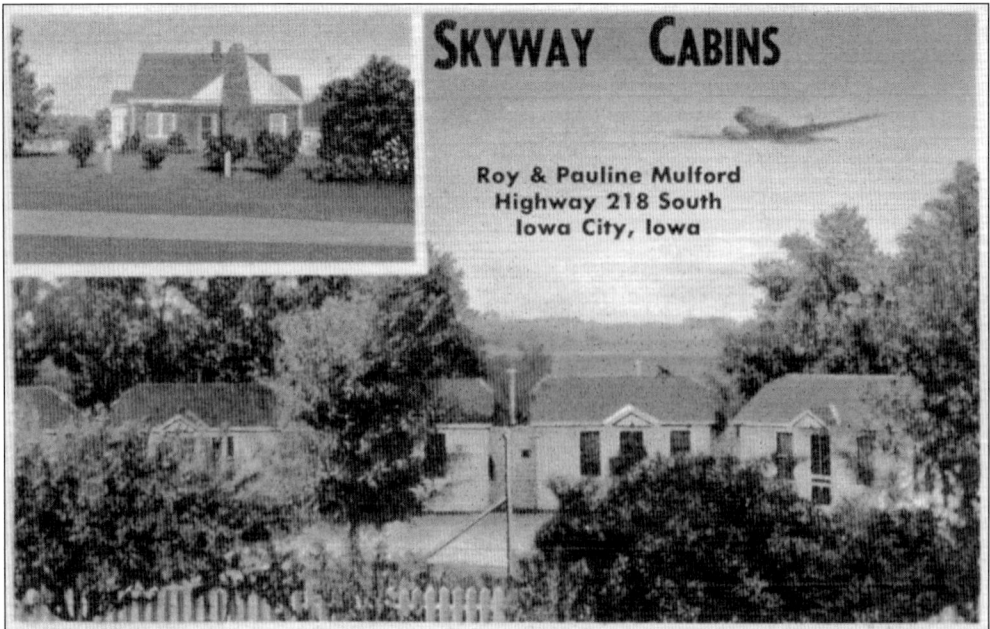

This 1940s postcard shows a DC-3 airliner roaring above a home and rentals adjoining the airport. A multi-floor motel using flight motif now inhabits the site.

Eight

THE COMMON GOOD
PO, COURTHOUSE, SCHOOLS, FIREMEN, AND MILITARY

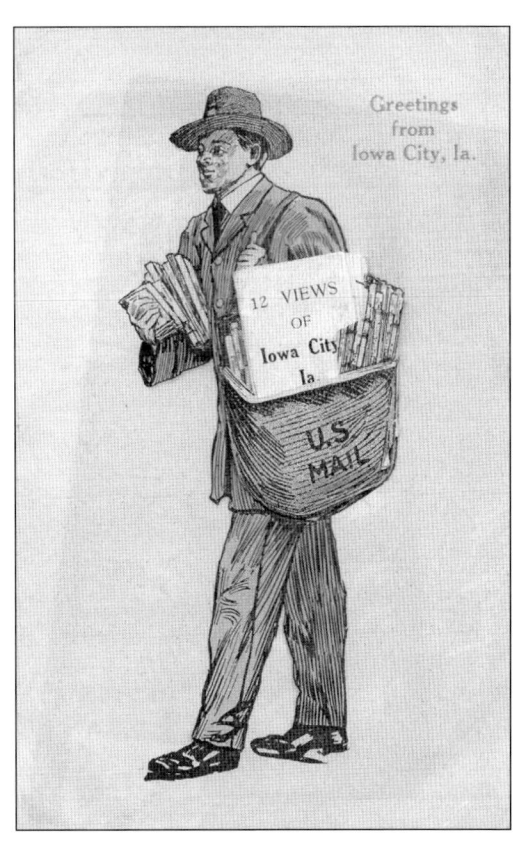

A 1908 carrier carts an accordion-folded strip of images.

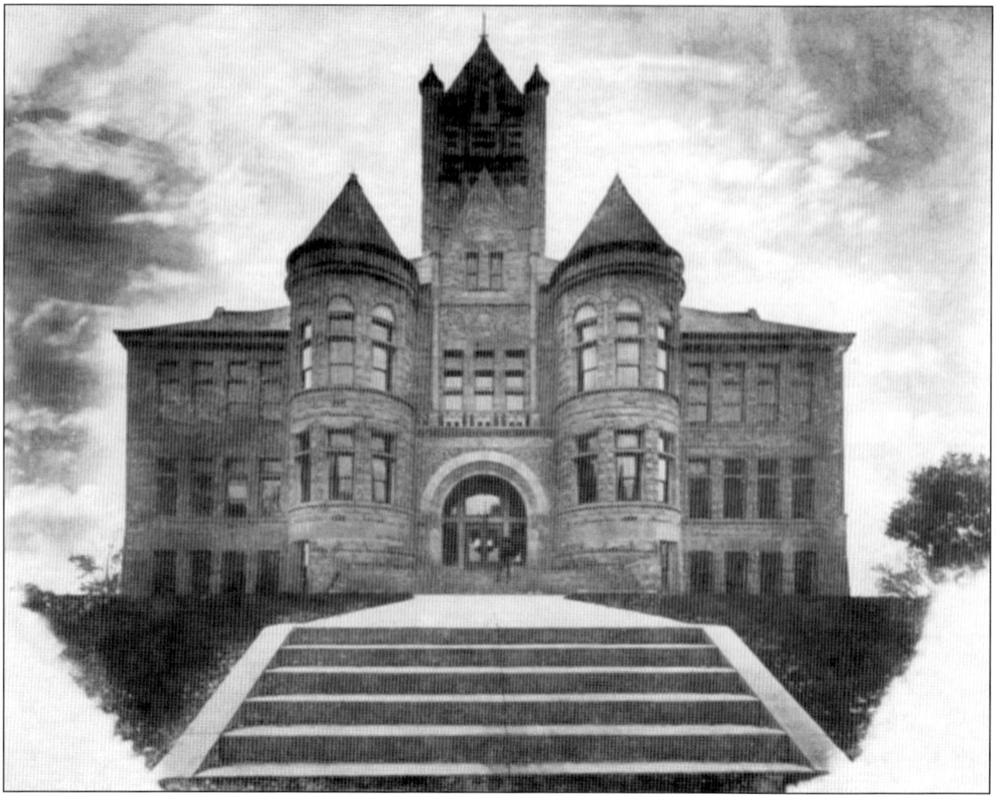

A spooky, sinister, and foreboding air hangs over an artsy 1905 image of the Johnson County Courthouse. It was constructed in 1901, after fire razed its predecessor, the ornate Gothic Revival three-story seen below. Erected in 1859, it was nicknamed "Trimble's Smokehouse" for its builder and a penchant for filling with smoke from its own wood-fueled stoves. It was the county's third effort after an 1839 wooden wilderness cabin at a site called Napoleon, and an 1842 stone predecessor in Iowa City.

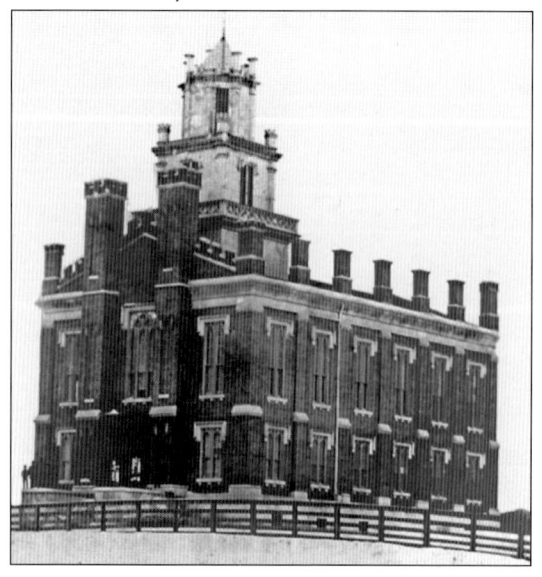

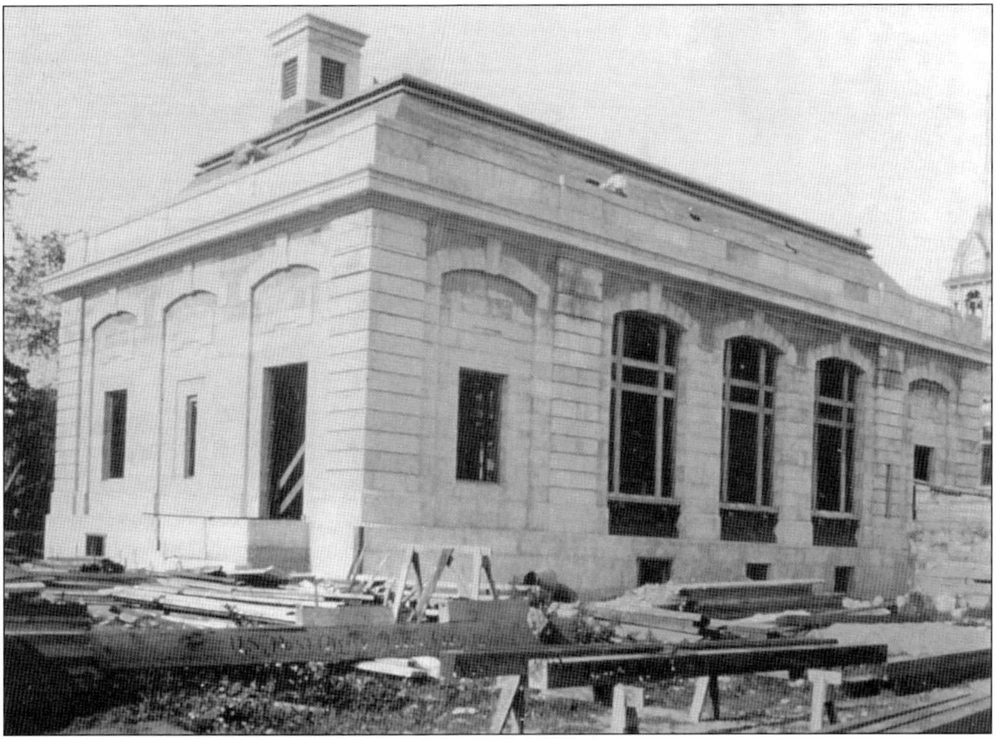

Built in 1904 by Jacob Hotz who earlier had erected the Johnson County Courthouse, the first federal building constructed specifically for postal use in Iowa City shows above with work underway. The post office had previously been in rented quarters, both in a store where the university business college now sets, and on the Iowa Avenue and Clinton Street corner now serving Iowa Book across from Pentacrest.

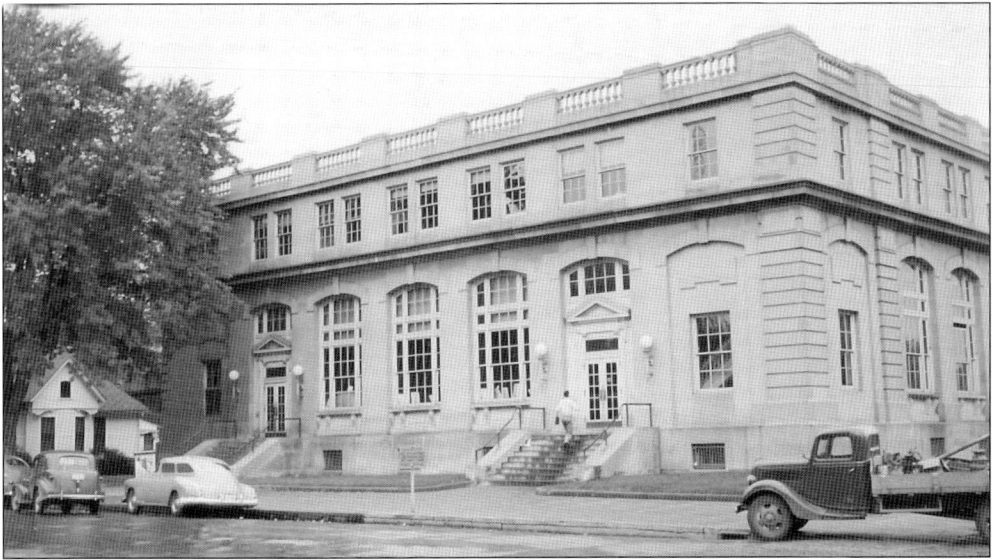

Reorientation from south to west, plus quadrupling its size, produced the postal facility imaged above in 1935. This is now the senior center after a new post office was built in 1974.

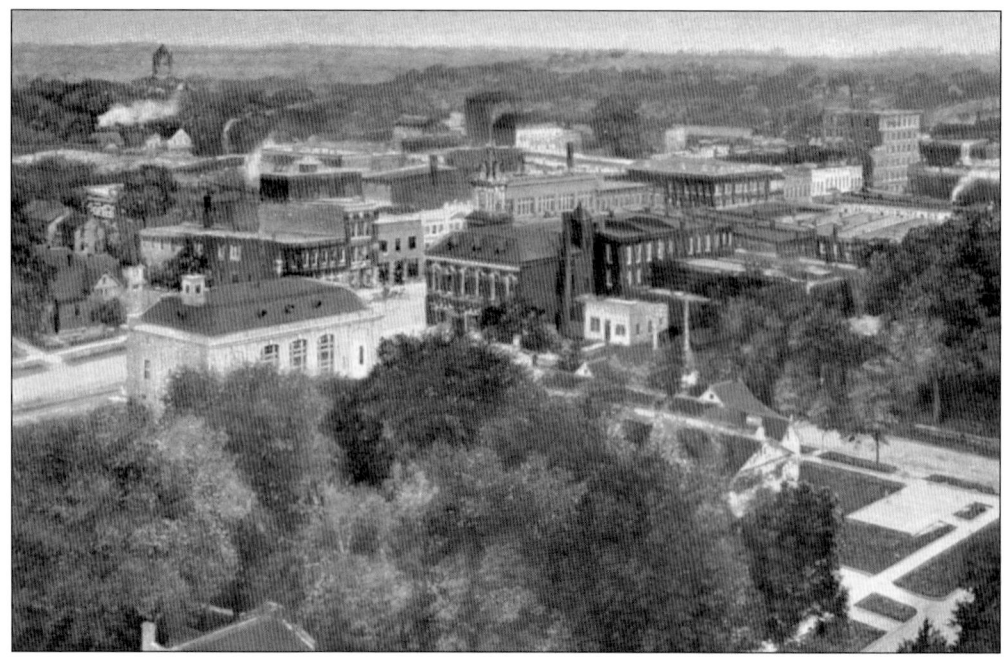

A span from the 1904 post office just beyond the trees at left to the six-floor Johnson County Savings Bank at right, and stretching to the 1901 Johnson County Courthouse on the left horizon, is recorded in this bird's-eye view, made about 1912, probably from a UI laundry chimney. The next year, the first six floors of Hotel Jefferson came to the site of Metropolitan Hall, which shows as the dark building left of the bank.

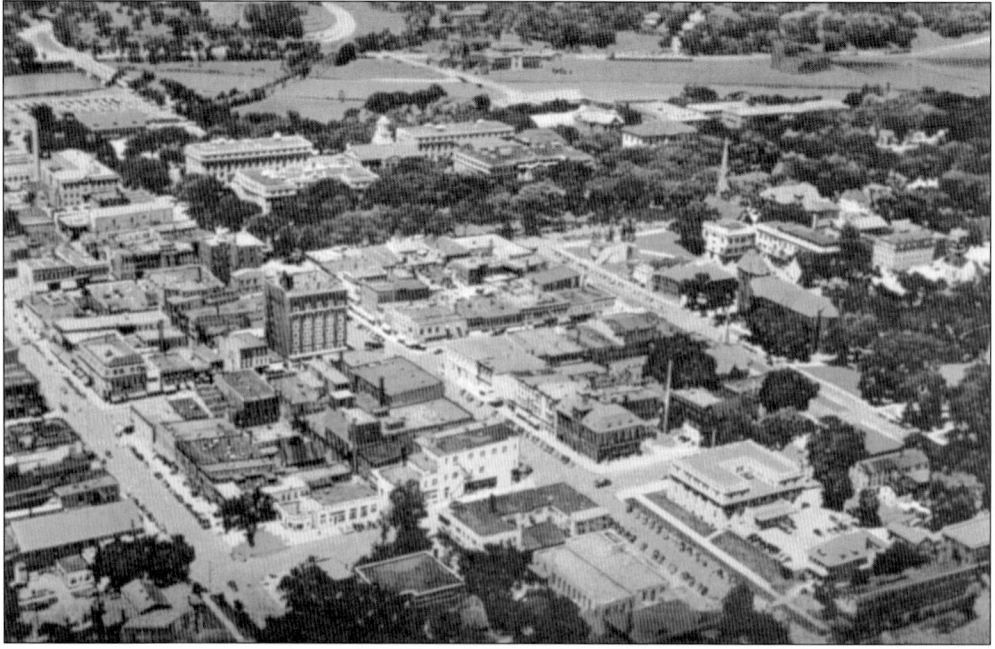

This aerial image of central Iowa City taken during the mid-1940s shows the Jefferson Hotel as the tallest downtown structure, with Pentacrest visible beyond it.

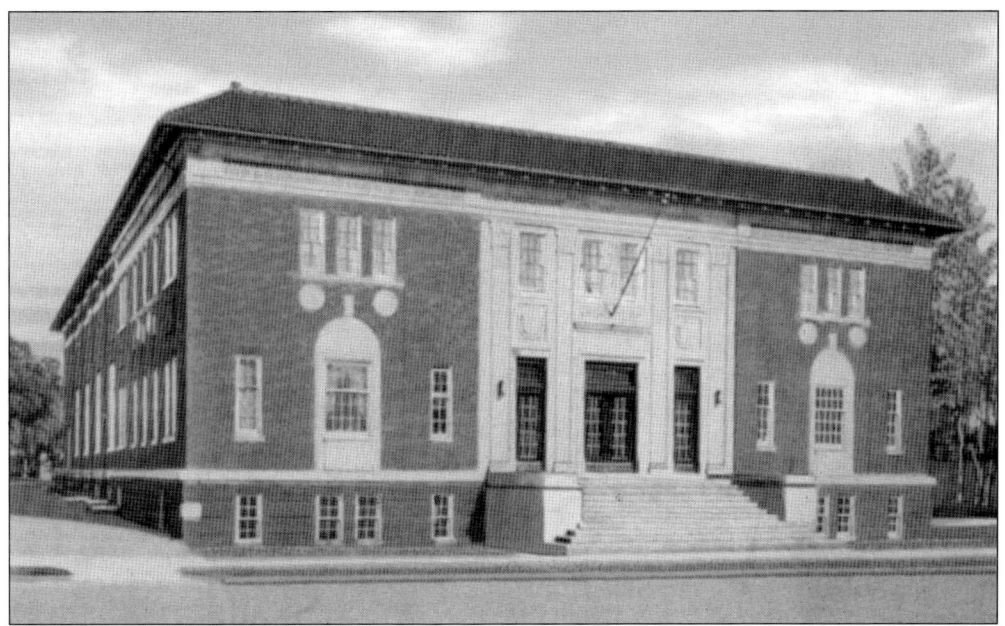

Kinnick Stadium and the American Legion building above share the unofficial title of worst timing possible for construction—both on the very eve of the Great Depression, which effectively bankrupted both. Lenders couldn't figure out what to do with the football stadium when bonds weren't paid, so they let it ride a decade until it could be redeemed. This building landed in the hands of Iowa City under a deal with the Legion to convert it into a community center, with legionnaires receiving a room for their office. After a January 1955 fire, it was replaced onsite by the current recreation center downtown.

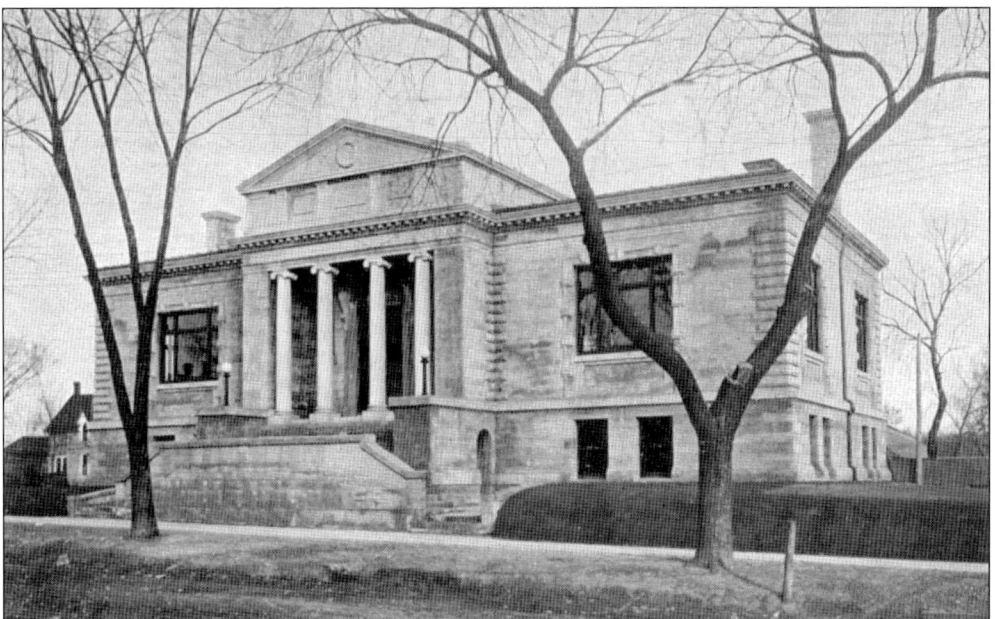

Iowa City's first public library outside rented quarters, this image presents a new 1904 facility financed largely by a grant from the Andrew Carnegie Foundation.

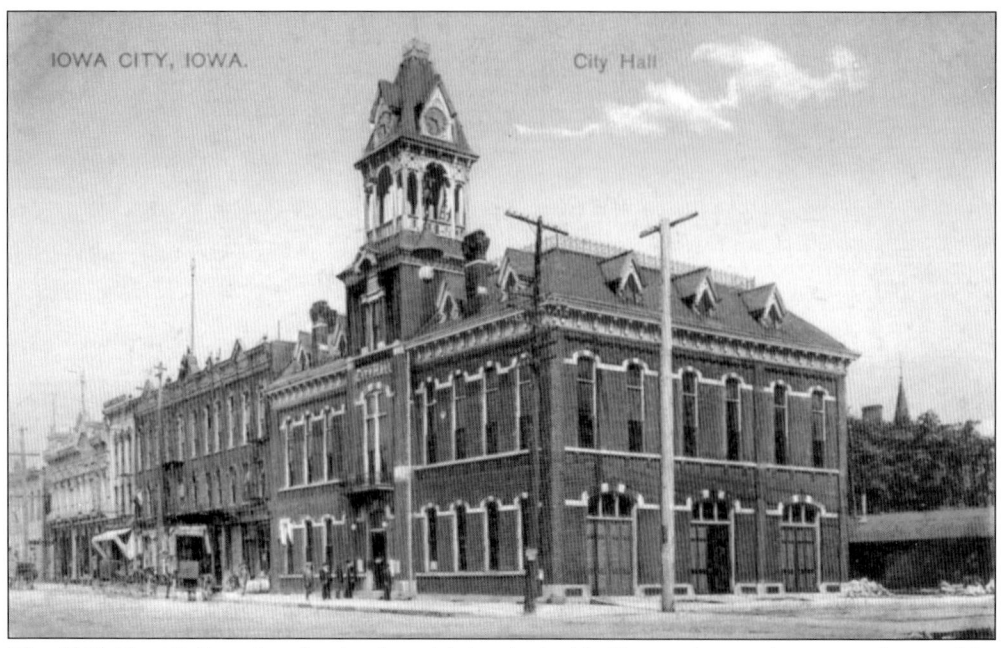

The 1881 City Hall reaches for the sky with its clocked belfry on the northwest quadrant of the Washington and Linn Streets intersection in this century-old image. The first floor was occupied by city offices on the left half, and by fire equipment behind the three doors on the right. The council chamber and fire quarters were up a flight of 23 or 24 steps to get to any public meeting held in the chamber. Public restrooms were provided in the basement—without a coin slot on the doors as at Hotel Jefferson where kids used them anyway by slipping in under the doors.

A regular meeting of volunteer firemen is called for 7:30 p.m. on January 6, 1913, at City Hall by the postcard notice reproduced above and addressed to Willie Tomlin.

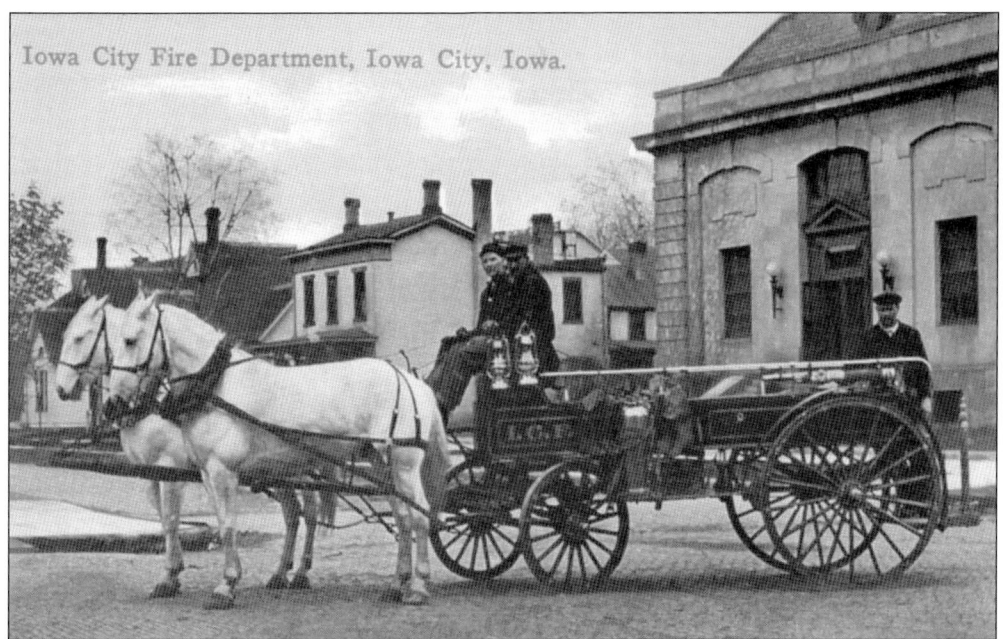

Snowball and Highball, a matched pair of white Percherons imaged about 1910 in the Washington-Linn intersection outside City Hall, were popular among local firemen, kids, and adults alike. They participated in many parades, as well as in competitions held regularly among various fire companies and departments. After decades of service, they were retired about 1925 to a farm near Solon. Below, while also still using horses, Iowa City's first horseless engine was imaged during 1911, while James Clark (center) was beginning service as the first paid fireman. Behind the wheel is Herman Amish, with George Kaspar standing. All three were longtime firemen and served as chief, including Clark for 30 years. Slush is visible on the brick pavement.

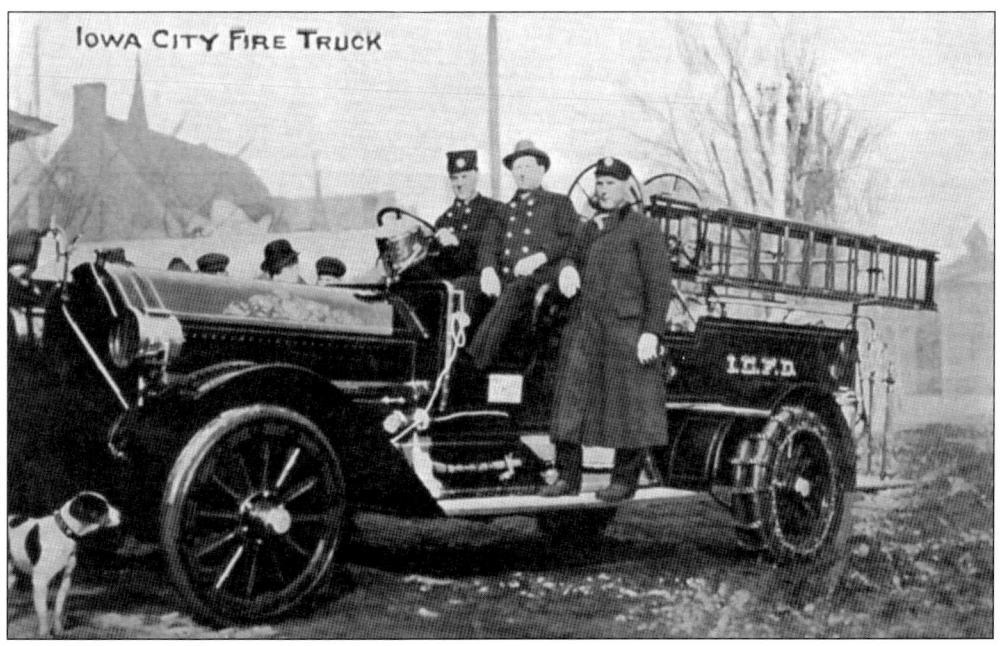

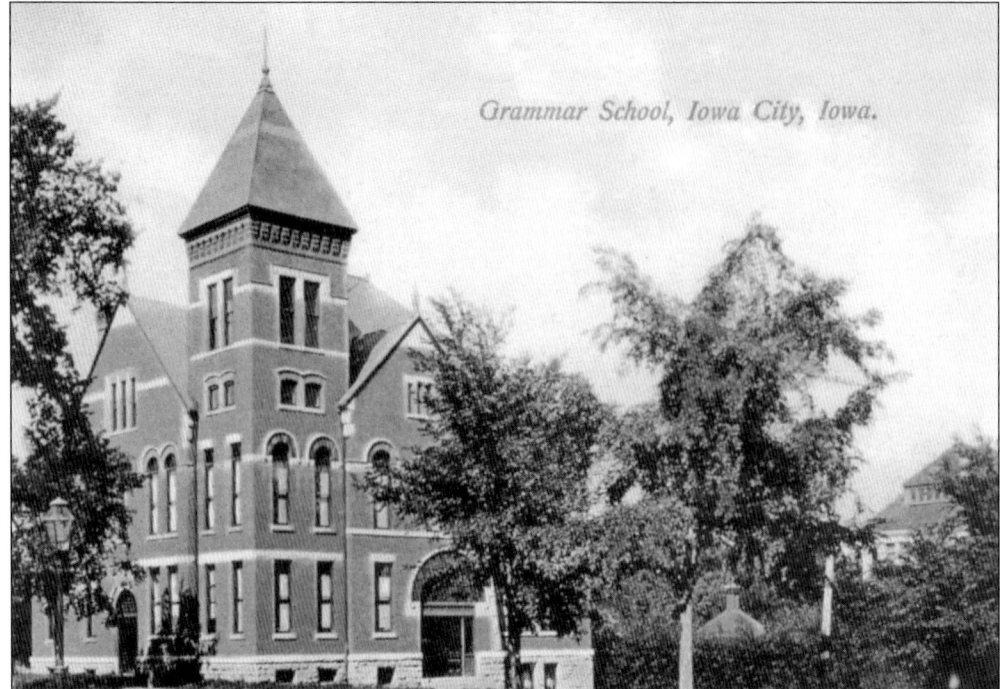

This 1892 building, constructed as the second City High to replace a wood-frame structure along Gilbert Street north of Iowa Avenue, is imaged above about 1906. It became the district's first junior high for grades six through eight, then called Grammar School, when a new City High was erected across the block, later called Central Junior High. This structure faced Jefferson Street at Van Buren, now the site of a Mercy Hospital parking ramp.

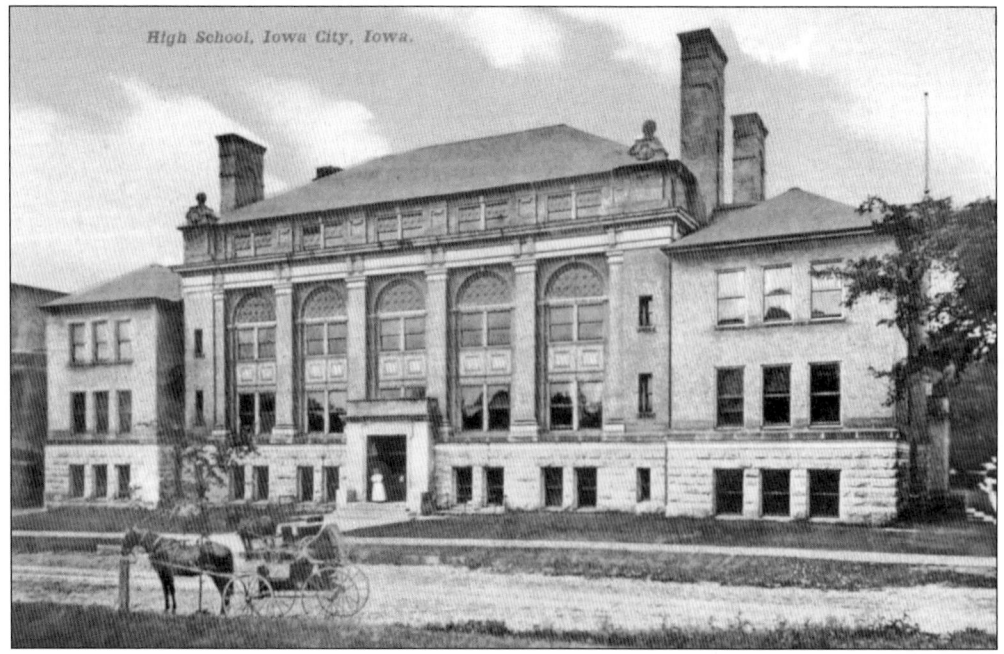

City High III, later Central Junior High, shines across Johnson Street about 1907.

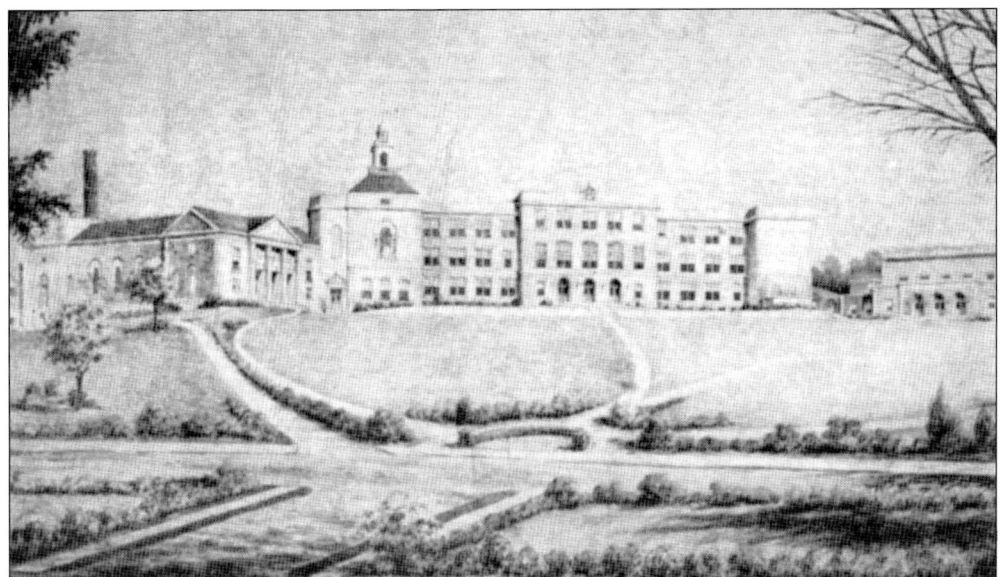

City High IV is imaged above from an architect's sketch placed on a 1938 postcard. Meanwhile, talk swirled around Iowa City about the school board planning a new senior high in a cornfield on the outskirts of town. It happened; an $800,000 building was opened in 1939 at the fairgrounds in what is now the Morningside Drive area. The fair moved on to its present site south of the airport. School financing included $358,000 in WPA money.

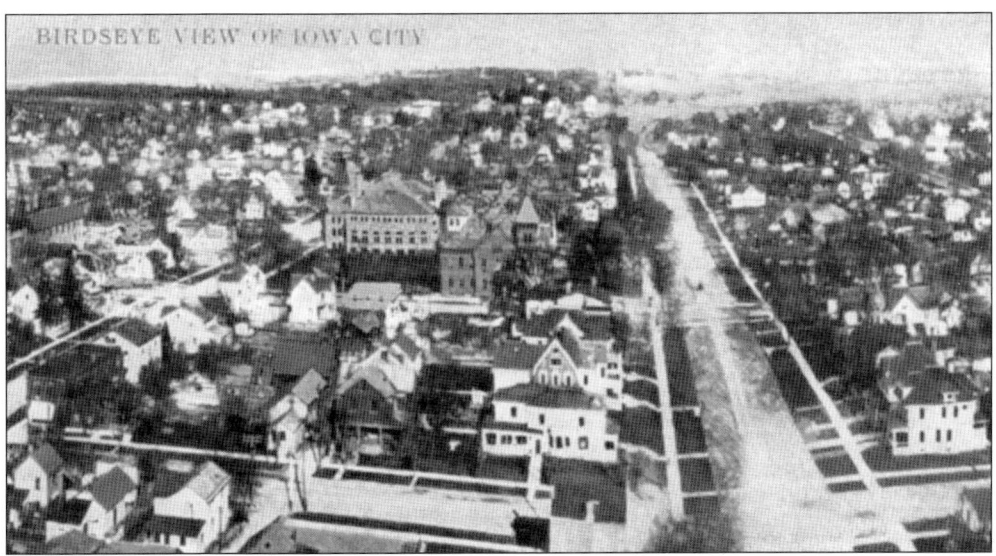

Jefferson Street, running east, is the dominant feature of this left third of a three-part postcard panorama taken about 1910 from the top of the St. Mary's Catholic Church steeple. Just left of Jefferson Street, near the center of the image, is the "school block," now home to the doctor's clinic across Market Street from Mercy Hospital. The Grammar School, City High, as well as infant Mercy Hospital, farther left, are visible. The dark building at lower left has housed John's Grocery since 1948.

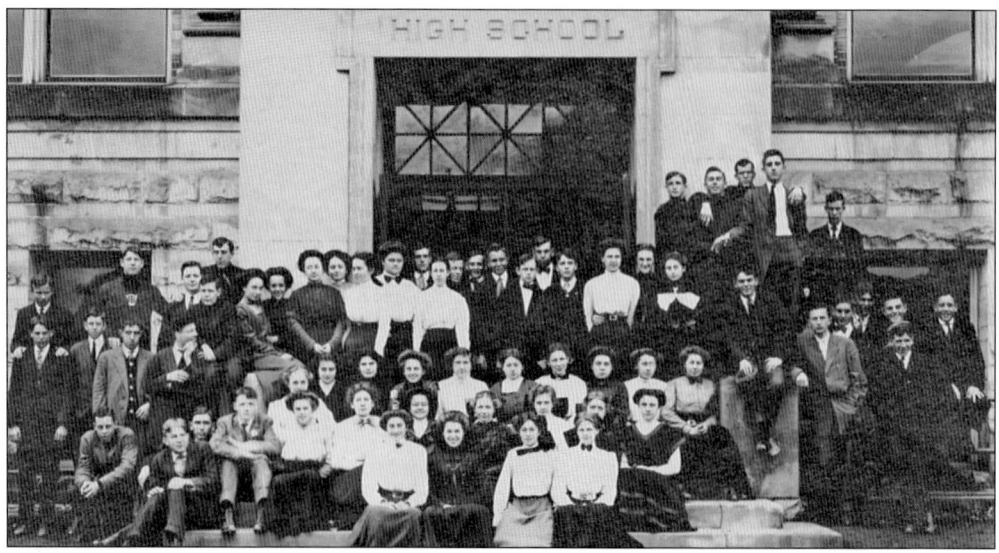

Sixty-three members of the graduating class of 1910 pose at the Johnson Street door of City High, later called Central Junior High, on a card mailed December 29, 1909. The card, from Leo, wished season's greetings to a cousin in Ohio. Leo writes: "I am sitting down and my head is all that shows." The public schools were founded by the city council in 1853 when it rented the two-story, 10-room Mechanics Academy building for $250 a year and hired several teachers and paid them between $150 and $400 a year. A school board arrived in 1858.

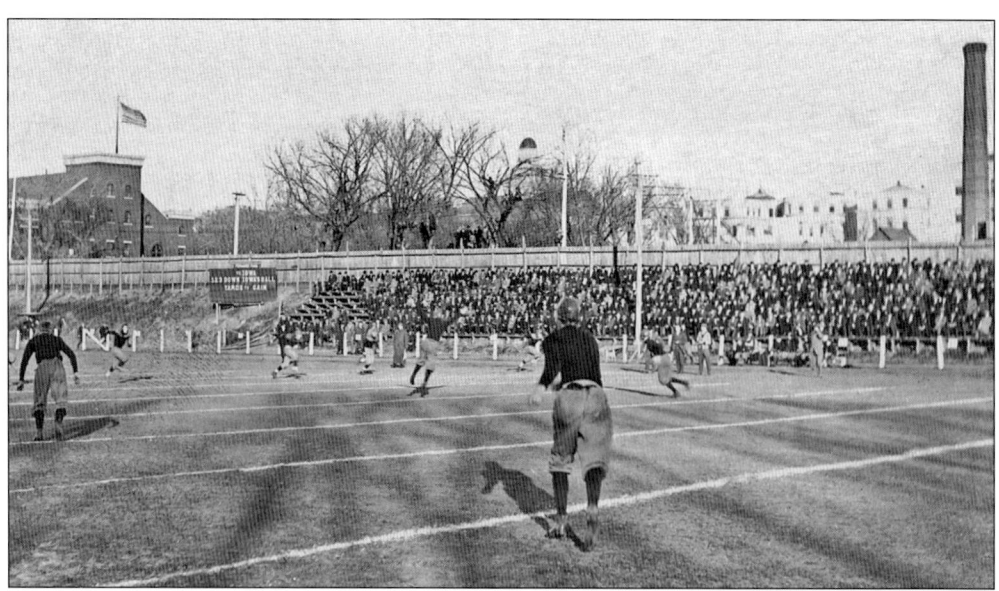

The 1911 Little Hawks of City High begin a punt return against Clinton High in a game played on the university's Athletic Park field along the river between Iowa Avenue and Burlington Street. Old Capitol is visible on the horizon, and the 1904 University of Iowa's Armory and Men's Gym peeks in from left. The chimney at right serves the UI power plant of that era, which set at the foot of Washington Street on a site now occupied by part of the university's engineering building. City High won the game 6-0.

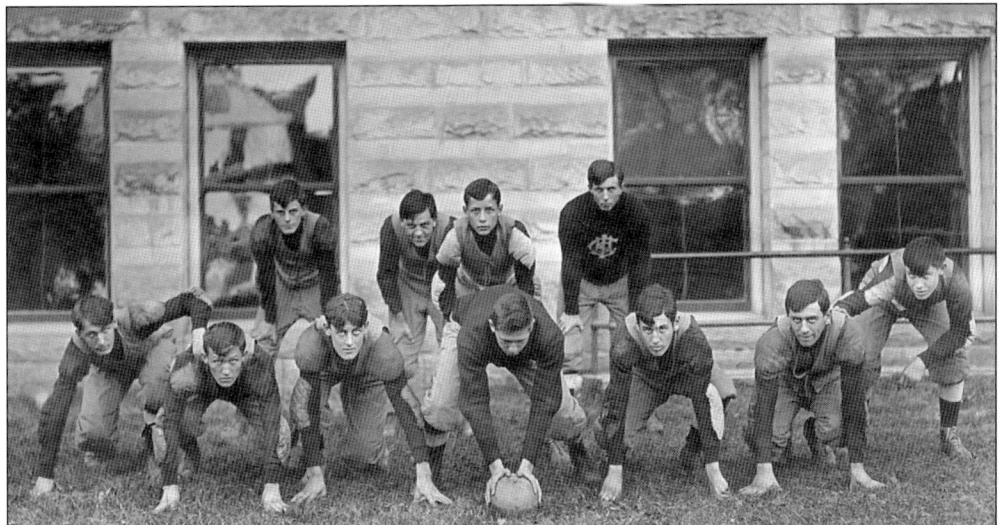

City High fielded this football group of Little Hawks during fall 1908, imaged on a card postmarked that October that was mailed to Gaza near Primghar in northwest Iowa. David wrote that the captain is the one with the ball. City High classes then met in a 1904 building along Market Street, constructed for $60,000. Demolition 80 years later cost twice as much, including trucking its debris and that from a gym addition to the Elks Club golf course and dumping it into a gully on the sixth fairway Mercy Hospital redeveloped the site after its purchase from the schools.

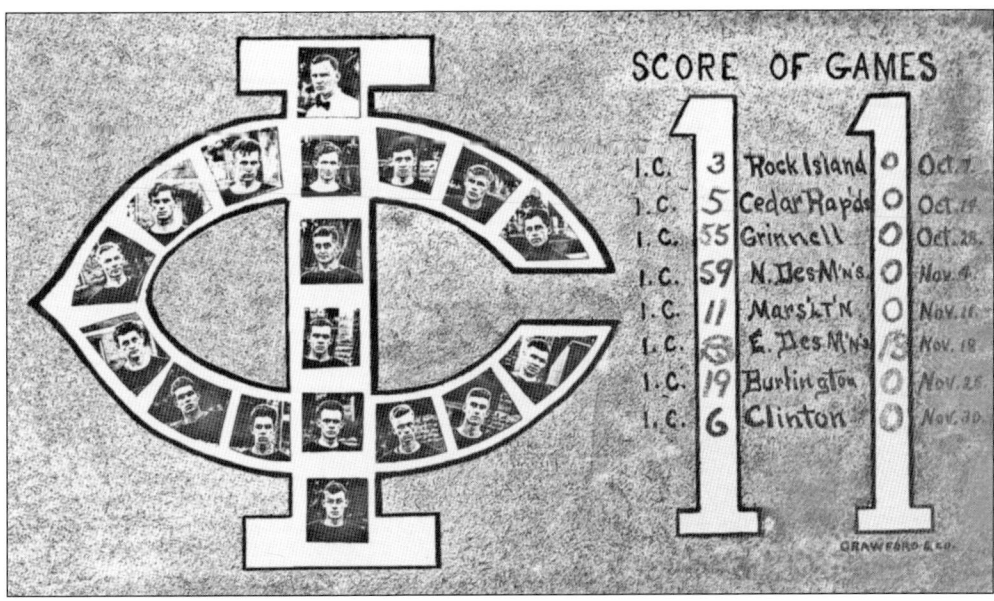

Little Hawk football excelled during 1911, when their record was 7-1, based on the scores written on the card below; however, one Des Moines score is unclear on the card. A contemporary newspaper article reports a 13-3 Des Moines win on "a sea of ice," with City High objecting to use of cleated shoes by Des Moines. In the other games, all played during October and November, City High blanked all comers. Its home games were played that year in the university's Athletic Park.

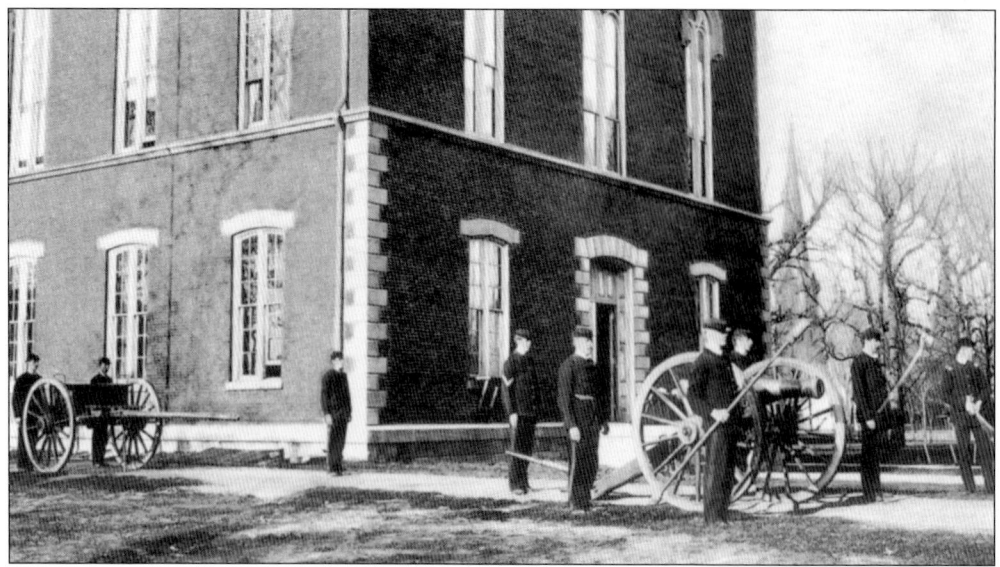

The south door of 1866 North Hall, immediately north of Old Capitol, provides a visual backdrop, about 1907, for a university student military corps in full-dress uniforms mustering Civil War artillery. The university has played a role in officer training from its infancy and benefited with facilities provided by military bucks. As early as 1888, the military paid in part for a three-level armory a few feet west of Old Cap, with its bottom level providing the first boiler heating plant for Old Cap. These cadets used a main floor armory, and engineering students used the top floor. A second armory came in 1904, and a third rounded-roof one in 1921, with all three now gone.

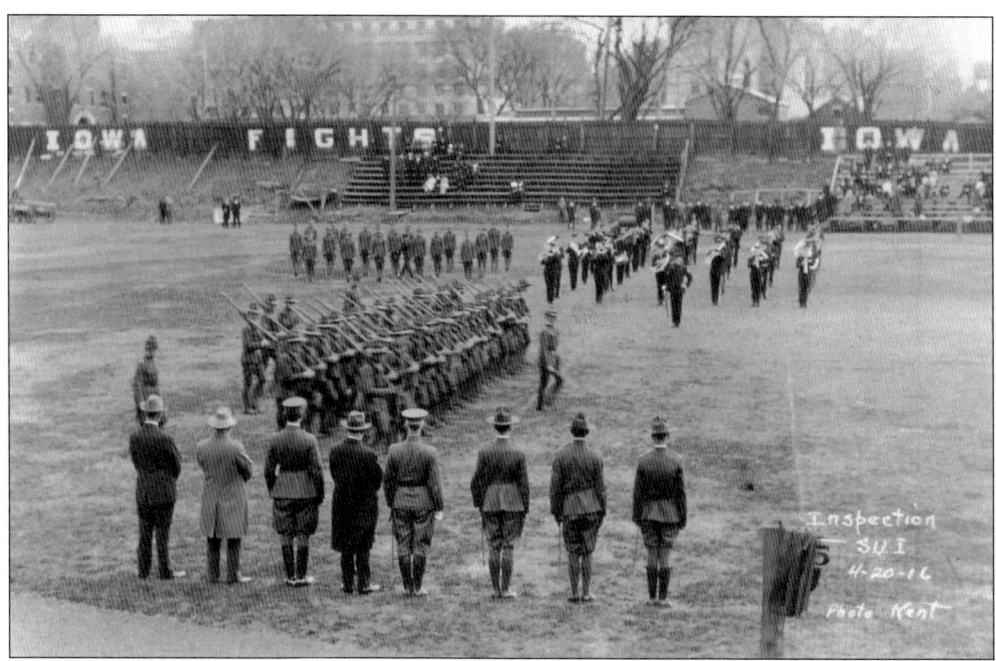

A 1916 Fred Kent photograph card shows an inspection call in UI's Athletic Park below Old Cap in spring 1916, when Thomas Macbride was the university's president.

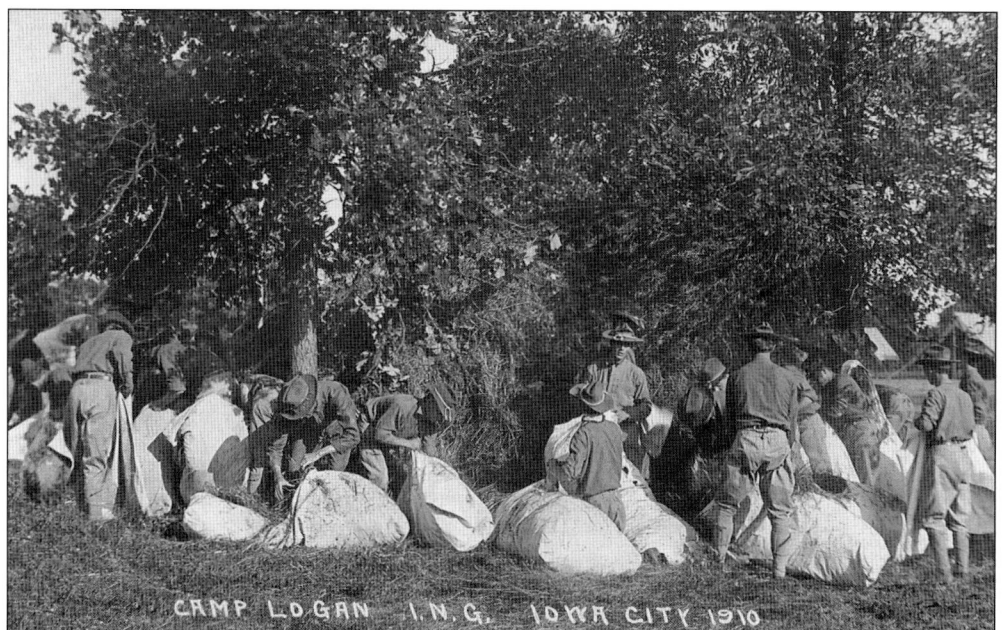

As early as the Civil War, Iowa City and university facilities aided in staging and training of military personnel. Above, Iowa National Guard participants prepare to break camp on a fairgrounds spot they named Camp Logan for their summer training exercises. During the Civil War, when Iowa supplied the Union cause with a record number of troops in proportion to its population, a large Johnson County contingent was feted at Metropolitan Hall, where Hotel Jefferson now stands, before forming up and marching to the Rock Island Railroad depot for transport to the war front.

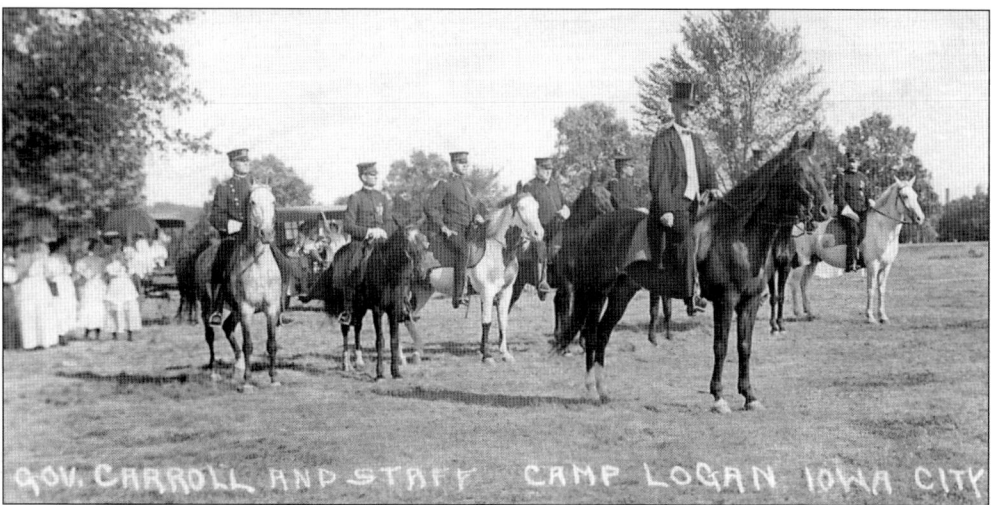

Gov. Beryl Carroll (1860–1939), a popular two-term Iowa governor and Davis County newspaper editor and publisher at Bloomfield, sits tall in the saddle in formal dress with high top hat, as he joins military staff in reviewing summer camp training units at Camp Logan in Iowa City on a sunny summer morning during 1910.

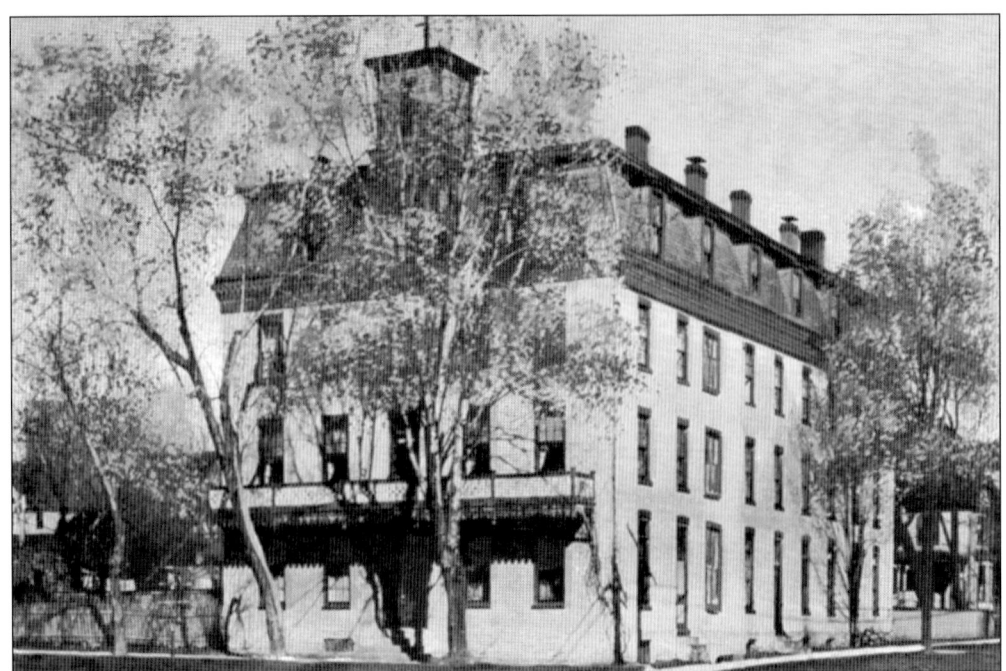

Svendi Hall was born about 1850 as Park Hotel to serve legislators, government officials, and hangers-on meeting and lobbying at Old Capitol, located two blocks away. Bought by St. Mary's Catholic Church, it served for a time as a convent and teaching facility before being sold. It is now fully renovated and serves as student apartments.

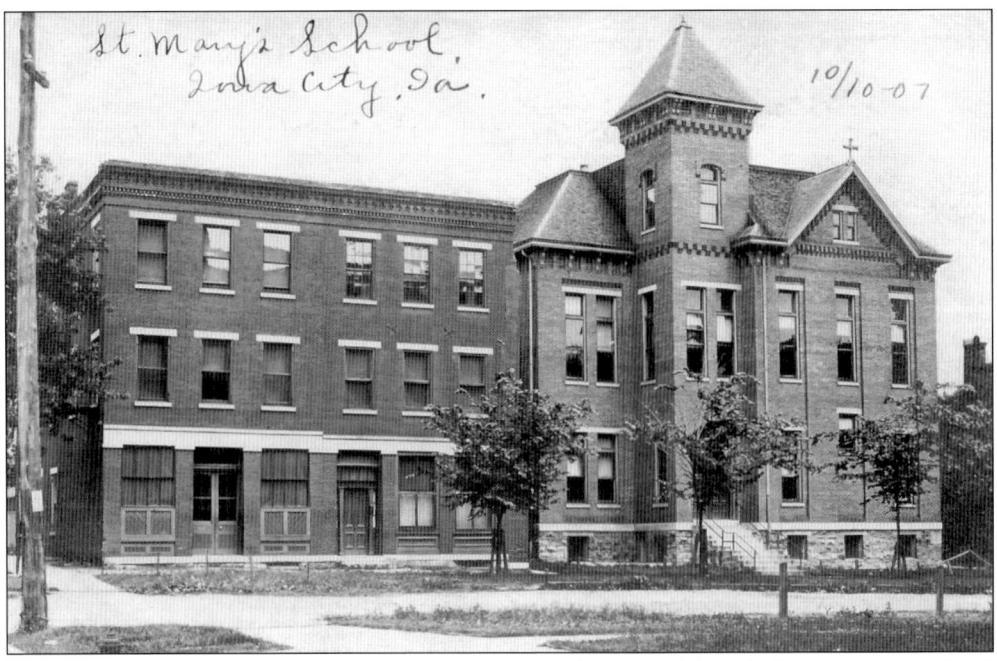

St. Mary's parochial school, shown in 1907, was an early successful Catholic venture into local schooling. This Clinton and Jefferson Streets corner site opposite Pentacrest now serves as a Catholic university student center. Regina is now the K–12 Catholic school.

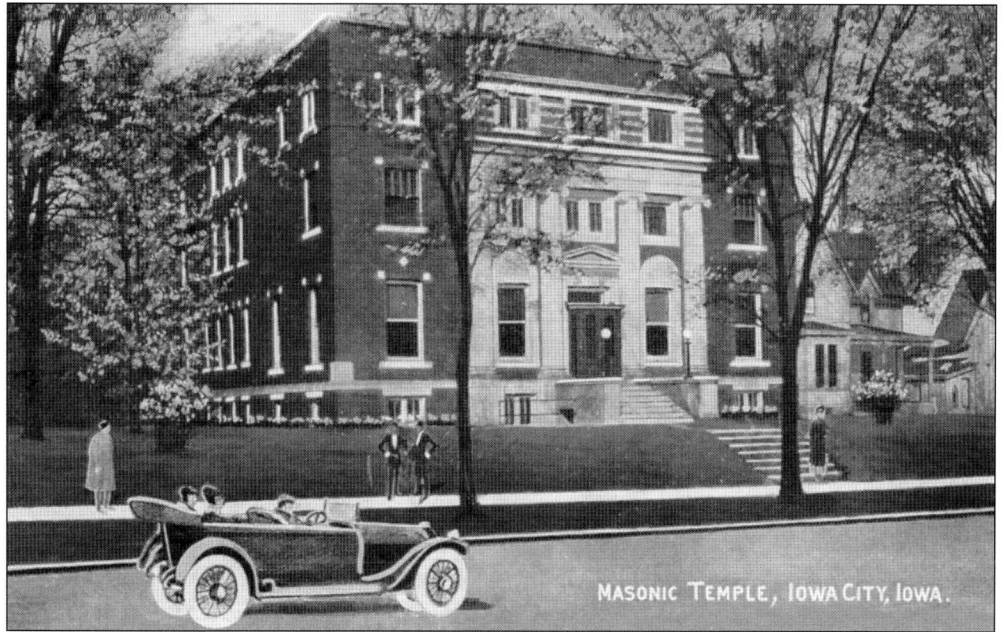

Iowa City Masons purchased a lot at the College and Clinton Streets intersection late in the 19th century, selling it to the CRandIC "Interurban" Railway for its depot at "a handsome profit," sufficient to purchase this lot at 319 College Street without financing. Here Iowa City Masonic Lodge built its hall during 1913–1914, as represented by this image on a card produced during 1915. The Beaux-Arts, brick and stone structure cost $35,000.

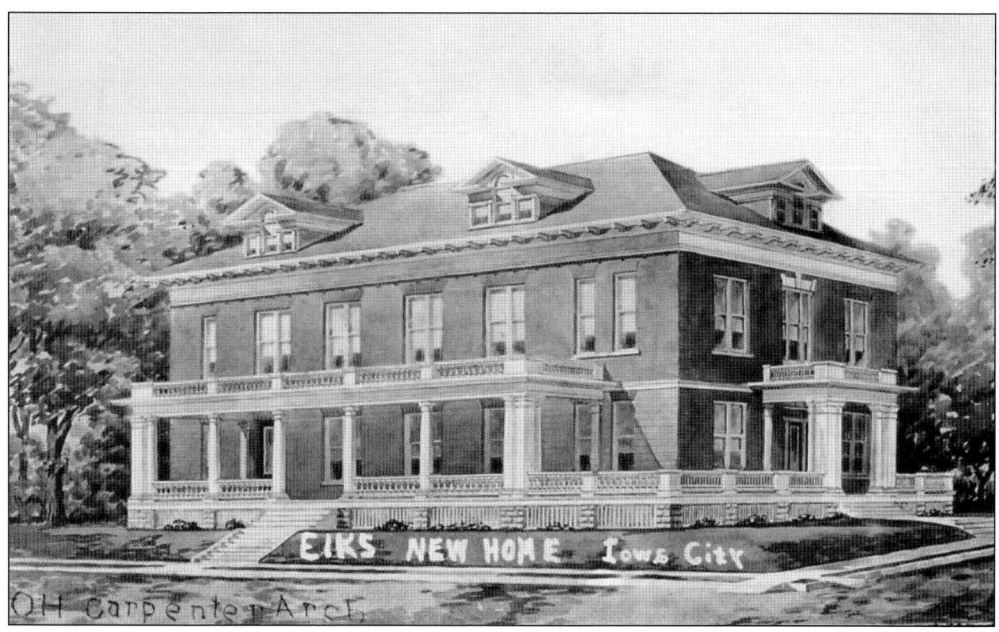

An east-facing summer porch welcomed Elks Club members to their new clubhouse in this image, soon after its 1909 construction. The genteel porch was lost to a 1939 expansion of the structure east to Gilbert Street. It faces toward Washington Street.

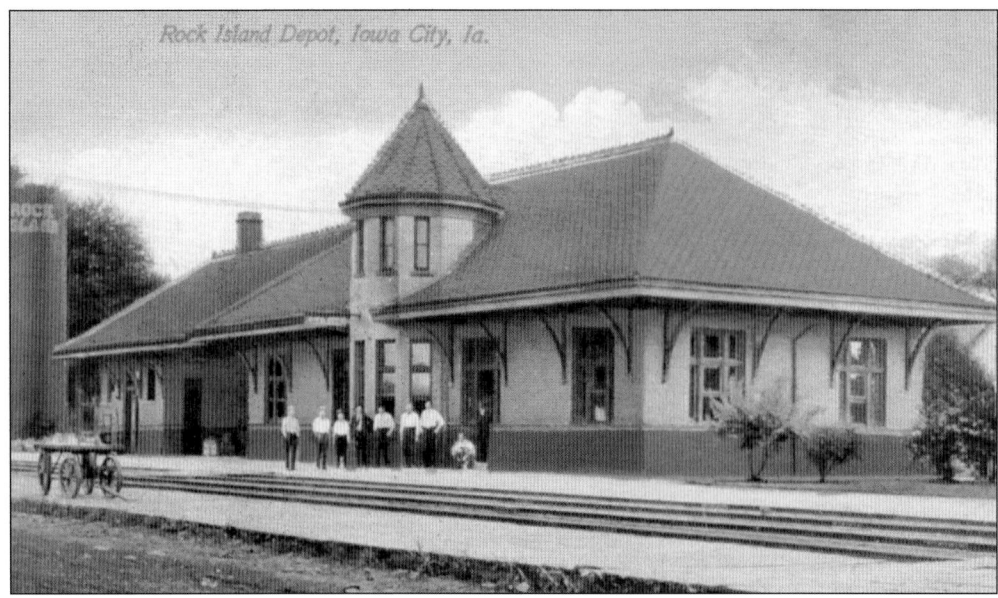

The Rock Island Railroad depot stands stoic in this 1913 image with its station crew standing beside the exterior ticket window and office area, and the mail cart already on the outer platform for servicing the next train. This depot was built nearer the downtown area in 1898 to replace an 1855 facility a half-mile farther east, at the end of Johnson Street. The trolley company responded by installing tracks to this new site, and a hotel soon was open across the street, a structure that now houses rentals. The depot was sold out of the RI bankruptcy in 1981 and currently houses law offices.

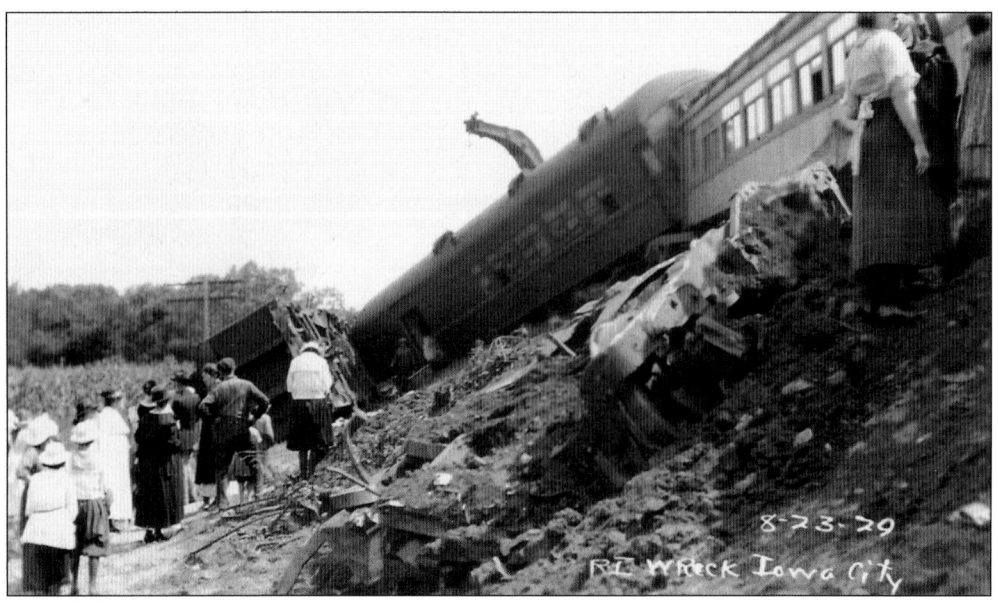

A 1920 Rocky Mountain Limited passenger train wreck, just west of Iowa City, was recorded by ubiquitous photographer Fred Kent. Many were injured, none fatally.

Nine

SIGHTSEEING
OUT AND ABOUT, INCLUDING TWO DOUBLE-PAGE SPREADS

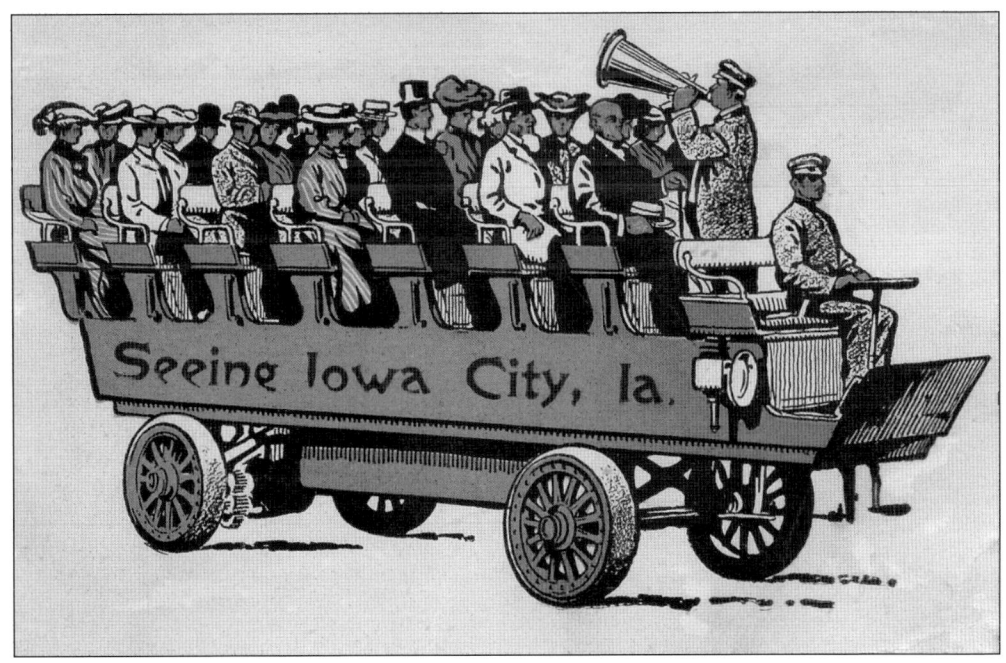

The 1907 folded card shown here contains an accordion-folded strip of 22 postage-stamp-sized images.

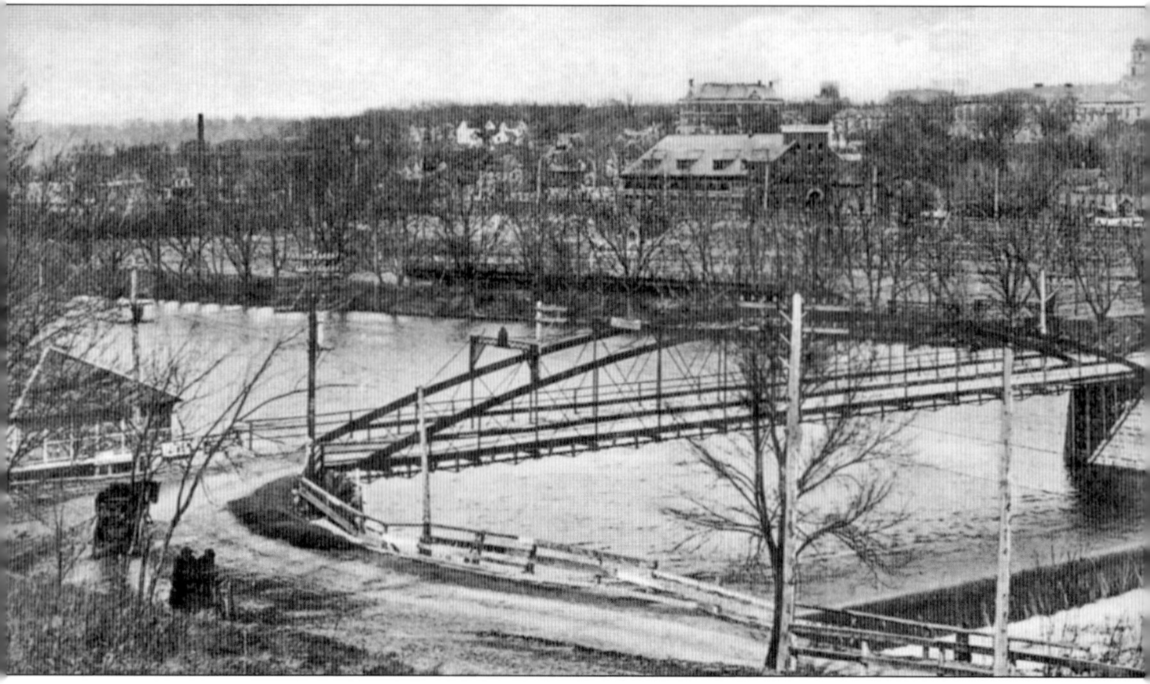

Above, two carriages, seen at left, approach the 1860 Burlington Street Bridge in a panoramic scene from a double-postcard image. The picture was easily dated by the roof being built on the hydroelectric powerhouse at right, erected during 1906. The university's Athletic Field spans the

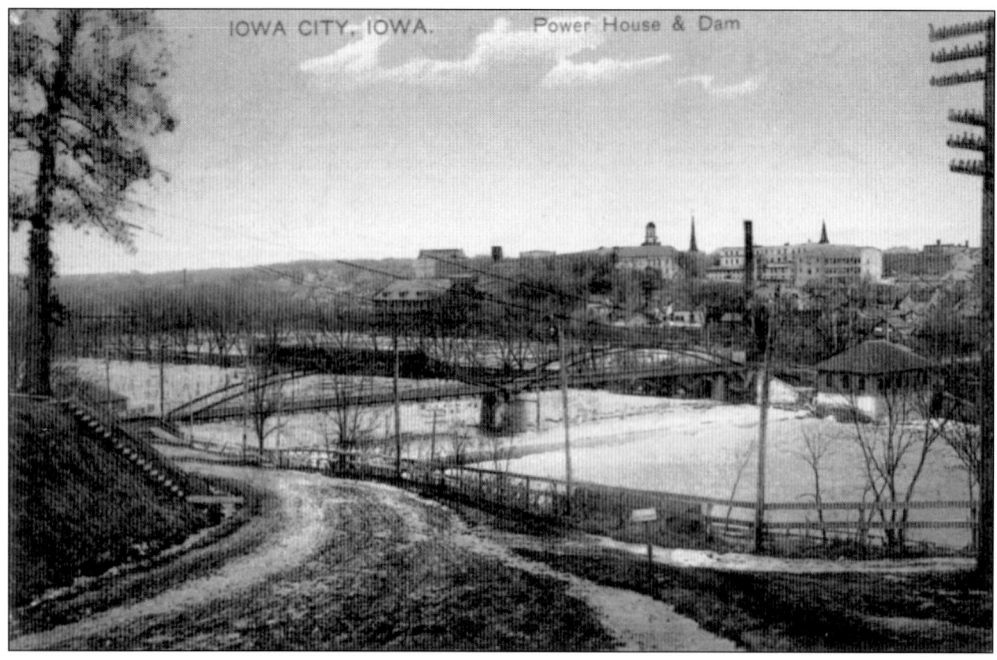

Above, the Iowa City-Williamsburg-Victor (IWV) Road drops down what now is the law school bluff in a 1907 scene lost to the Riverside Drive widening, which closed this road.

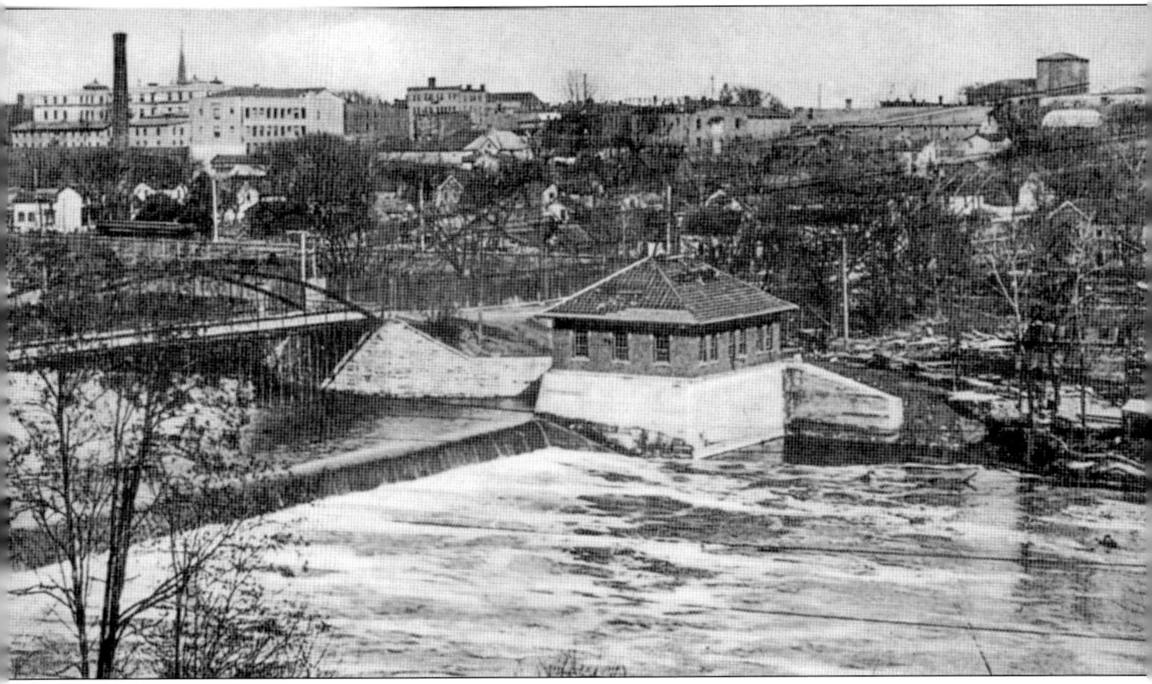

image from Burlington Street to Iowa Avenue at far left. Among many uses, it served football games until Kinnick Stadium was constructed during 1929. Old Capitol crowns the scene.

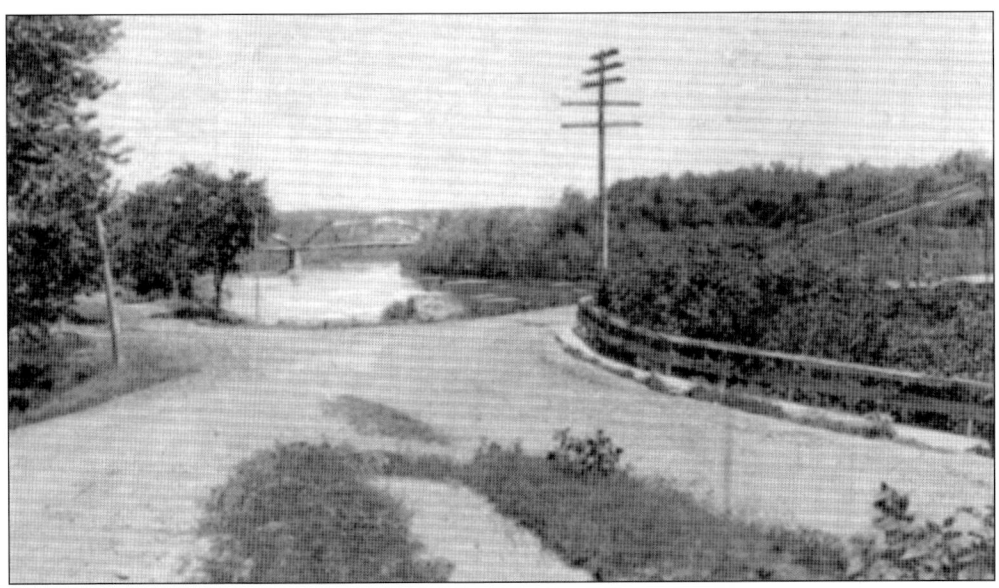

The IWV Road, down from the lower left, joins Riverside Drive, at the lower right, at the east end of the Burlington Street Bridge in this 1905 image. It shows what today is one of the busiest intersections in Iowa City. The old Iowa Avenue bridge is on the horizon.

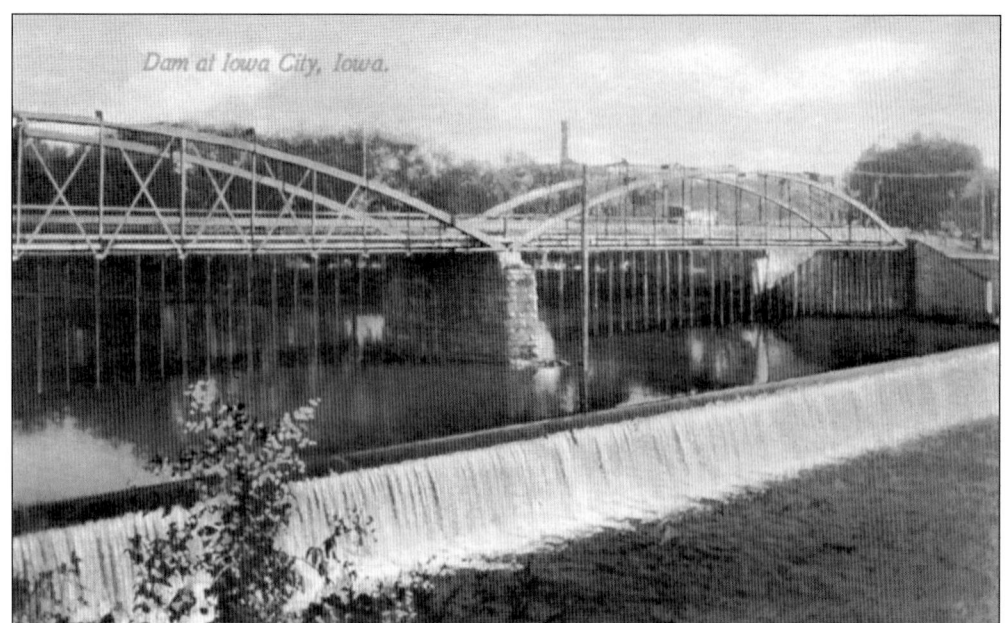

If a boater were caught in the flow of water toward the dam, he might save himself by grabbing one of the chains hanging every few feet along the full length of the Burlington Street Bridge, shown in this 1911 image. A herd of cattle collapsed this bridge in 1863; but it was salvaged, re-erected, and served another 52 years.

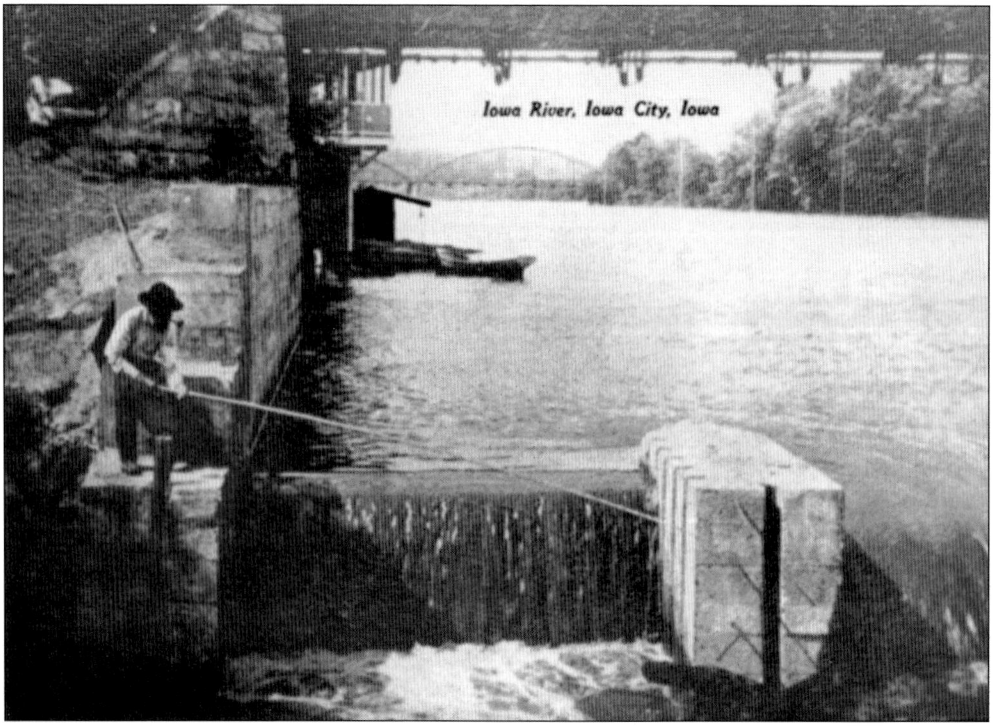

A fisherman plies his craft at a fish ladder below the Burlington Street Bridge in this 1907 image. Sum Place, a public eatery and boat rental, is seen upstream.

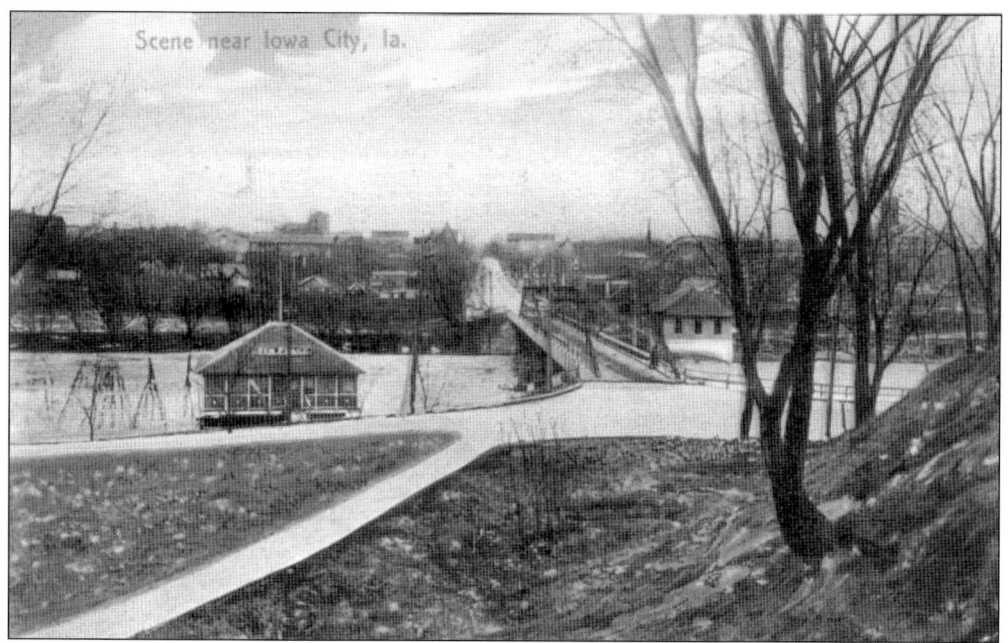

Sum Place stands in this 1910-era image at the foot of the Grand Avenue buggy trail, offering grub and boat rentals across the Burlington Street Bridge from most of town.

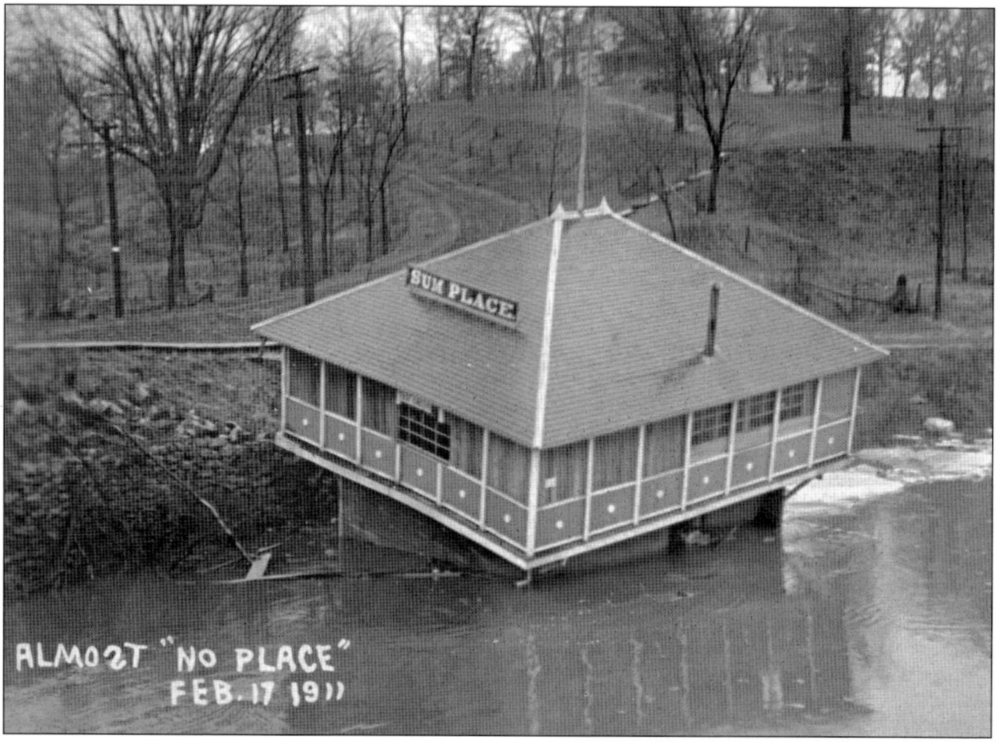

Noted local photographer and naturalist Fred Kent (1894–1984), for whom a major Johnson County park is named, displays his renowned sense of humor in his title on an image taken after a local flood. The facility, below Hillcrest dorm hill, was never rebuilt.

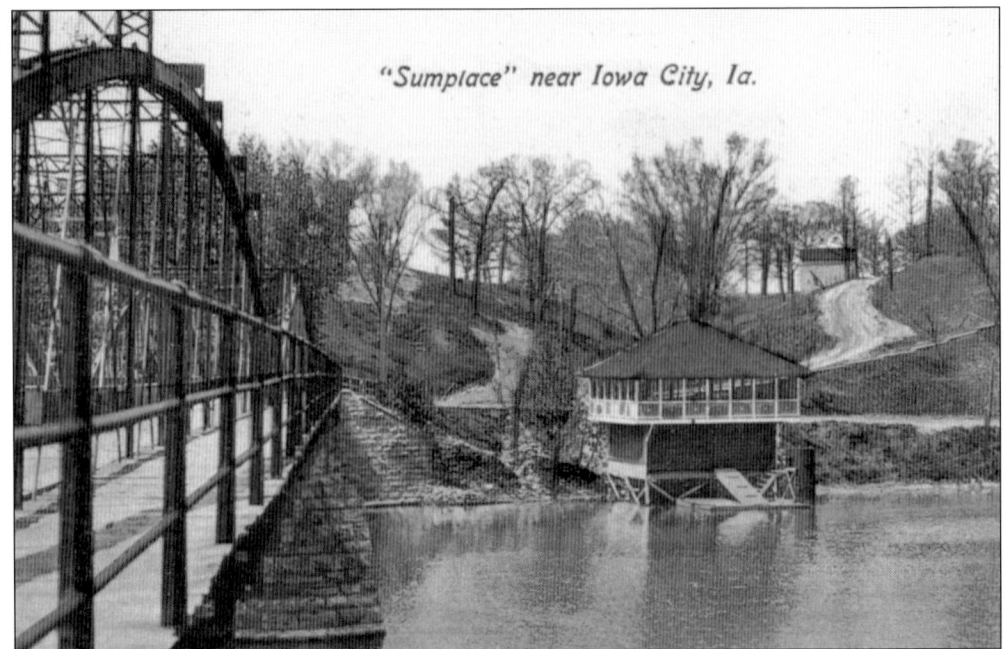

Sum Place dominates this 1910 postcard view across the 1860 Burlington Street high-truss bridge with a sidewalk cantilevered outside the main trusses. Buggy trails mark the Grand Avenue route up the bluff now serving the law school and Hillcrest dorm.

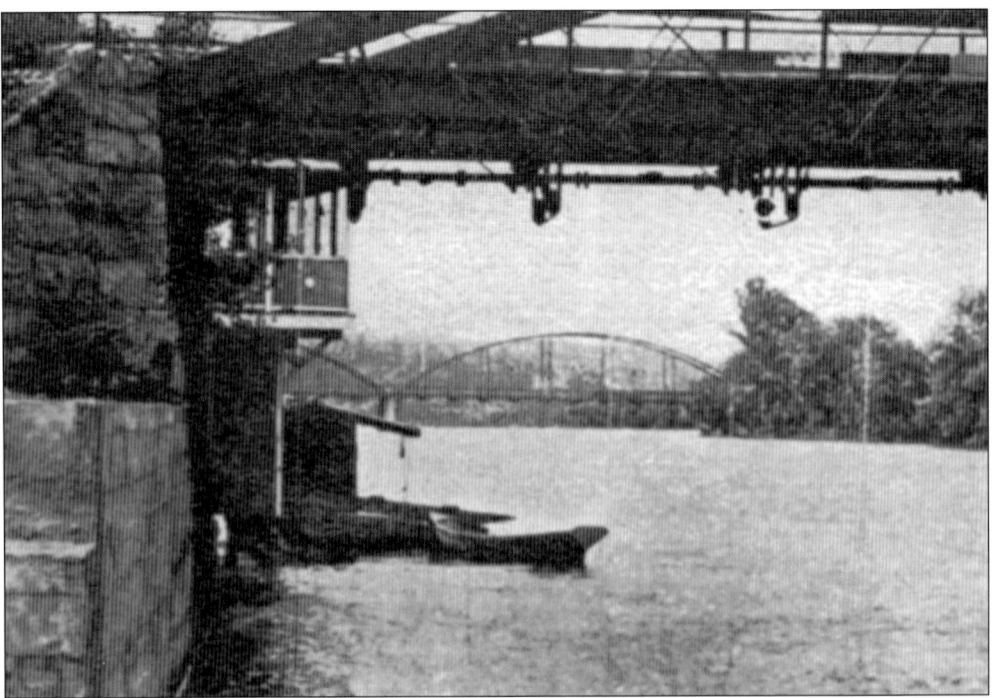

Centennial Bridge at Iowa Avenue shows below the stringers of its sister at Burlington Street in this Iowa River view recorded during 1907. The Sum Place dining and boat rental facility guards the left portion of this postcard image.

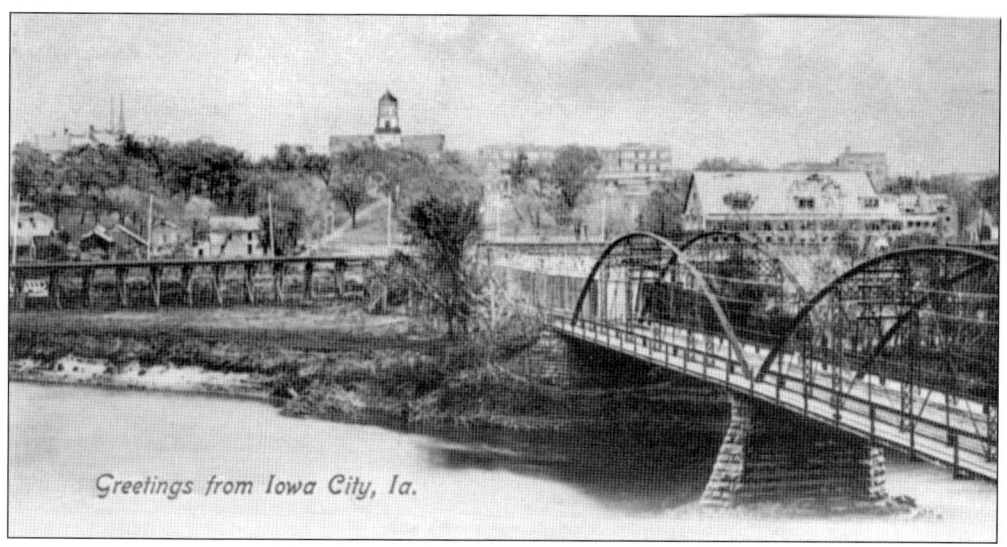

An image taken about 1908 from the west river bluff, now serving the university's College of Nursing building, presents Centennial Bridge at Iowa Avenue, as well as the CRandIC "Interurban" Railway high trestle, which today has been replaced by an earthen embankment blocking river flow, which the railroad engineers in 1903 had deemed desirable. Rinella Grocery sat along Iowa Avenue at its Madison Street corner below Old Capitol, providing its name to the neighborhood seen above, which is now called Hubbard Park on the campus adjoining Iowa Memorial Union.

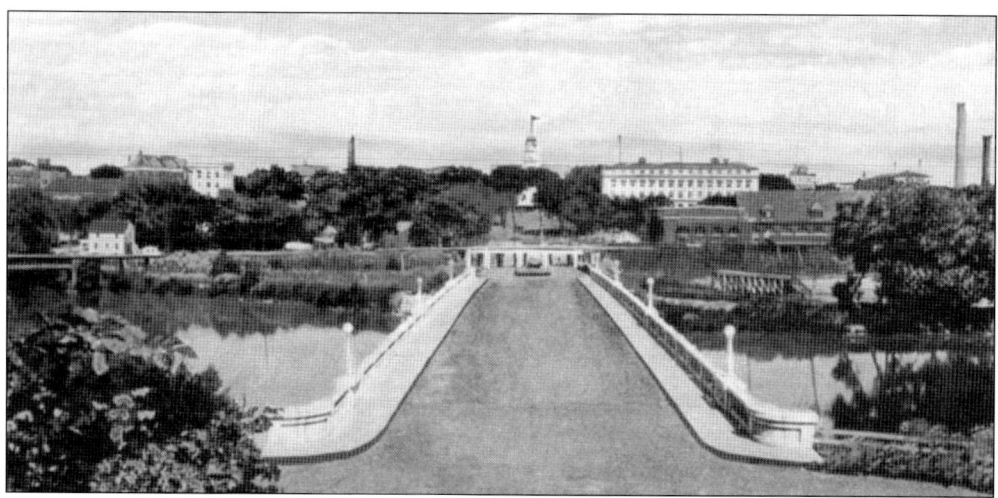

The 1915 Iowa Avenue span dominates this 1920s image, which also shows the street in its reconstructed boulevard form and a new CRandIC overpass. The Rinella neighborhood, occupying the area left of Iowa Avenue, was purchased as part of the IMU planning during the teens and 1920s. It is now an open green named for Philip G. Hubbard, who was associated with UI from his 1940 student days through his 1991 retirement, except for time out for military service during World War II. He was an engineering professor, vice president of student affairs, and finally dean of academic affairs.

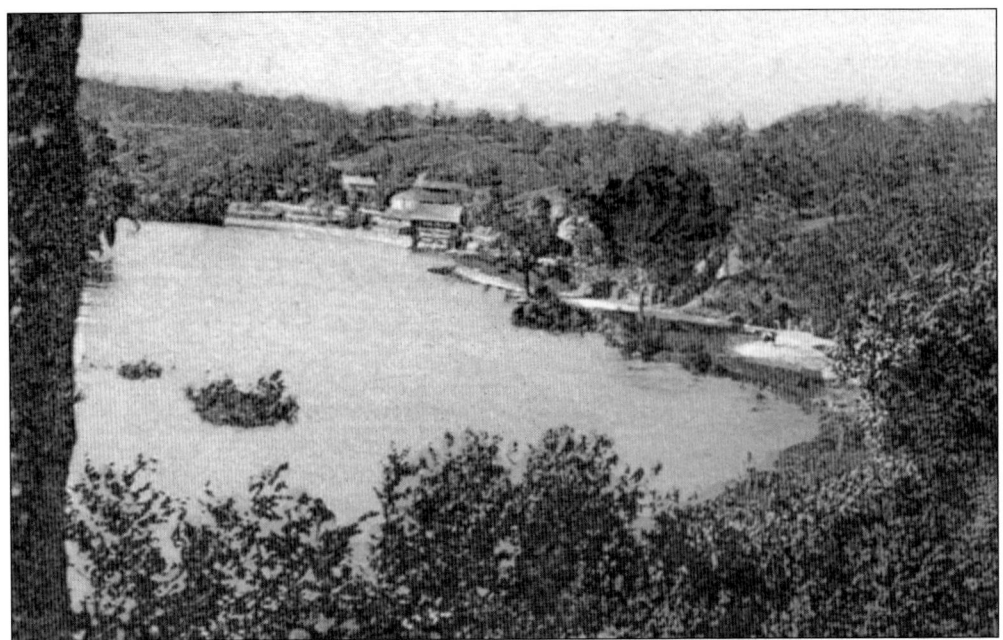

Pausing on Observatory Hill a century ago would have produced this view upstream at Terrill Mill, with Dubuque Street meandering along the right shoreline. The river has since been rechanneled to widen the area available for a divided four-lane Dubuque Street thoroughfare running to Interstate 80. There is not even a single commercial spot along its 2-mile run between the downtown and freeway. This image may have been made with construction underway on the hill. The UI president moved there in 1909.

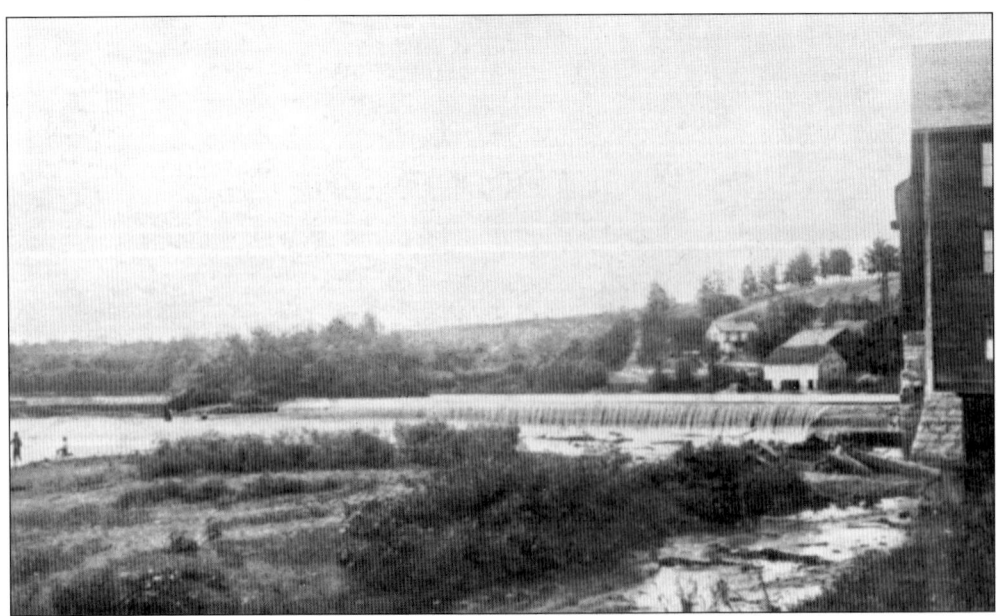

Both dams at Terrill Mill show in this 1908 image from Dubuque Street near where the Mayflower dorm now rests. The mill began operations during 1844, some eight months after a gristmill began grinding grains into flour at the Coralville dam site.

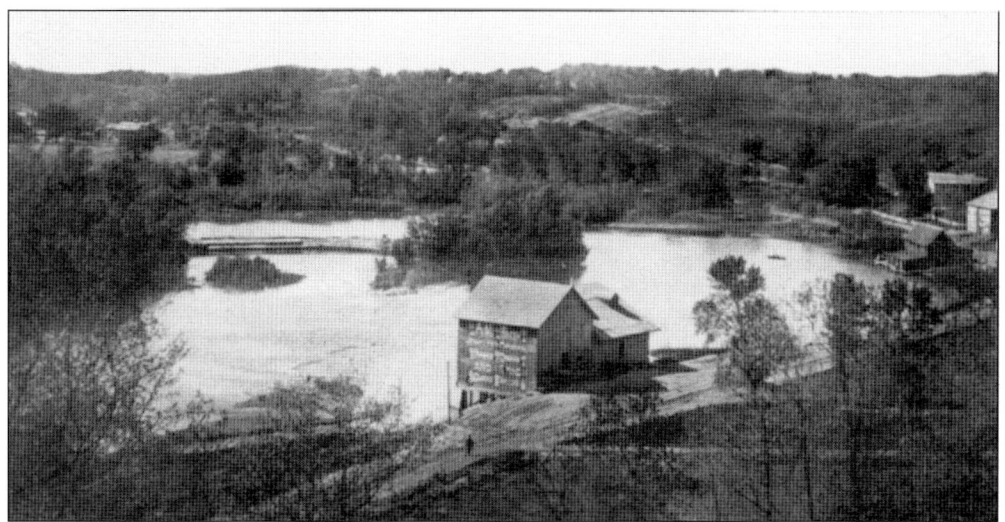

From the Sigma Pi fraternity house bluff, Terrill Mill is nestled in the Iowa River valley in this scene appearing on a postcard mailed during 1907. The mill's main dam, which runs from the island, is hidden by the millhouse. The river now passes entirely through the area of the shorter visible dam at left. The old main stretch is now landfill under Dubuque Street, under Terrill Park's skateboard court, and under the university athletic department's new women's scull training center and boathouse.

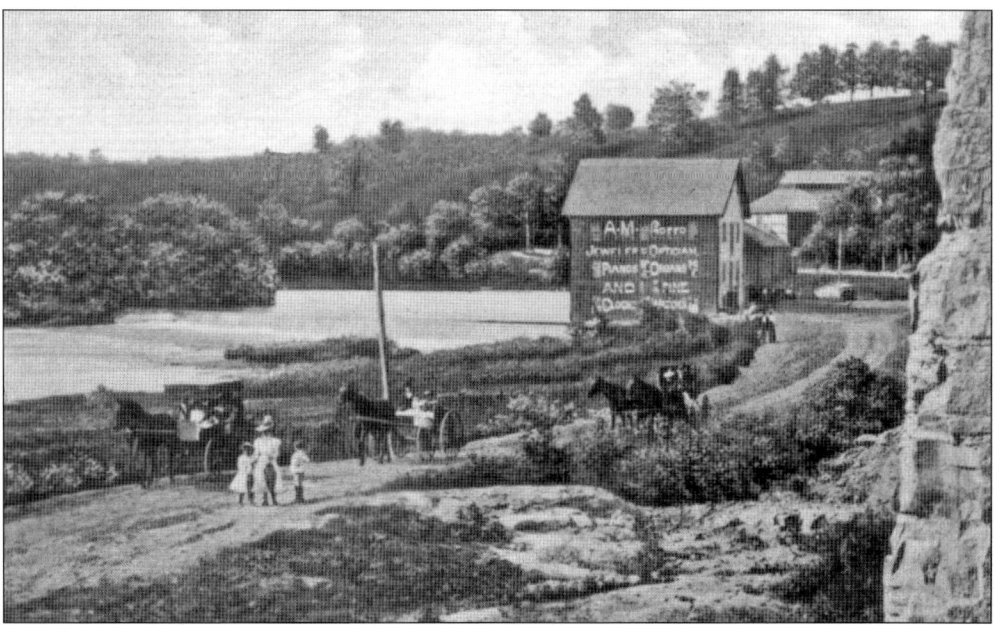

Above, an ad for A. M. Greer jeweler and purveyor of pianos and organs blares from the wall of Terrill Mill, as Sunday strollers hike and ride along Dubuque Street about 1910. The dams were washed away by floods, and the site was sold by daughter Mary Terrill Sanders about 1906. The sale included the Terrill mansion, which became home to the notorious Mayflower Inn, where ladies and booze flowed forth during Prohibition.

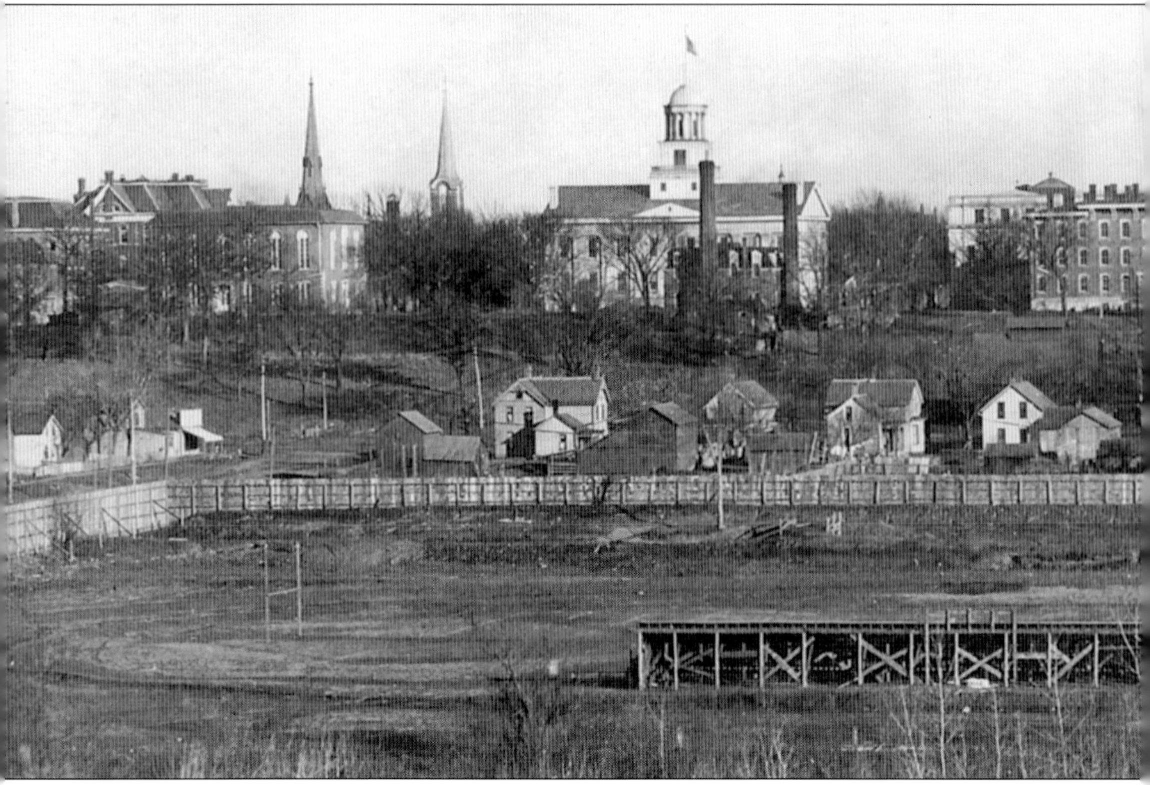

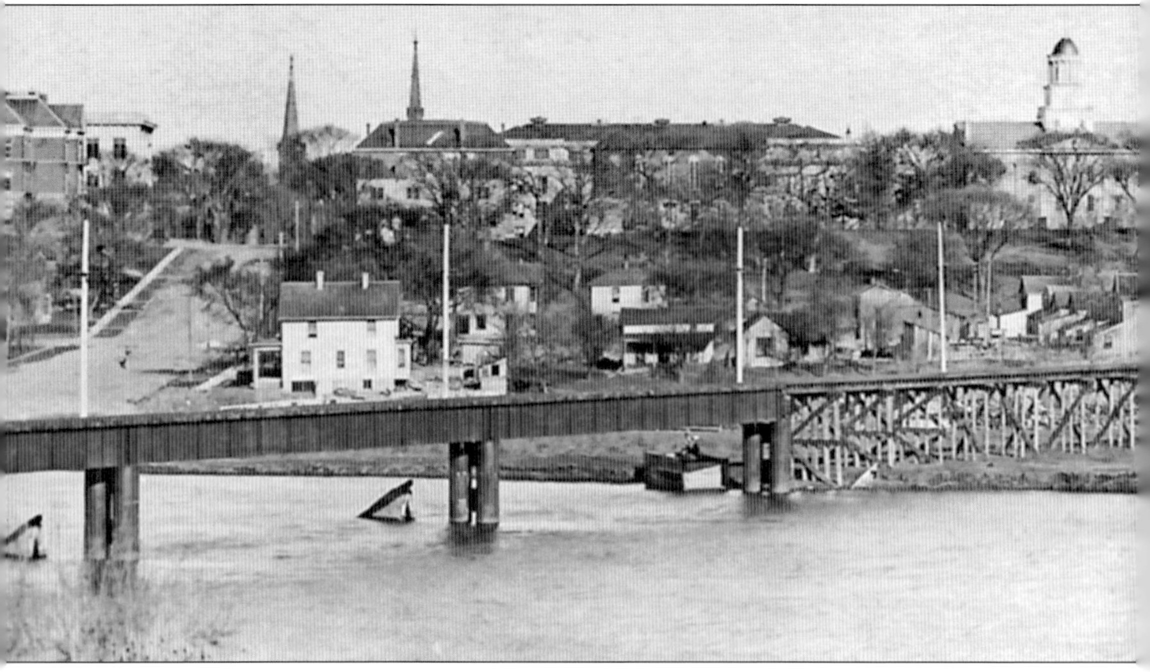

Above, another central campus view is seen during 1905 or 1906 and shows the railroad, built during 1904; the Armory and Men's Gym at lower right, erected in 1904; and the engineering building above the gym, added in 1905. The transformation of Pentacrest has begun with new

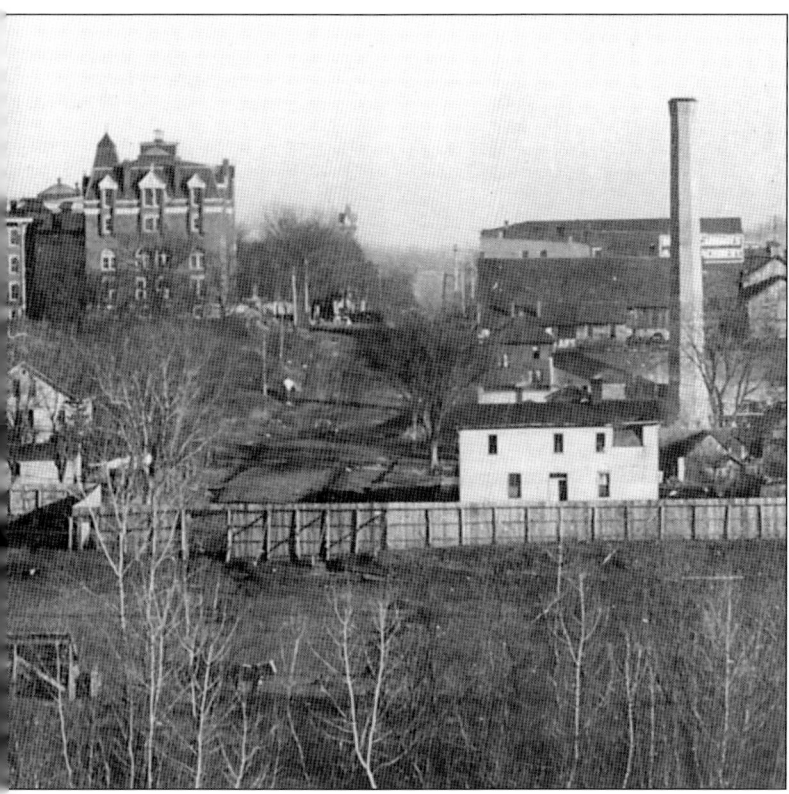

At left, a fascinating 1900 panorama displays the entire red brick Pentacrest, along with the expanse of Athletic Park and adjoining residential areas. From left, Old Dent, Calvin, and North Hall are left of Old Cap, with South Hall and the medical building, razed by a 1901 fire, shown at right.

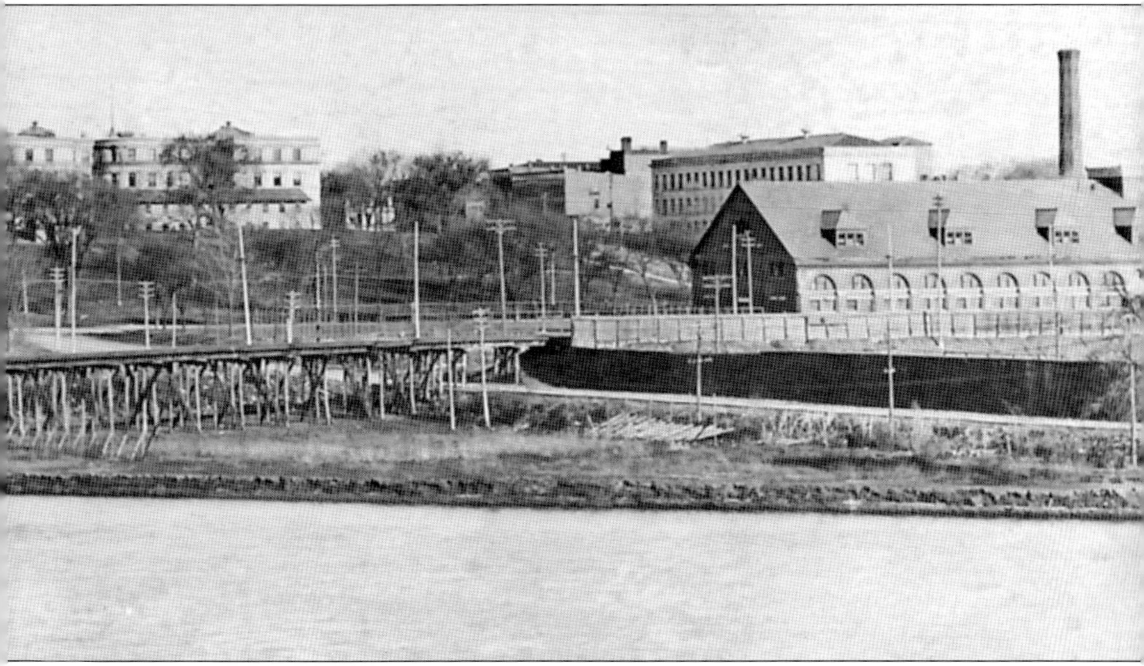

Schaeffer and Macbride halls visible, with the fire-razed South Hall and medical building replaced by the "Sheep Shed" in front of Schaeffer, and Calvin moved across Jefferson Street.

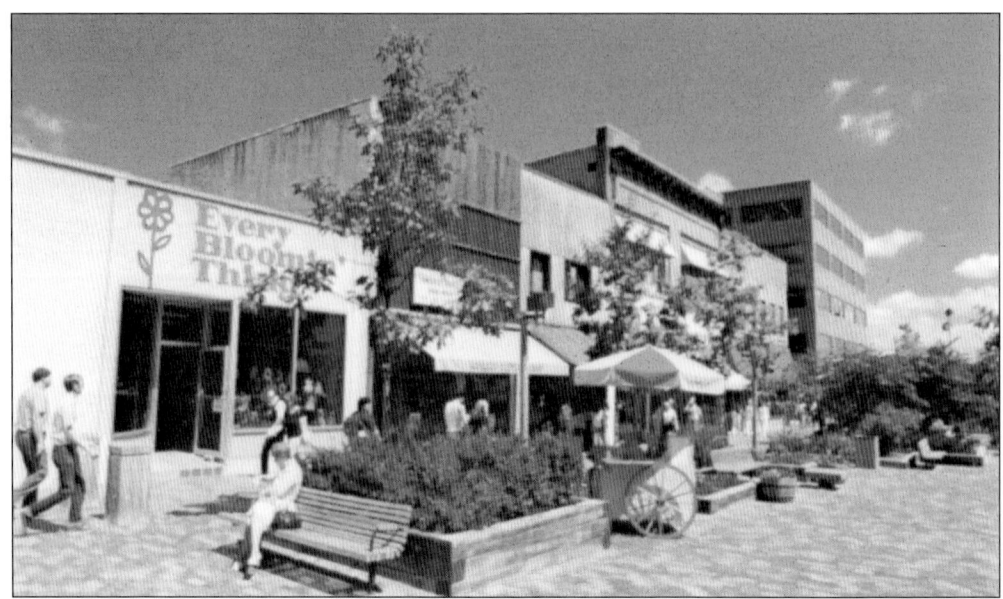

An early 1980s card presents this view of a pedestrian mall that now occupies three blocks of downtown Iowa City, a creature of a 1960s urban renewal plan that also resulted in the Sheraton Hotel building and adjoining Plaza Towers properties. It also was responsible for the Old Capitol Towne Center enclosed two-square-block mall and the Plaza Center One office tower shown at the far end of this streetscape by John M. Zielinski.

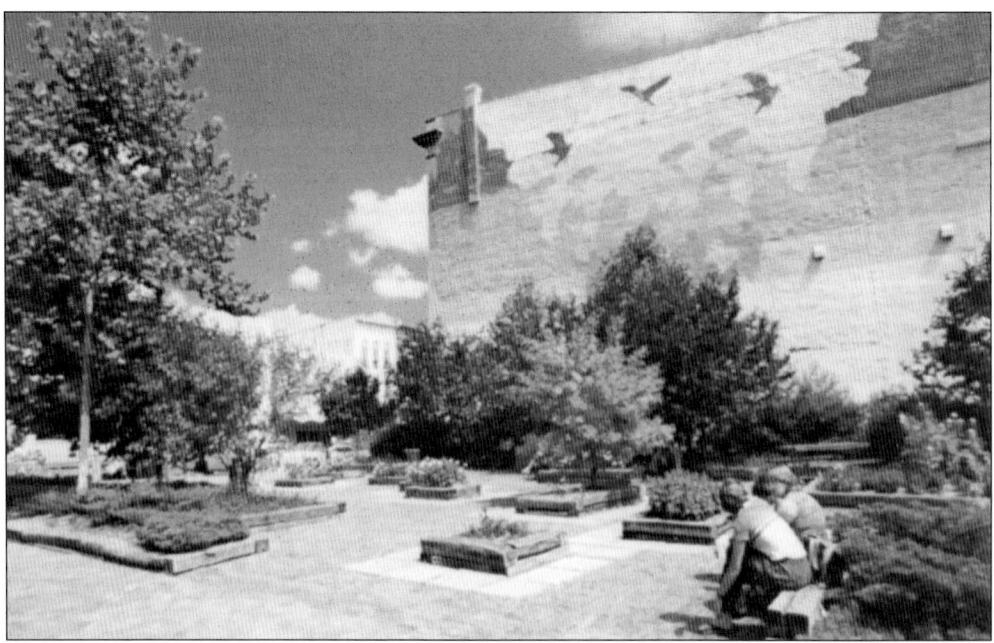

Another early 1980s view along the pedestrian mall by heralded Iowa photographer John M. Zielinski presents "Black Hawk Mini-Park" at the north pedmall entrance. A huge, now-nonexistent mural called the Spirit of Black Hawk depicted transformation of the Native American from a figure in his native dress into a soaring hawk seen at top.

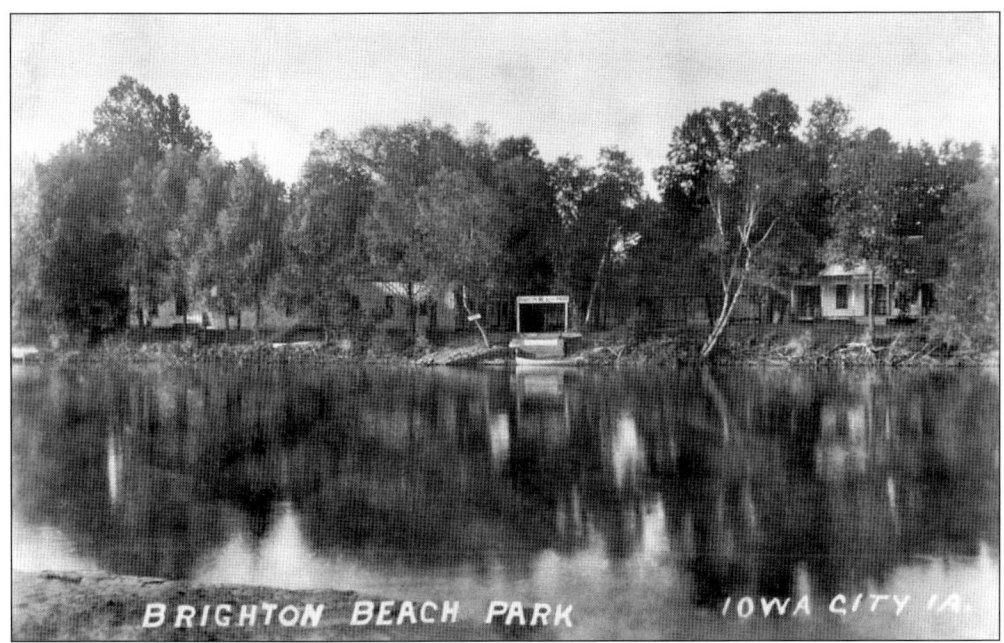

Brighton Beach was a commercial venture along the north shore of the Iowa River, not far upstream from the new university boathouse across the river from City Park. Swimming in the river was widely enjoyed during the era before heavy loads of farm chemicals choked river life and discouraged swimming. Just upstream from Rocky Shore Drive, Black Springs Beach was another spot widely used a century ago.

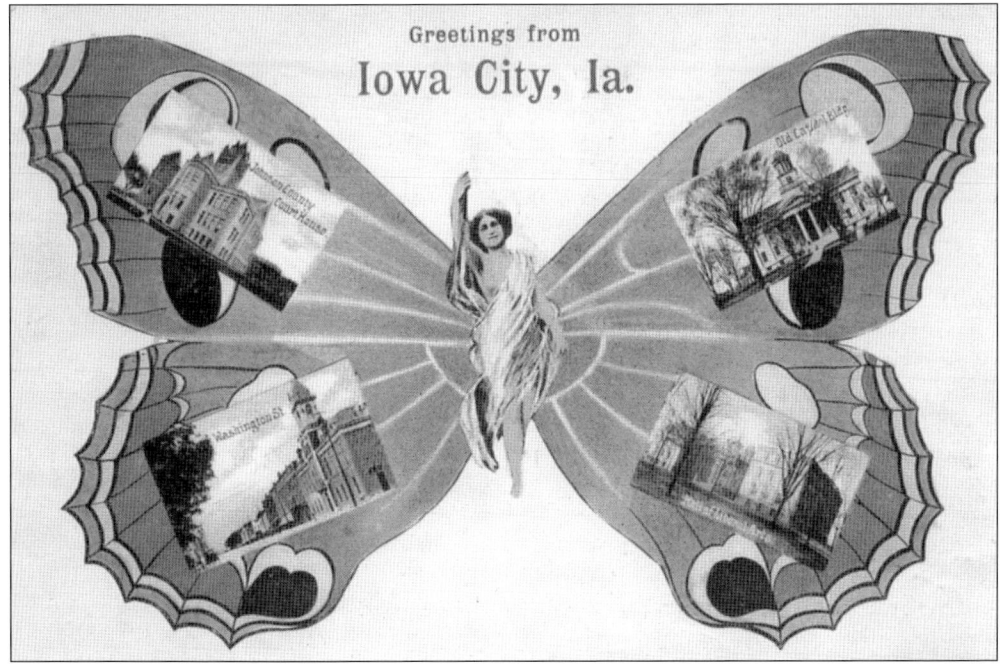

Carrie J. Wieneke ran Arcade Books on Washington Street a century ago, designing some of the outstanding postcards of the era. Her taste and flair are reflected above.

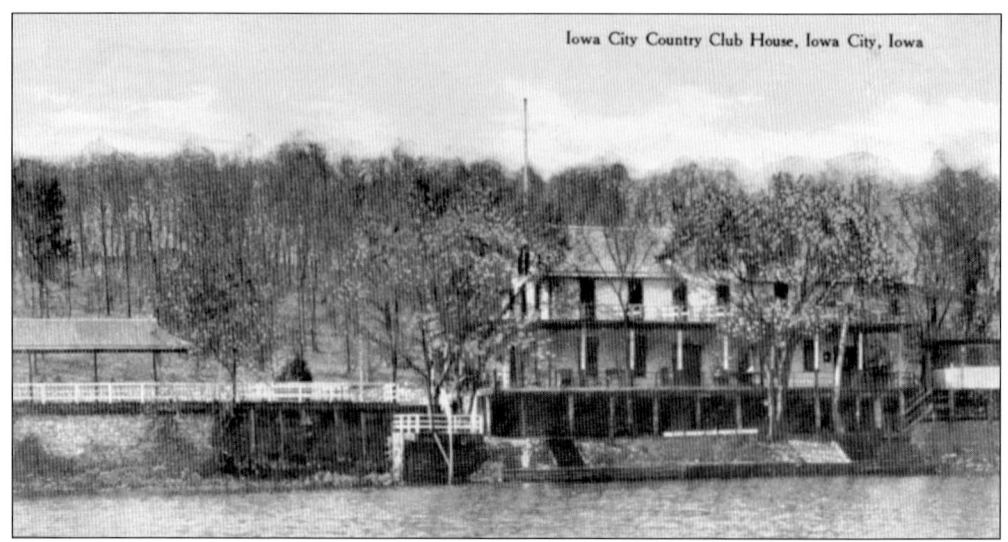

Formed in 1899 by a group that initially called itself the Iowa City Golf Club, the Iowa City Country Club flourished for nearly two decades in this facility, until it was washed down the Iowa River by the historic local flood of 1918. The club had arranged with successful local nurseryman Patrick Regan to lease his 100-acre farm north of the Iowa River near City Park for $500 during 1900, provided he would install and maintain a golf course. The plan also included moving the house, imaged both above and below, to the site. He also agreed to install indoor facilities with a water supply, which meant having a well dug, a routine undertaking given the location and the era before extensive groundwater pollution. The private club became a popular spot among the well-healed local citizenry. Below, the curved stone wall at left is still visible today along the north riverbank just upstream from City Park.

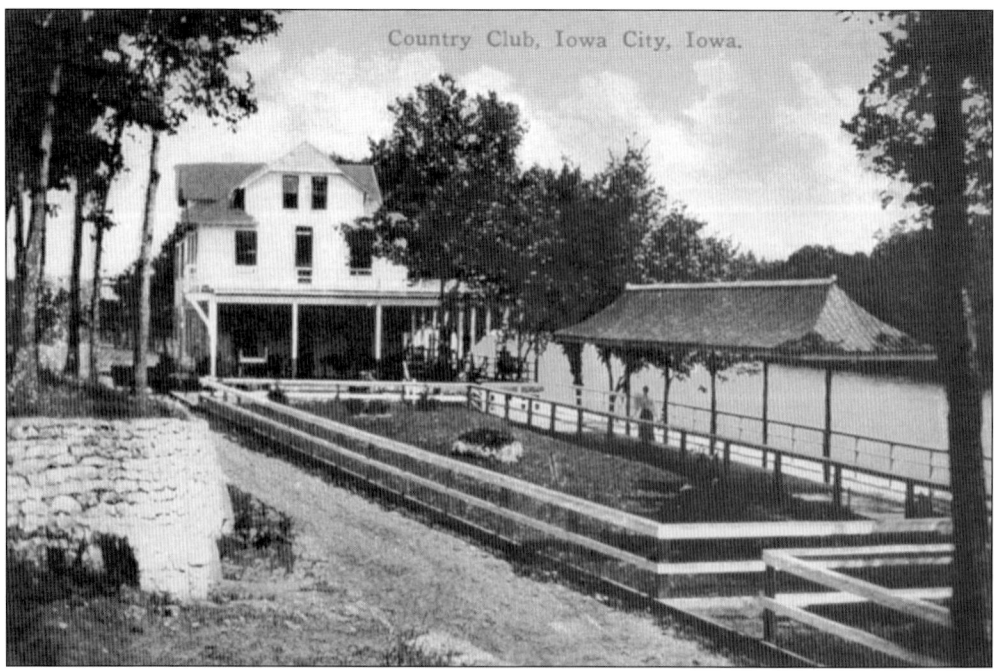

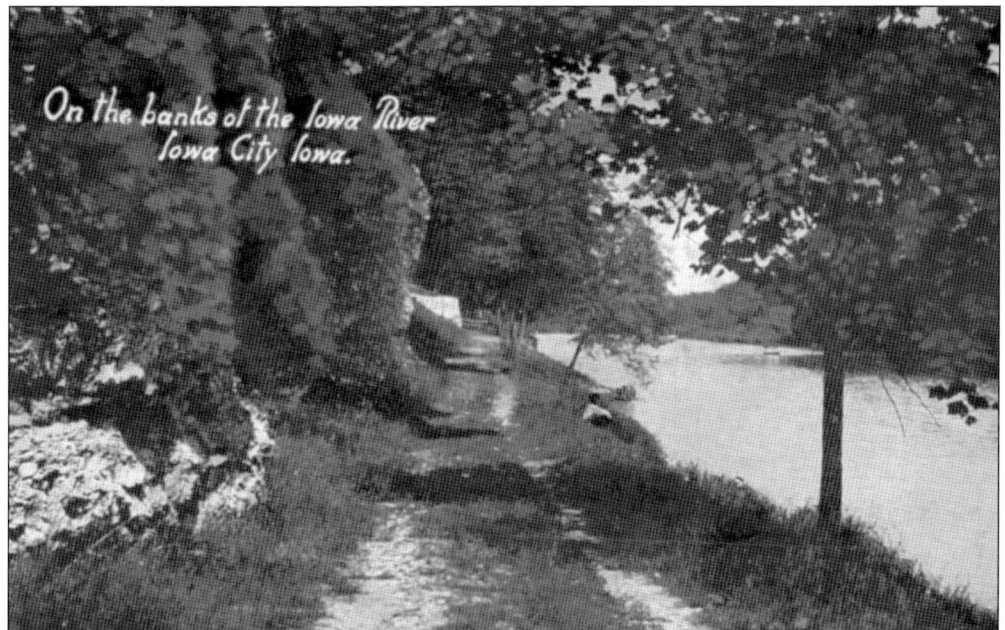

The road to the Iowa City Country Club is recalled above, in a postcard mailed during 1912, as a trail along a limestone outcrop just beyond the club site. It carries a lasting local tale since it is now preserved in a street name. During the 1908 U.S. presidential campaign against William Jennings Bryan, president-to-be Howard Taft spoke at the country club. Afterward, he asked his driver to let him try out the motorcar. Wags named the road Taft Speedway, as it is now officially named a century later.

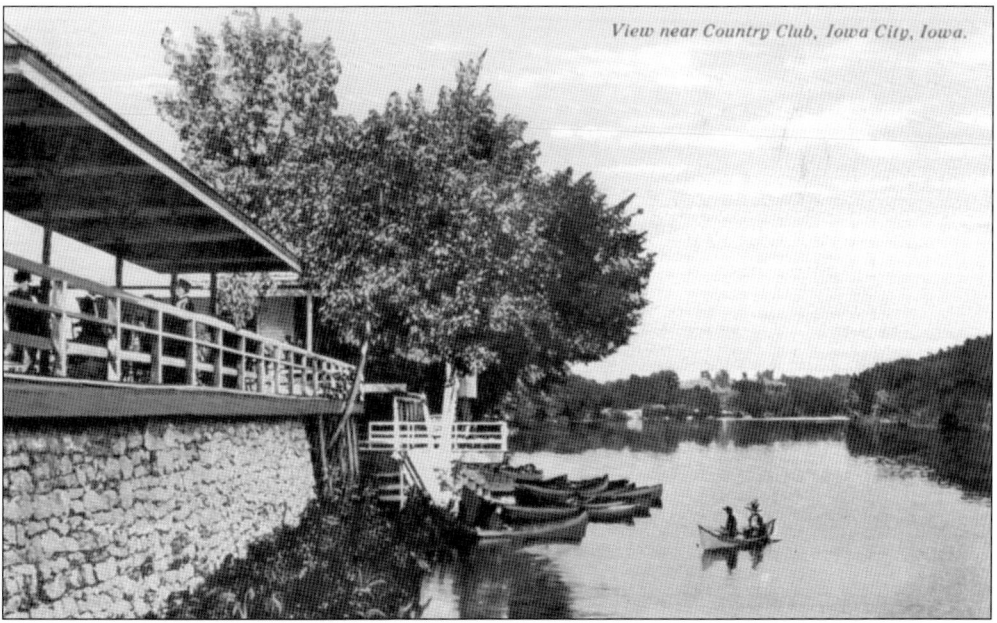

Boats for fishing or pleasure riding were available at the country club dock. After the 1918 flood, it was rebuilt uphill. The Elks Club bought the course in 1947.

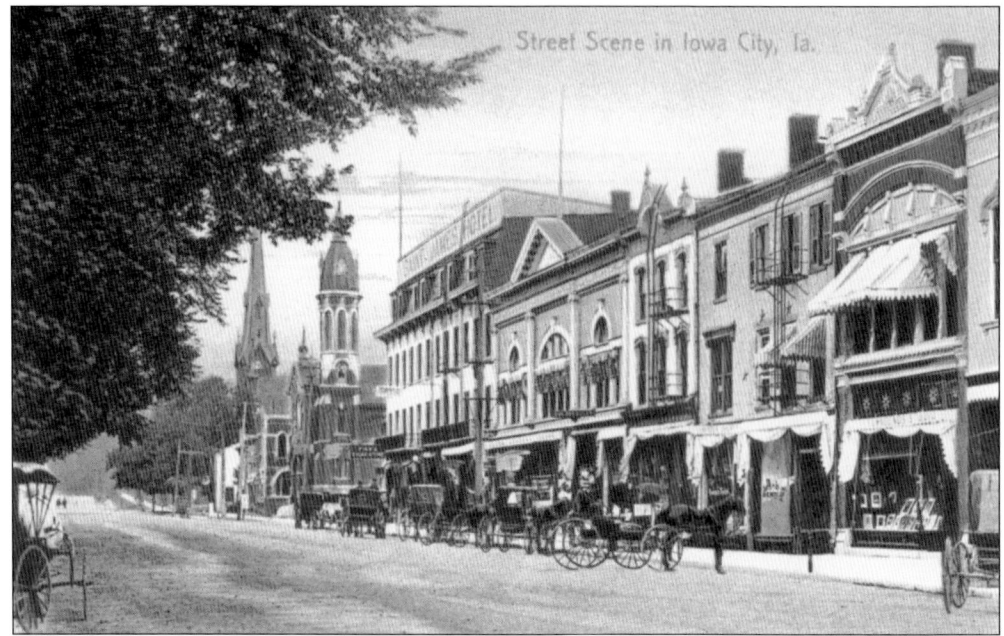

Charm, beauty, and even dignity spring forth from this century-old Clinton Street scene, a favorite of the author. The four-story St. James Hotel structure, near the center of the image, and the onion-domed Universalist Church building beyond it, both constructed during 1872, are gone. The other structures all survive, sans canvas awnings, pretty much with the same general appearance despite repeated remodeling. The card was created by Carrie J. Wieneke, printed in Germany, and mailed during 1909.

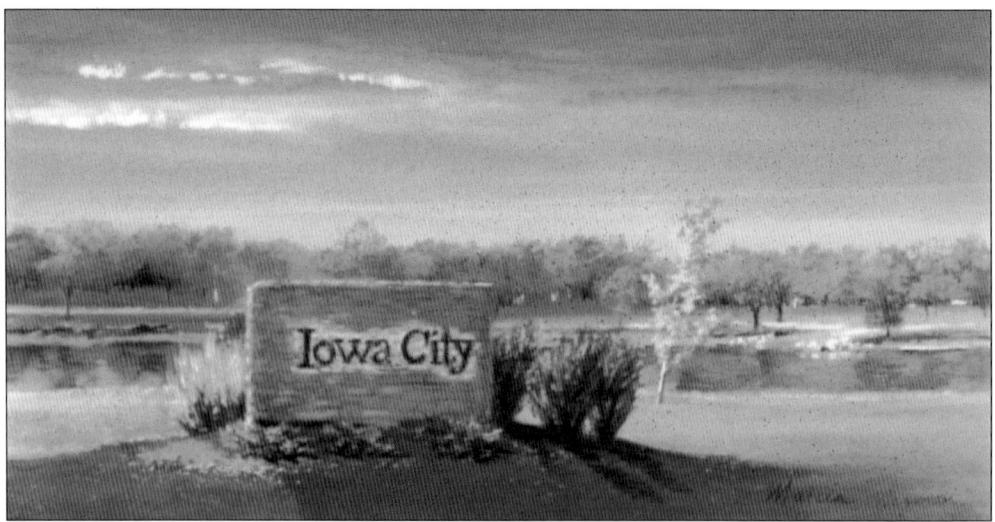

Above, pastel-painted by heralded local artist Marcia Wegman during 2003 titled "Iowa City Evening" is presented on a 2006 postcard. It depicts one of the city's welcoming entrance signs located across the Iowa River from City Park at sunset. Now city-owned and displayed at City Hall, the sky is filled with rosy hues, the trees in glorious fall garments, and, altogether, it is stunning. Ms. Wegman said she now paints "much better works."

Ten

LIES AND SHENANIGANS
PHONY IMAGES, INCLUDING "NIGHT" SCENES

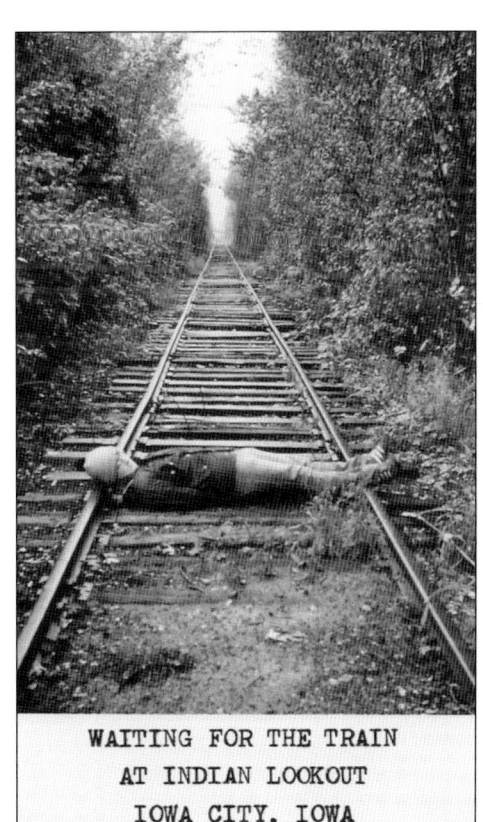

The source of this 1950s-era card is unknown.

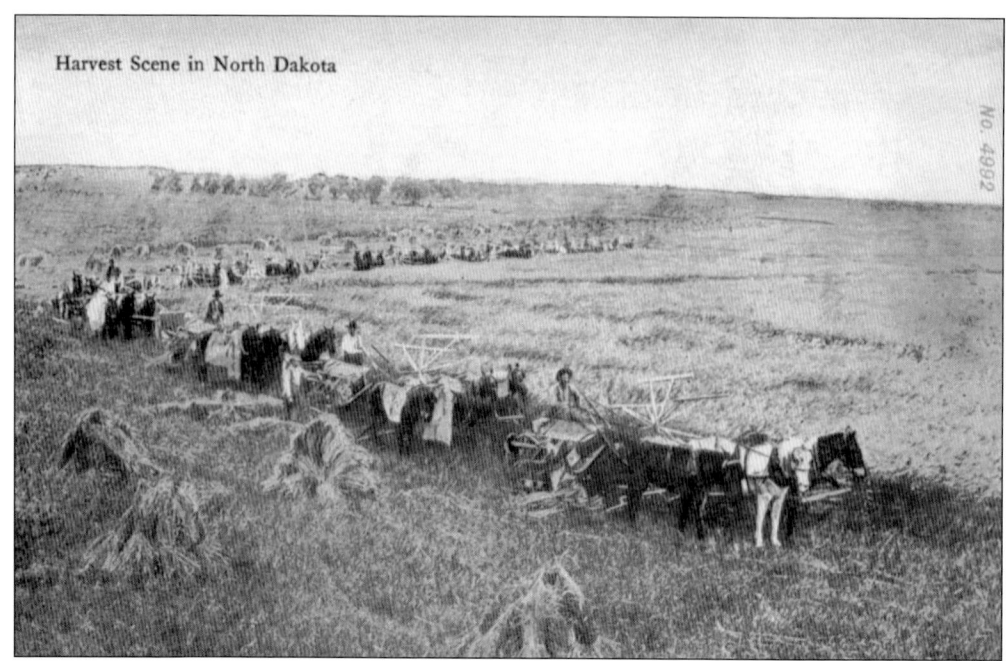

Harvest Scene in North Dakota

Here are two postcards that contradict each other. The postcard above gives North Dakota as home to the harvest scene, which carries an apparent image "No. 4992" just above the horizon at the right edge of both cards. The exact same image below uses "Johnson County, near Iowa City, Iowa" as the homesite. It carries a postal cancellation dated September 9, 1909. Also, the correspondent for the "Iowa City" card writes, "looks as if Johnson County was trying to make fun of Washington," obviously thinking the scene looks like yet a third location. Although many old postcards list a printing source, of course, none is listed on these.

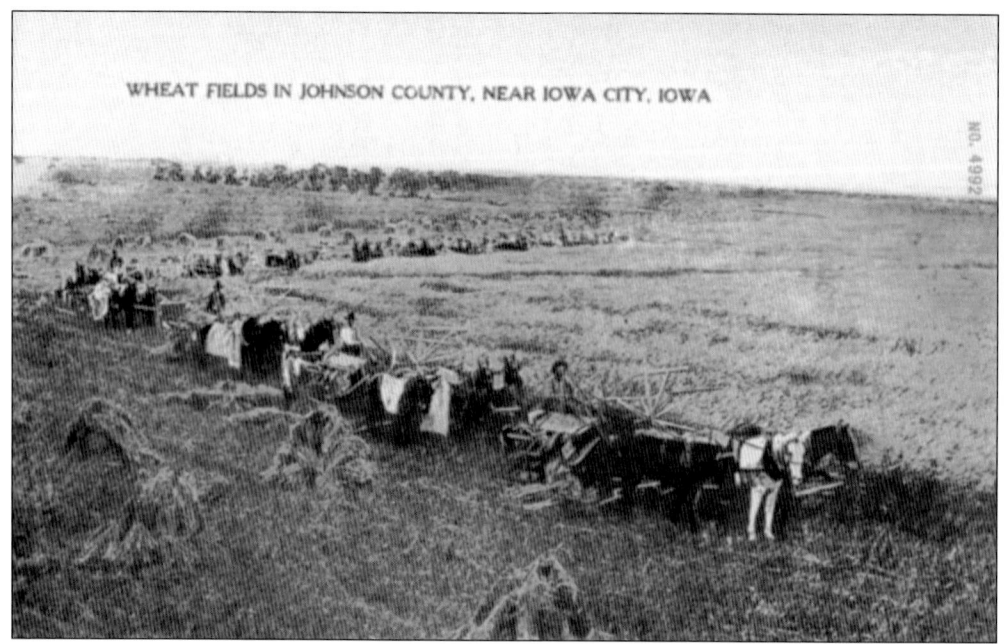

WHEAT FIELDS IN JOHNSON COUNTY, NEAR IOWA CITY, IOWA

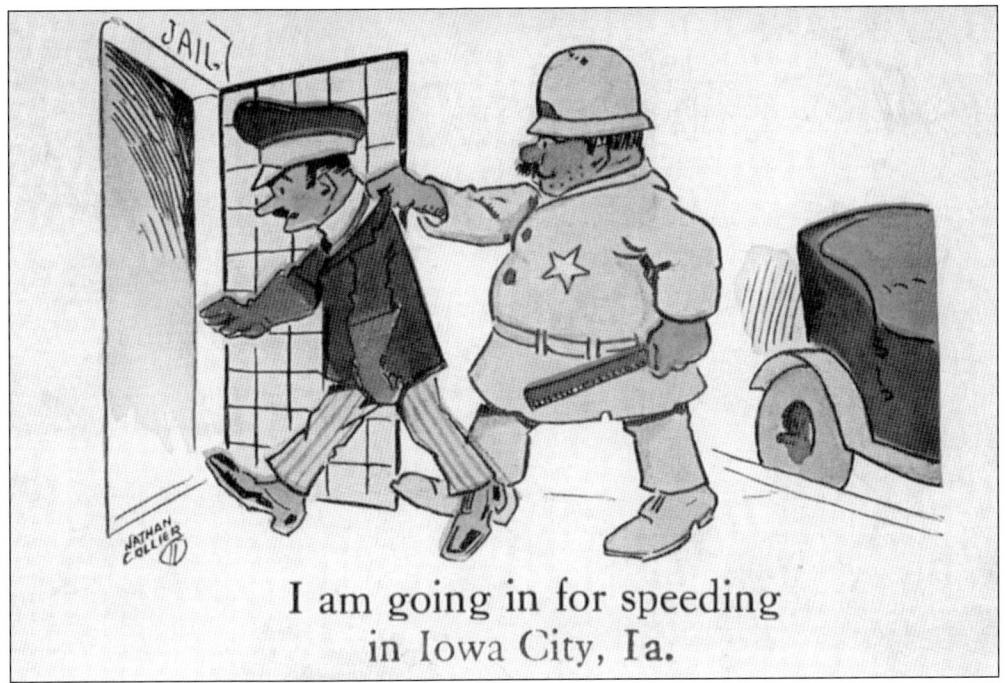

During several decades of the early 20th century, cartoon humor sprang forth on postcards regularly, like this example postmarked at Iowa City on April 6, 1912. From rolling out the carpet, to potty humor, romantic themes, and much more, cards that cost a penny to mail during that period brightened many a day.

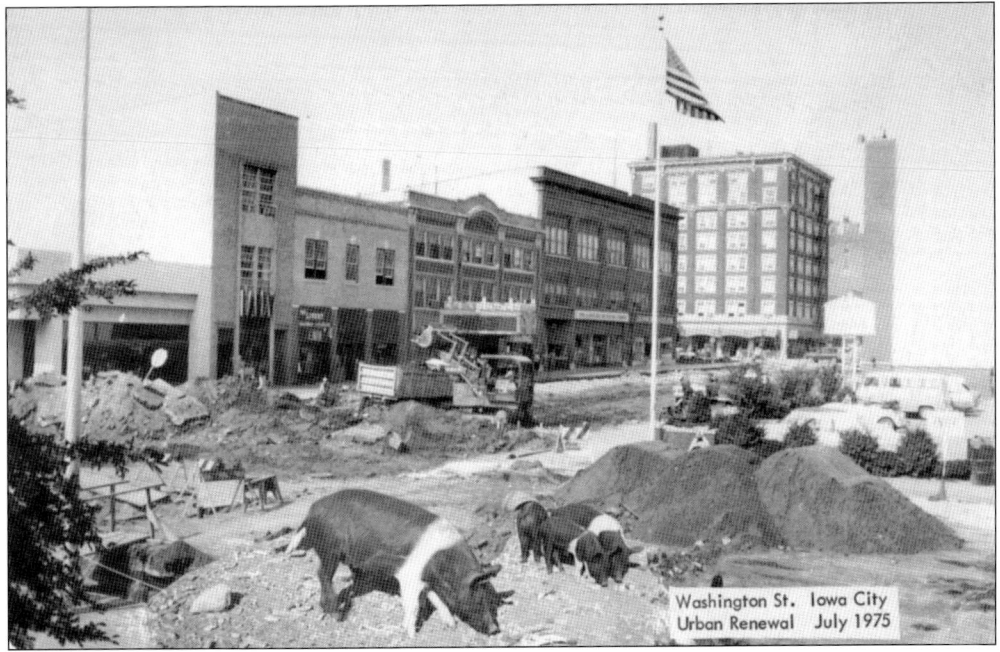

A downtown urban renewal project executed during the 1970s was the brunt of much talk. Above, photographer Fred Kent superimposed hogs into urban renewal street work.

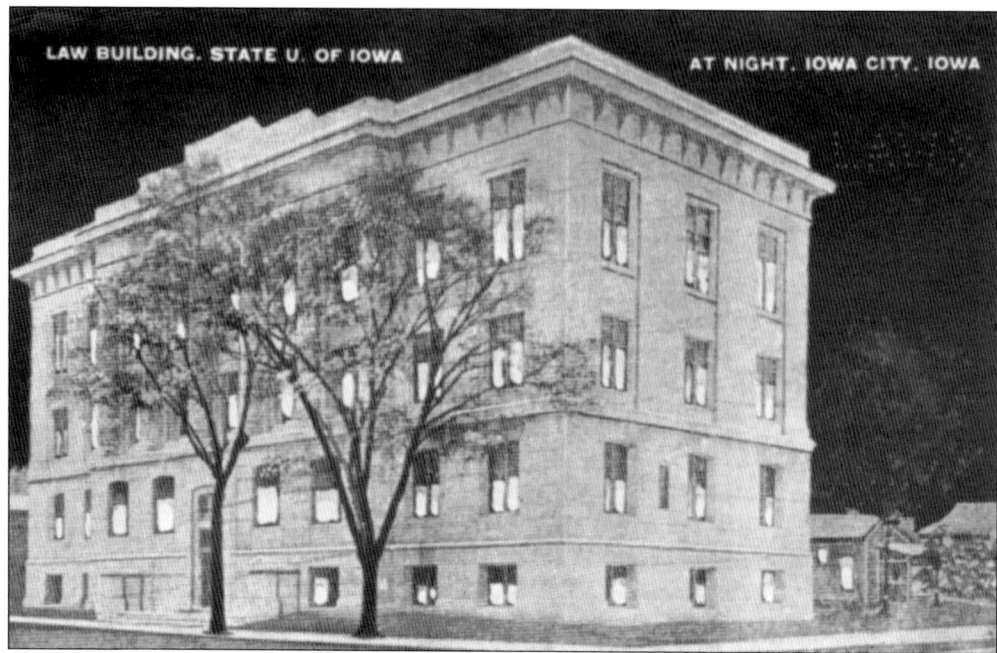

Above, the new 1910 College of Law building is offered in a folder of "Night" cards, which also provides a view of the 1909 university president's house below. Both are courtesy of fake photographic darkroom trickery. They appear in a folded double pseudo-envelop containing a strip of nine accordion-folded cards. Each is printed in an enlarged 4-by-6-inch size, while regular cards typically are 3.5 by 5.5 inches. The cover states the whole pack could be mailed for 1¢, or 2¢ with a message.

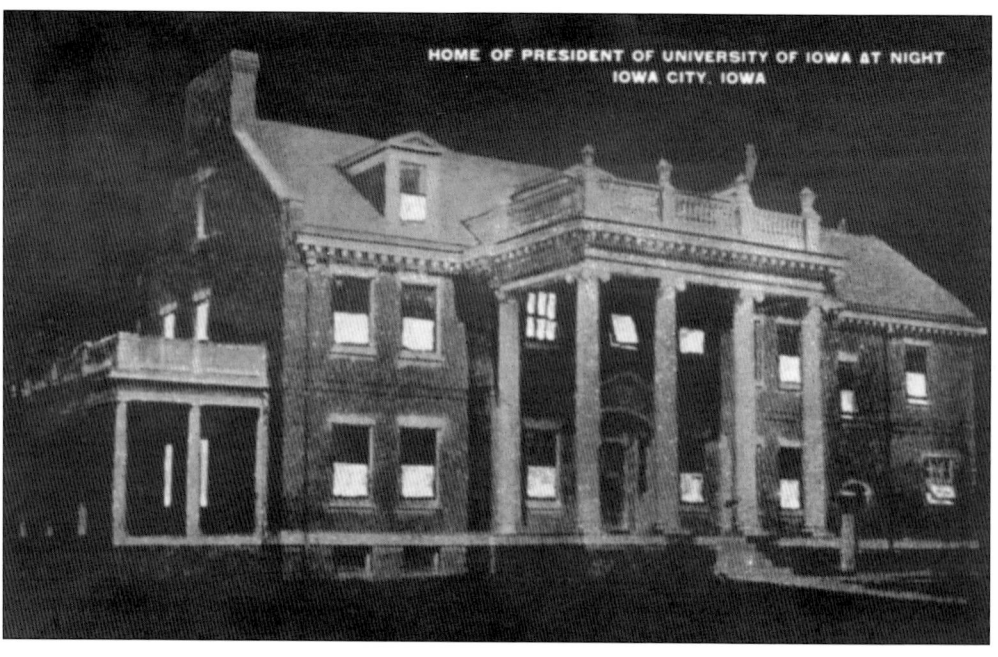

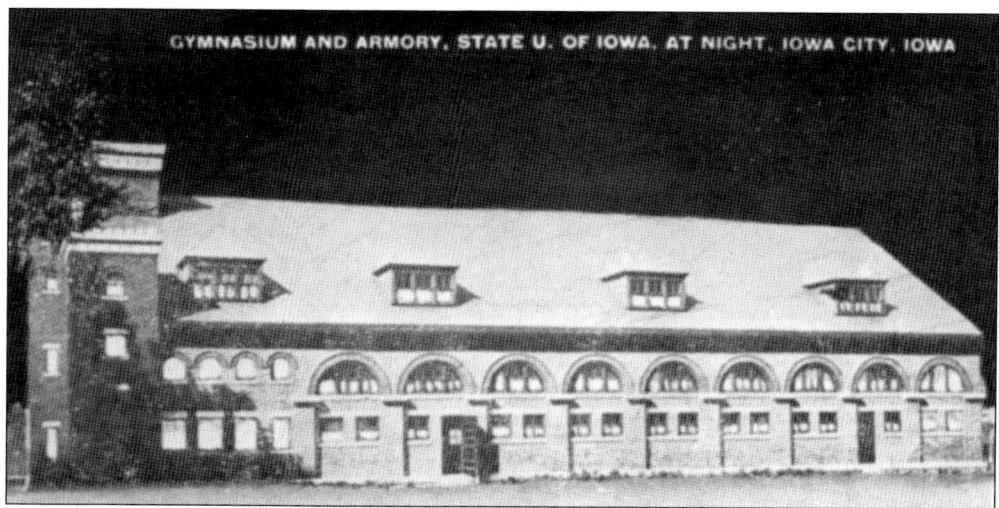

Above, a 1904 profile of the Armory and Men's Gym is offered by a folder of "Night at Iowa City" cards sold in the 1910 era. A saltwater pool addition to the Iowa Avenue face (right) came in 1915. The building was a campus chameleon during the 20th century, used as cadet armory, formal ballroom, concert hall, and basketball court, plus graduation forum and 1918 flu infirmary where several died. Its later use was as library annex, since it neighbored Main Library across Washington Street until its 1985 demolition.

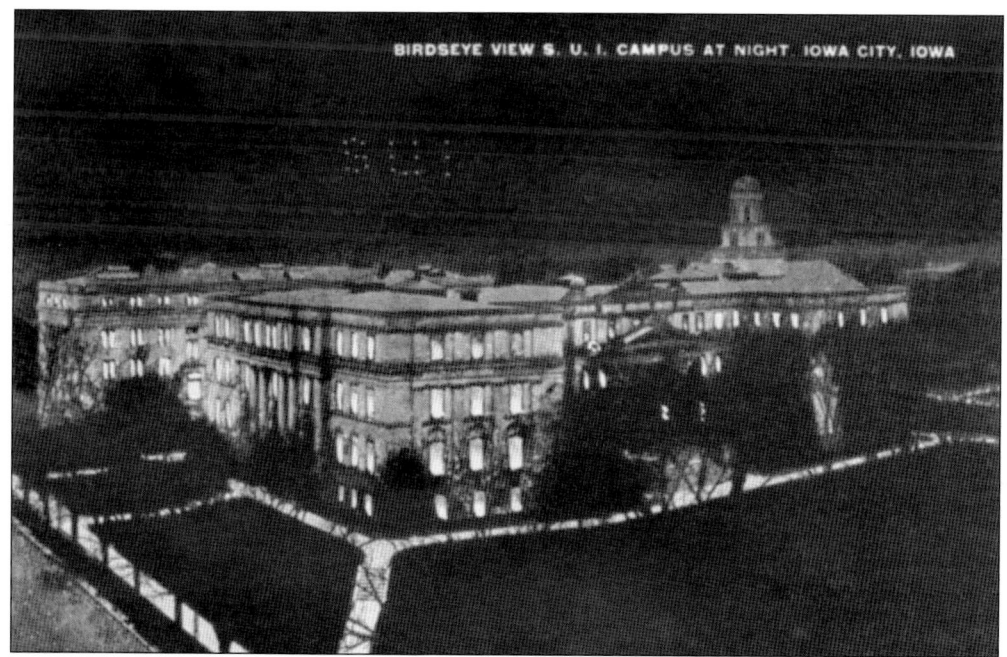

An "SUI" constellation seems to shine in the sky below the printed word "Birdseye" in this night image of the Pentacrest, showing Schaeffer Hall in the foreground with McLean Hall behind and Old Capitol at right. During most of the 20th century, the university was called SUI for State University of Iowa, before the word "state" was phased out during the 1960s to help avoid confusion with Iowa State in Ames.

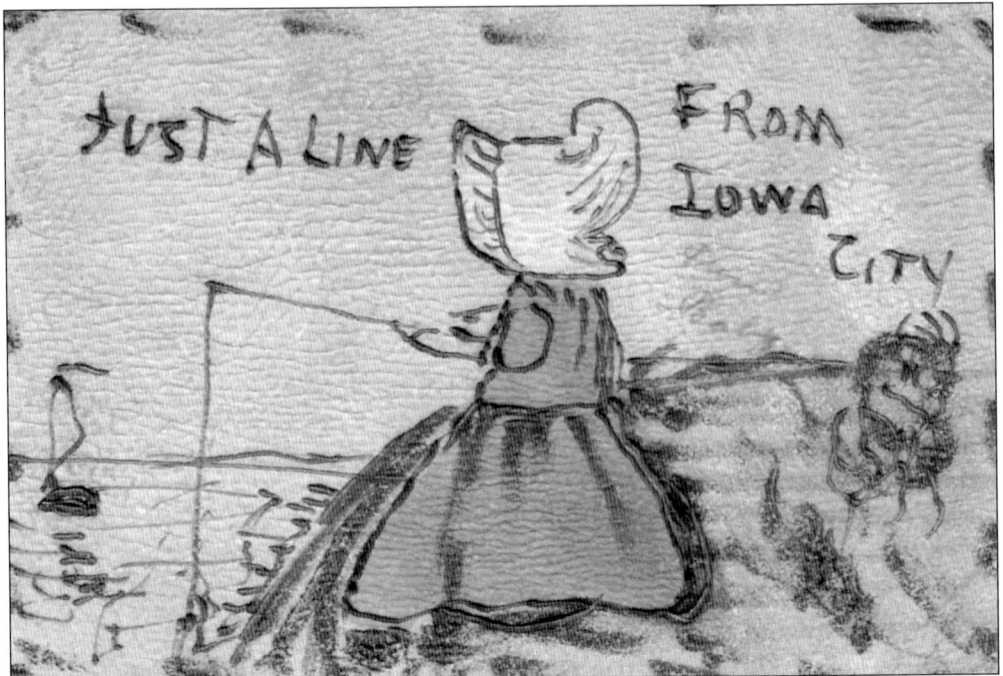

Postcards printed on leather were all the rage during the first decade of the 20th century, before an apparent change in postal regulations ended the practice, since they were so pliable that they had to be canceled by hand. Both front and back faces of a 1906 example appear on this page. It is signed above as "From Baby" faintly visible below "From Iowa City." It was canceled both in Iowa City and at its destination post office in Pekin, Illinois. "Baby" paid a message-added rate of 2¢ postage.

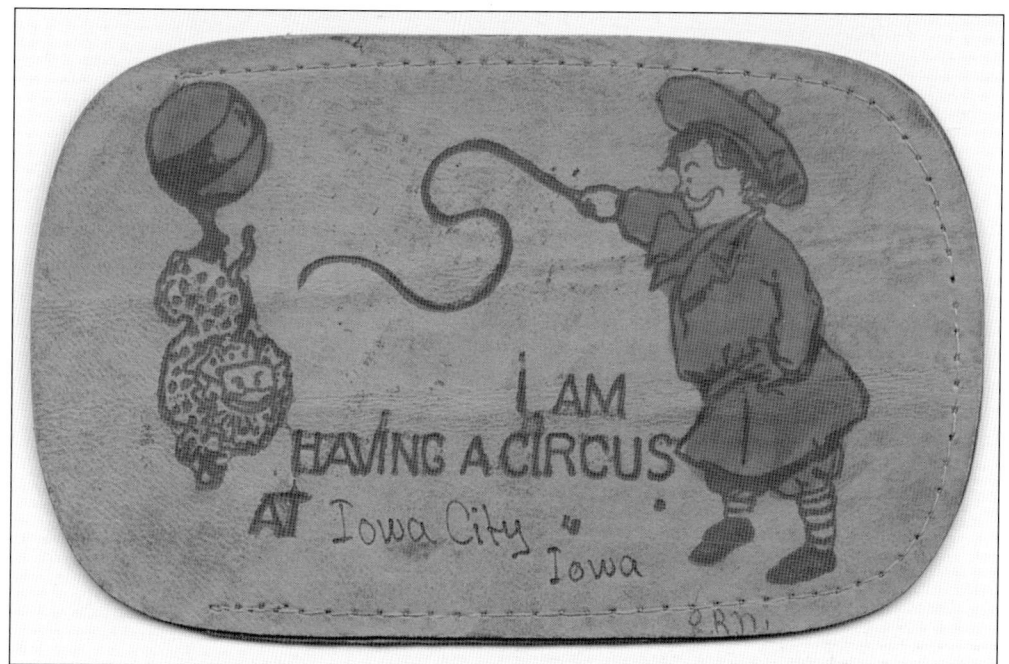

The leather card shown front and back on this page is two pieces stitched together, but open at one end, to form what seems to be a case for eyeglasses. It carries an Iowa City cancellation and a 1¢ postage stamp. It was sent to neighboring town West Liberty after the sender "P.R.N." printed the words "Iowa City, Iowa." The sender's initials are seen below the feet and tiny stitching holes. The same image appears on a flat leather card without being an apparent glasses case, which is not shown.

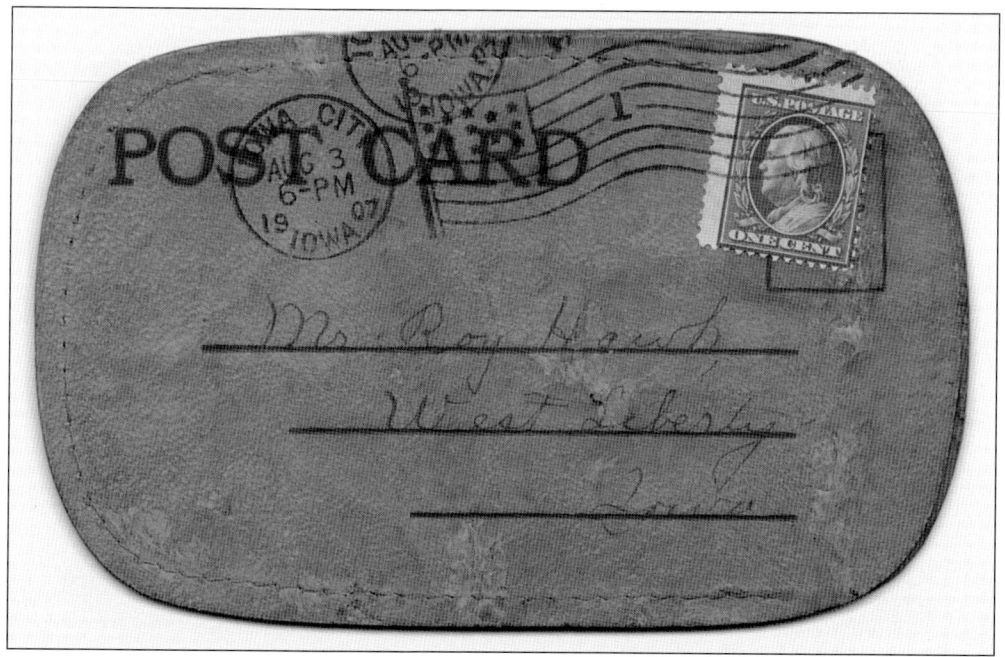

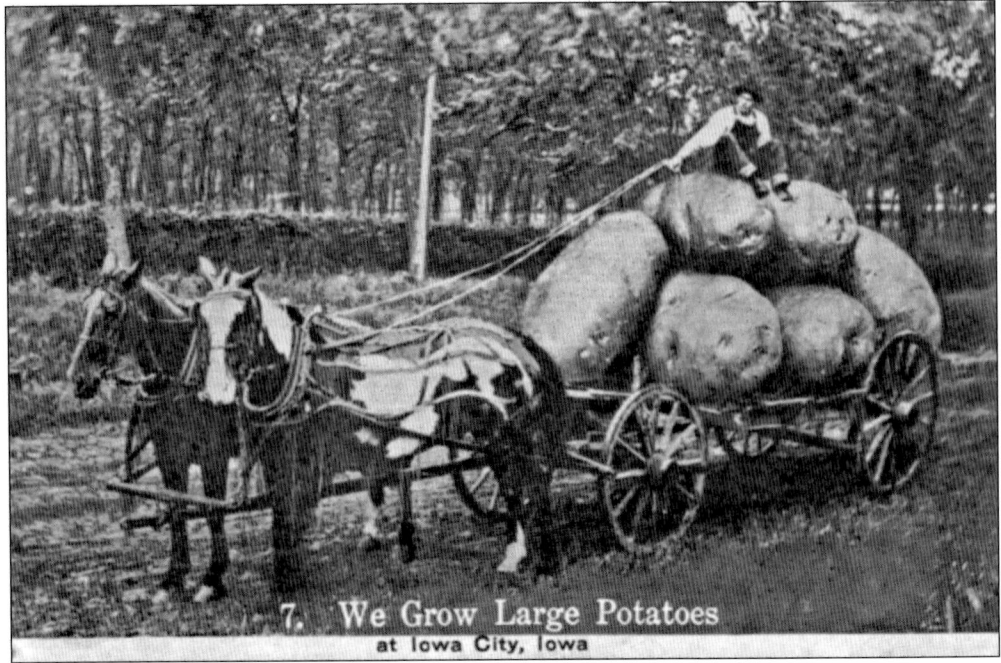

7. We Grow Large Potatoes
at Iowa City, Iowa

Misleading postcards like those showing the oversized potatoes above and the fish below were good clean fun purveyed during the first quarter of the 20th century in widely sold cards with just the town name changed at the bottom. Even today, "jackalope" cards, providing an image of a rabbit with antelope horns, are sold in Montana and Wyoming. Note the numbers at the beginning of the title on these cards, mailed in 1914, which indicate an apparent series of many such images.

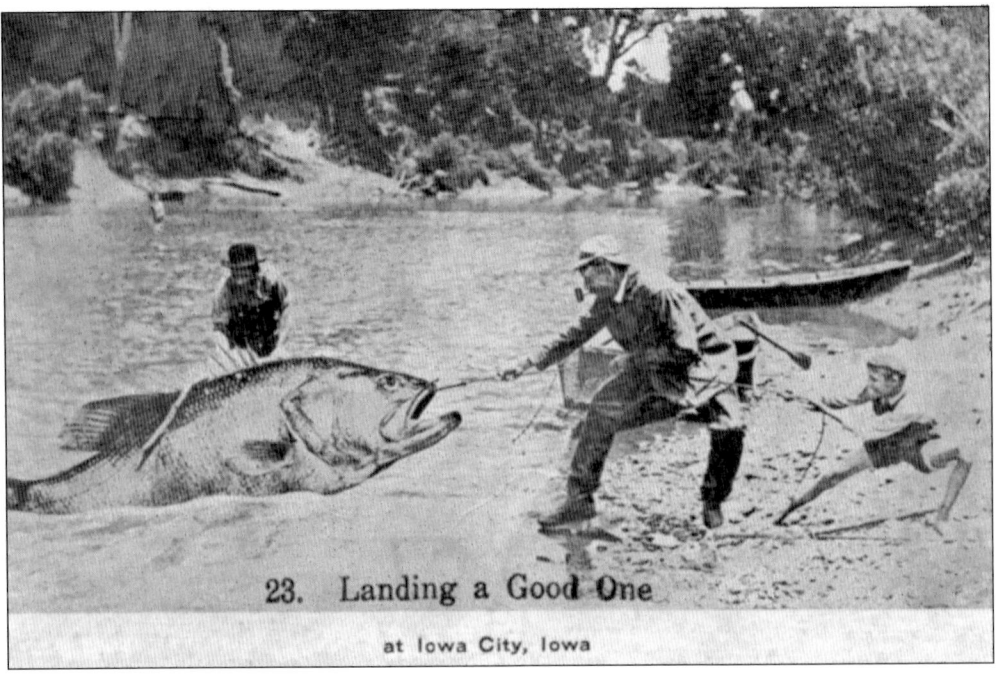

23. Landing a Good One
at Iowa City, Iowa

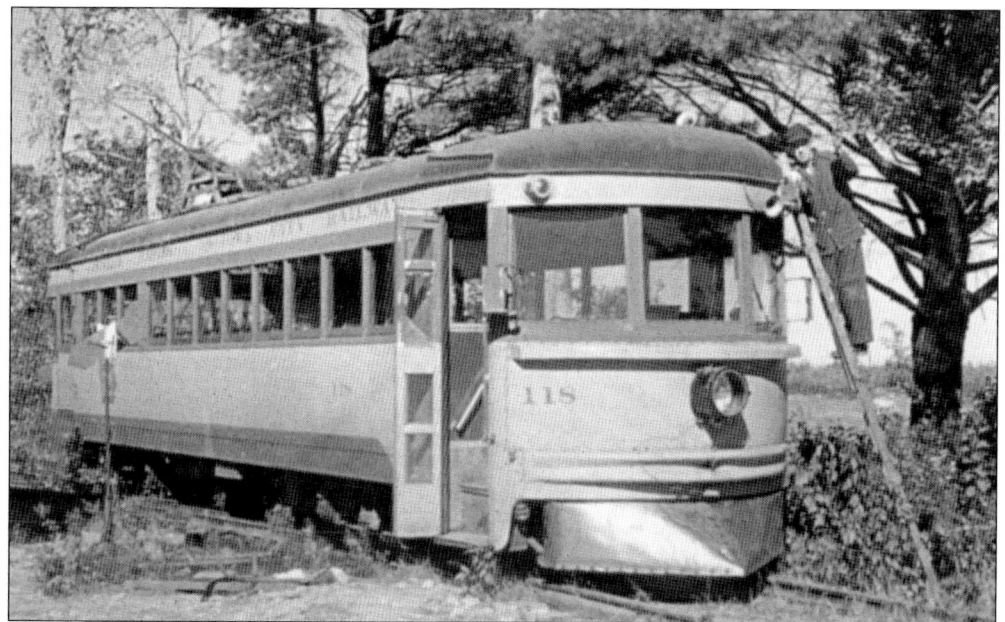

Retired CRandIC "Interurban" car No. 118 rests at its final stop, the Trolley Museum in Kennebunkport, Maine. The 1950s-era card claims the car "outraced an airplane in 1930," perhaps over a rural section of its 27-mile Iowa City to Cedar Rapids route. Dissatisfied with clutter, the author digitally processed the image seen below. The resulting "lie" reveals inconspicuous detail, such as the electric arm on top, which slid along an overhead cable providing a continuous electric power source.

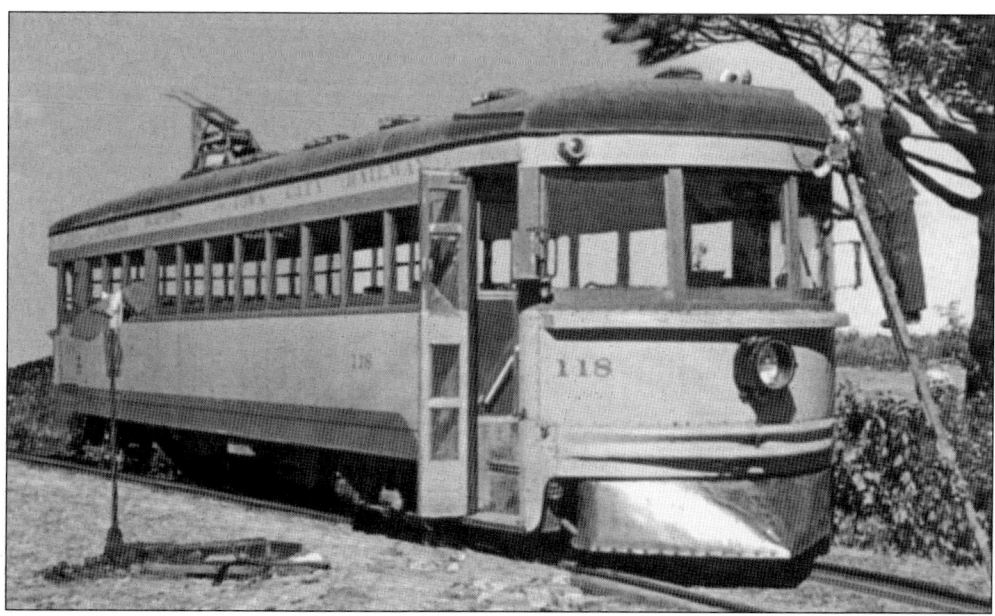

Fun journey. I hope you've enjoyed coming along as much as I've enjoyed preparing it for Arcadia Publishing. Perhaps we'll journey together again. I'd like that. Bob Hibbs, Iowa City.

Index

Alamo Motel, 81
American Legion, 89
Amish, Herman, 91
Anciaux, Joe, 27
Armory, military, 96
Armory and Men's Gym, 94, 110, 121
Athens of Iowa, 8
Athletic Park, 42, 44, 94–96, 102, 103
Betty's Flowers, 49
Blue Top Cabins, 79
Boerner Drug, 53
Brighton Beach, 113
Burlington Street Bridge collapse, 104
Butler's Capitol, 72
Butler's Landing, 76
Calvin Hall, 111
Carnegie library, 89
Carroll, Beryl, 97
Carroll, Len, 52
Central Jr., 13, 92, 94
Chautauqua, IC, 34
Children's, 16, 71
City Hall—1881, 5, 59, 64, 90, 91, 93, 94, 113
City High, 13, 37, 92
City Hotel brothel, 72
City of Literature, 26
City Park, 19, 42, 43, 50, 69, 72–75
Clark, James, 91
Coast and Sons, 25
Coldren Opera, 63
Congress Inn, 81
Coralville, 68, 69
Coralville dam, 108
Coralville Strip, 68, 78
Country Club, 114, 115
Courthouse, 86–88
CRandIC, 14, 44, 62, 99, 107, 110, 125
Creekside Park, 49
Currier dorm, 36
Curtis Florists, 49
Deadwood Tavern, 58
Donohue, John, 28

Donohue, Walter, 28
Dostal, John, 13
Dresden China, 30, 31
Economy Advertising, 48
Elks Club, 50, 99, 115
Englert Theatre, 38, 39
Epstein's Books, 58
Ewers Shoes, 58
Fairgrounds, 37, 93
Fire Department, 90
First Methodist, 19, 73
First National, 54, 63
First Presbyterian, 18
Fish ladder, 104
Foster Livery, 38
Franklin, John, 45
Gehry, Frank, 7
Goosetown, 52
Grammar School, 92
Greer jewelry, 109
Hall's gifts, 49
Ham radio, 36
Ham's Hall, 52
Hancher, Virgil, 41
Harris, Jim, 26
Hawkeye Lodge, 79
Hawkeye Special, 70
Herky Hawk, 45
Hillcrest dorm, 71, 105
Hills Bank, 80
Hinrichs, G., 56
Hoepfner, Craig, 36
Hohenschuh's, 28
Hotel Jefferson, 25, 28, 39, 59, 82, 88, 90, 97
Hotz, Jacob, 87
Hubbard, Philip, 107
Huddle, The, 83
Indian Lookout, 117
Iowa Book, 64, 87
Iowa Chick Hatchery, 49
Iowa Memorial Union, 40, 61, 107
Iowa National Guard (ING), 97
Iowa State Bank, 39, 55, 60, 62
Irish, Elizabeth, 26

Isensee residence, 80
IWV Road, 102, 103
Joffrey Ballet, 7
John's Grocery, 13, 93
Johnson, Leora, 29
Johnson, Richard, 7
Johnson County Fair of 1853, 10
Johnson County Bank, 39, 55, 59, 88
Jolliffe, Elwin, 52
Kaspar, George, 81
Kent, Fred, 37, 44, 96, 100, 105, 119
Kinnick Stadium, 7, 40, 42, 44, 45, 53, 70, 89
Klondike Bill, 46
Kobe's Motel, 78, 81
Lee, J. Walter, 50
Littrell, Ralph, 49
Law Commons, 40
Law School, Old, 120
Lensing, Mike, 28
Little Hawks, 94, 95
Lone Tree, 34
Loghry's Drive-In, 70
Louis, Bud, 67
Lourdes Hall, 13
Lover's Leap, 76
Macbride Hall, 11, 46
Macbride, Thomas, 96
Main Company, W. F., 48
Manville Heights, 34, 62, 73
Marriott Hotel, 76
Masons, 52, 99
Mayflower dorm, 108
Mayflower Inn, 109
Mazzuchelli, Fr., 20
McCollister, James, 52, 53
McGruder, John, 27
McInnerny's bar, 7
McLean Hall, 121
Mechanics Academy, 12, 94
Medical Building, 111
Melody Mill Café, 78
Mercy Hospital, 12, 13, 92, 93, 95
Methodist Church, 19

Metropolitan Hall 59, 88, 97
Miller, Russ, 79
Motel Iowa, 80
Mulford, Pauline, 84
Mulford, Ray, 84
Murals, Pelzer, 82, 83
Napoleon, 86
Nonpareil dance, 52
North Hall, 10, 96, 111
North Liberty, 14
Novy, Milo/Libby, 52
Nursing 9, 71, 107
Oakdale Campus, 14
Oakland Cemetery, 62
Oathout's, 28, 84
Observatory, 11
Observatory Hill, 72, 73, 108
Old Brick Church, 18
Old Capitol, 9, 10, 17, 20, 21, 36, 37, 56, 60, 61, 72, 94, 96, 98, 103
Old Capitol Inn, 81
Old Dental, 111
Old Lime Kiln, 51
Opera House Bar, 63
Park Hotel, 98
Park Road bridge, 72
Paul-Helen, 38, 39
Pedestrian Mall, 112
Pelzer, Mildred, 82, 83
Penney, JC, 63
Pentacrest, 9, 46, 58, 60, 64, 71, 87, 88, 110
Phillips Hall, 61, 62
Pine Edge Motel, 80
Plaza Towers, 82, 112
Post Office, 87, 88
Prairie Lights, 26, 31
President's House, 10, 72, 108, 120
Proctor & Gamble, 8
Public Library, 89
Rate gloves, 51
Rebel Motel, 84
Recreation Center, 89
Red brick campus on Pentacrest, 110
Regan, Patrick, 50, 114
Regina school, 98
Reichardt's, 63
Reid, Hiram A., 56
Rex mascot, 44

Rinella Grocery, 107
River Heights, 72
Rock Island depot, 62, 97, 100
St. James Hotel, 61, 64, 116
St. Mary's Church, 13, 19, 20, 73, 93, 98
St. Mary's School, 98
St. Patrick's, 22
Sanders, Mary Terrill, 73, 109
Schaeffer Hall, 11, 111
Schuttler Hotel, 38
Sears, 63
See Us Increase, 35
Senior Center, 87
Shakespeare Festival Stage, 7, 74
Sheep Shed, 111
Sheraton Hotel, 112
Siesta Motel, 78
Sigma Pi house, 109
Skyway Cabins, 84
Smith, Larry, 79
Snowball and Highball horses, 91
Solon, 81
South Hall, 10, 111
Spencer, Dick, 45
Stadium Park, 45
State Hygienic, 14
Steindler, Arthur, 16
Stewart's Shoes, 25
Sum Place, 104, 105
Summerwill, Ben, 55
Svendi Hall, 98
Swan, Chauncey, 18
Taft Speedway, 115
TB hospital, 14, 15
Thomas Hardware, 63
Terrill Mill, 69, 108
Tornado, 2006, 22, 84
Tomlin, Willie, 90
Townsend, T., 18
Traffic light, first, 82
Train wreck, 100
Travel Lodge, 81
Triangle Club, 40
Trimble's Smokehouse, 86
Turkish Bath, 27
Unitarian Church, 62
Unity Hall, 61

Universalist Church, 61, 62, 116
University Heights, 53
University Hospitals, 8, 12, 16, 17, 60, 78
University Theatre, 41
Urban renewal, 119
Van Meter Hotel, 60
Varsity Ballroom, 52
Varsity Heights, 71
Van Allen Hall, 11
Yocum's, Curt, 70
Volunteer firemen, 90
Wallick's, 27
Wards, 63
Wayne Feeds, 49
Weber, Irving, 7
Wegman, Marcia, 116
Welch, Willard, 30, 31
West Liberty, 123
Whetstone's, 58, 60
Wieneke, Carrie, 113
Wildman, Ralph, 79
Wildman, Ruby, 79
Wilson, Keith, 49
Writers Workshop, 26
Woolworth's, 58
Wurlitzer jukebox, 78
Yell Leaders, 44
Yetter's, 24
YM-YWCA, 63
Zielinski, John, 112
Zion Lutheran, 22

www.arcadiapublishing.com

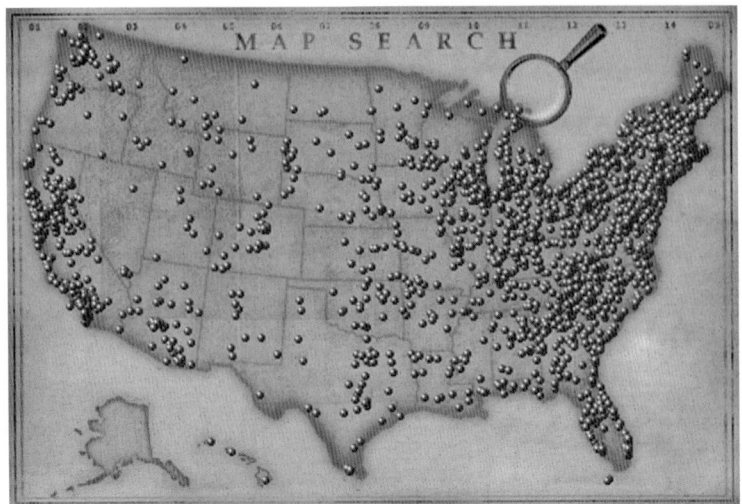

Discover books about the town where you grew up, the cities where your friends and families live, the town where your parents met, or even that retirement spot you've been dreaming about. Our Web site provides history lovers with exclusive deals, advanced notification about new titles, e-mail alerts of author events, and much more.

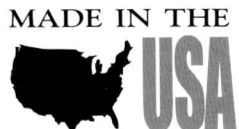

Arcadia Publishing, the leading local history publisher in the United States, is committed to making history accessible and meaningful through publishing books that celebrate and preserve the heritage of America's people and places. Consistent with our mission to preserve history on a local level, this book was printed in South Carolina on American-made paper and manufactured entirely in the United States.

This book carries the accredited Forest Stewardship Council (FSC) label and is printed on 100 percent FSC-certified paper. Products carrying the FSC label are independently certified to assure consumers that they come from forests that are managed to meet the social, economic, and ecological needs of present and future generations.

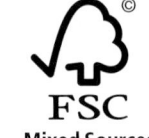

FSC
Mixed Sources
Product group from well-managed forests and other controlled sources
Cert no. SW-COC-001530
www.fsc.org
© 1996 Forest Stewardship Council

Find Your Place in History.